RECASTING THE MACHINE AGE

Recasting the Machine Age

Henry Ford's Village Industries

HOWARD P. SEGAL

UNIVERSITY OF MASSACHUSETTS PRESS
Amherst and Boston

LC 2004030727
ISBN 1-55849-481-2

Designed by Steve Dyer
Set in New Caledonia
Printed and bound by The Maple-Vail Book Manufacturing Group

LIBRARY OF CONGRESS CATALOGING-IN-PUBLICATION DATA

Segal, Howard P.
  Recasting the machine age : Henry Ford's village industries / Howard
P. Segal.
      p. cm.
  Includes bibliographical references and index.
  ISBN 1-55849-481-2 (cloth : alk. paper)
1. Ford Motor Company—History.   2. Automobile industry and
trade—Location—Michigan—Case studies.   3. Industrial location—Social
aspects—United States.   4. Labor unions—Michigan—History.   5.
Technology—Social aspects—United States.   6. Ford, Henry, 1863–1947.
7. Industrialists—United States—Biography.   I. Title.
HD9710.U54F682 2005
338.7'6292'0973—dc22

                                                    2004030727

British Library Cataloguing in Publication data are available.

All illustrations unless otherwise credited are from
the Collections of The Henry Ford.

This book is published with the support of a generous grant from
the University of Maine.

FOR MY MENTORS

In Honor of Solomon Wank and James Banner

and

In Memory of Norman Smith and Melvin Kranzberg

Henry Ford would be less than the man he is if, walking by the River Rouge, he did not thrill at the sight of his huge plant growing huger and huger by the day. But the old man's dearest dream is no longer of piling building on building in metropolitan congestion. A farm boy who has kept his love of the land, Ford now visions the "little factory in a meadow" as the future shape of American industry. . . . Ford will furnish land for use by those who do not have farms or gardens. Henry Ford is convinced that, for happiness and security, the worker of the future must divide his time between factory and farm.

—*Life*, May 30, 1938

CONTENTS

ILLUSTRATIONS FOLLOW PAGES 50 AND 74.

PREFACE AND ACKNOWLEDGMENTS

I HAVE SPENT A GOOD DEAL OF MY ACADEMIC LIFE ON THIS topic, infinitely more than I could ever have imagined when I decided to write the first book-length study of Henry Ford's nineteen village industries. True, I have written other books and articles since the earlier versions, but the project has been with me long enough, and it is time to send it out into the world.

As *Recasting the Machine Age* contends, Henry Ford's motives for building and funding the village industries are multiple and murky. By contrast, my reasons for writing this book are few and clear. They reflect the circumstances of my being geographically close both to those nineteen sites and to the most important primary and secondary sources about them. Soon after I began teaching the history of technology at the University of Michigan's College of Engineering in 1978, I took several undergraduate classes to the Ford Museum and Greenfield Village (then collectively and officially known as The Edison Institute) in nearby Dearborn in order to raise their technological literacy and my own. For this initial acquaintance with the vast number of tools and machines collected by Ford and his associates, and for preliminary discussions of the vision(s) behind them, I am indebted to the late Peter Cousins, then Curator of Agriculture; to John Bowditch, then Curator of Industry; to John Wright, then Director of Education and Public Programs; and to Steven Hamp, then my graduate student and eventually the president of the Institute, now renamed The Henry Ford.

Each time I walked around the Ford Museum and Greenfield Village, I was struck by Ford's paeans to American history—which, contrary to popular accounts, he did *not* denounce as altogether "bunk"—overlooking the contemporary track for testing the latest Ford Motor Company vehicles. But nothing appeared to connect them. One did not have to be as insightful as Henry Adams in *The Education of Henry Adams*, contemplating the respective moral as well as material power of the Virgin Mary at the great medieval cathedral at Chartres and the forty-foot-high dynamos at the 1900 Paris Exposition, to wonder how the past and the present could be so physically close yet so intellectually apart. How could Ford simultaneously look forward and backward? Once I started learning about the village industries, I asked myself, why would the person most responsible for America's large-scale, centralized manufacturing and production facilities and processes wish to provide small-scale, decentralized alternatives to them? Why would the person most responsible for luring American workers to the urban locales of most of those major factories wish to provide rural alternatives to them?

When, in 1980, I joined the fifth annual "100-mile, four-county guided tour" of ten of the nineteen sites, sponsored by the Institute, things made more sense to me. The tour was led by the world's foremost expert on Henry Ford, business historian David L. Lewis of the University of Michigan's School of Business Administration, who had written several articles on the village industries but had no plans to publish a book on the topic. Instead, from that day on, he repeatedly encouraged me to pursue my research and was always available to answer questions. As the notes to my book indicate, his writings have been invaluable to my work. Eventually I benefited from his further assistance when, unknown to me at the time, he agreed to serve as one of the two readers for the University of Massachusetts Press.

In the early 1980s, before the dissolution of my unit at the University of Michigan (the Humanities/Engineering Department), I made many visits to the Ford Archives at the Edison Institute. By that point Steve Hamp had become Director of Collections and Chief Curator of Archives and Records; he was always helpful in getting me access to materials as efficiently as possible. Cynthia Read-Miller, still Curator of Photographs and Prints, was equally supportive and greatly assisted my search for pertinent photographs from the archives' massive collections. The late David Crippen, Curator of Special Collections and of Automotive History, was enormously helpful not only in locating and evaluating endless primary and secondary sources but also in trying to help me make sense of Ford's complexities and seeming contradictions. The late Ford Bryan, a former Ford Motor Company spectrochemical analyst who, in retirement, wrote seven fine books on Henry Ford (a distant relative) and the company, was also very helpful as our paths crossed in the archives. Finally, Judith Endelman, currently Director of Historical Resources and Chief Curator, joined the museum after most of my research was completed but assisted me in countless ways as I finished the manuscript. In addition, Darleen Flaherty, then Archivist of the Ford

Industrial Archives in Redford, Michigan, assisted my investigation of holdings there, as did independent researcher Eleanor Poteracki of Detroit.

I made much briefer but invaluable visits to both the Walter Reuther Library of Labor and Urban Affairs, part of Wayne State University in Detroit, and the Rockefeller Archive Center in North Tarrytown, New York, and I am most grateful to these two institutions for the research grants that allowed me to do so. At the Reuther Library I came upon materials in the Joe Brown Collection that illuminated organized labor's increasingly critical views of Henry Ford, the Ford Motor Company, and, most important here, the policy of corporate decentralization. Without these materials, my analysis of the village industries would likely have been one-sided and inaccurate. At the Rockefeller Archive Center—so ably directed by fellow historian of technology Darwin Stapleton—I came upon materials in the Rockefeller Family Archives that illuminated the profound difference between a pioneering "living history museum" such as Colonial Williamsburg and the village industries. That in turn clarified for me Henry Ford's sense of a "usable past" as compared with the conception of John D. Rockefeller, Jr.—the principal benefactor of Colonial Williamsburg—and of certain other early and middle twentieth-century Americans.

I thank the many Michigan local historical societies, museums, and newspapers that responded to my inquiries over the years and that frequently provided valuable information about their respective village industries. The Plymouth Historical Museum with its excellent permanent exhibit on the village industries, which I visited in 1999, had the greatest number of materials. Beth Stewart, director, and Bruce Richard, former president of the Plymouth Historical Society, have been especially helpful to me over the years. Richard had worked at the village industries, and his written and verbal reflections on those years were extremely helpful.

So, too, were the reflections of the other former workers with whom I communicated and whose responses greatly enhanced my book's accuracy and analysis. My most extended interview was with Kenneth Edwards, chief clerk of all the village industries from 1943 to 1946 and, before that, a worker and then clerk at the Milan plant. By extraordinary coincidence, Edwards's daughter was a University of Maine grants administrator who in that capacity knew of my research. On June 13, 1988, while visiting her, Edwards kindly allowed me to interview him at length. His varied experiences at the various sites were unique and his responses most informative.

Nancy Darga, now retired as Manager of Design for the Wayne County Division of Parks, has answered many questions over several years and has updated me repeatedly on the status of the surviving village industry sites and on both the Ford Heritage Trail and the Automobile National Heritage Area.

As my book developed, I had the opportunity to give lectures to a number of different audiences over the years. In addition to various historical society annual meetings, I thank several institutions for inviting me to speak: Harvard University's History of Science Department (especially Everett Mendelsohn) and its Charles Warren Center (especially Bernard Bailyn), Colby College (especially James Fleming and Leonard Reich), Cornell University (especially Ronald Kline), Iowa State University (especially Alan Marcus), and Mount Holyoke College (especially Eugene Hill). As much as I resented the common a priori dismissal by some listeners of any favorable treatment of Henry Ford, I also gained much from having to defend my mixed assessment of him and his village industries before such skeptics. I also appreciated the more positive comments from other audience members who suggested, for example, comparisons of the village industries with other American and several non-American developments in the nineteenth and twentieth centuries. All these lectures and discussions forced me to think more deeply— and, in certain cases, to rethink—what the book was ultimately about and how it fit into our existing knowledge of Henry Ford, the Ford Motor Company, decentralized technology, and the history of technology overall.

No less important were the critical readings of a draft of the entire manuscript provided by two colleagues at the University of Maine, Nathan Godfried and Richard Judd, whose respective comments were invaluable. So, too, were those on chapters of the manuscript by fellow historians of technology: Daryl Hafter of Eastern Michigan University, Thomas Kinney of Bluefield College, Arnold Pavlovsky, and Rosalind Williams of MIT. A third member of the University of Maine History Department, Bird and Bird Professor Emeritus David Smith, provided illuminating materials about Henry Ford from the perspective of H. G. Wells, about whom David is among the world's leading scholars. A fourth member of my department, Libra Professor Stuart Bruchey, a distinguished historian of American business who had retired from Columbia University, assisted me greatly in placing Henry Ford and the Ford Motor Company in the context of the evolution of American business overall. Finally, a fifth member of my department, William TeBrake, himself an award-winning historian of medieval technology, helped me utilize the latest word processing, Internet, and other electronic means of research and writing.

In addition, reference librarian Melvin Johnson of the University of Maine's Fogler Library provided repeated assistance over the years as I sought to complete the book. I have never met a more helpful—or intellectually engaged—reference librarian anywhere.

Amy Bix of Iowa State University, the second reader of the manuscript for the University of Massachusetts Press, made extremely helpful suggestions for revision and improvement. So, too, did her colleague Alan Marcus, with whom I coauthored *Technology in America: A Brief History* (1989; revised 1999) and who for many years has been my foremost sounding board and critic for various projects.

In addition to the travel grants noted above from the Reuther Library and the Rockefeller Archive Center, I gratefully acknowledge research assistance from the American Association for State and Local History (Grant-in-Aid), American Council of Learned Societies (Grant-in-Aid), American Historical Association (Albert J. Beveridge Research Grant), National Endowment for the Humanities (Travel to Collections Grant and Summer Stipend), Phi Alpha Theta History Honor Society (Faculty Advisor Research Grant), Smithsonian Institution (Short-Term Visitor Grant), and the University of Maine (Faculty Summer Research Grant). Since most of these grants were awarded before personal computers and laptops, the Internet, and the World Wide Web permitted researchers to obtain materials without having to travel to archives and libraries and often to download information without having to photocopy or take copious notes, they were of especially great help to my research.

Beyond these short-term grants, however, I am forever grateful for longer-term grants from the National Science Foundation (History and Philosophy of Science Program, then directed by the historian of science Margaret Rossiter, Research Grants SES-8218636 and SES-84-8408874); the Earhart Foundation of Ann Arbor, Michigan (then directed by the historian Antony Sullivan); and the Harvard University Andrew Mellon Faculty Fellowship Program (directed by the historian Richard Hunt until its eventual closure). These grants enabled me to complete my research after I no longer lived in Michigan and to write early drafts of the book. My two pleasant years at Harvard's History of Science Department, which sponsored me for a year as a Mellon Faculty Fellow and then kept me on for a second year as a lecturer, were intellectually invigorating, thanks above all to Allan Brandt and Everett Mendelsohn and to the then department administrator, Betsy Smith.

An early version of part of the book manuscript appeared as a long article in *Prospects: The Annual of American Culture Studies* 13, superbly edited by Jack Salzman (New York: Cambridge University Press, 1988), 181–223. I appreciated the opportunity to contribute to such a significant publication.

Paul Wright, acquisitions editor at the University of Massachusetts Press, has endured with great patience and good cheer the repeated delays in my completing *Recasting the Machine Age*. As with my earlier Press books, *Future Imperfect* and the coedited *Technology, Pessimism, and Postmodernism*, so with this: he has been a professional in the best sense. So, too, have his colleagues, not least Carol Betsch, managing editor, and Bruce Wilcox, director of the Press.

My wife, Professor of English Deborah Rogers, has listened to me discuss this book far longer than either of us cares to recall, but she has never tired of encouraging me to make the published version the very best I can offer. For this—and for so much else unrelated to the book—I thank her more than I can possibly express here.

Our children, Ricky and Raechel, were both born well after I began the book and have related to it only insofar as we had a Ford station wagon for most of their young lives. I did repeatedly try to connect our vehicle to anything remotely historical about Henry Ford, Ford Motor Company, and the village industries. But it was, alas, almost always in vain.

This book is dedicated to four persons who had little to do with its actual research and writing but much to do with my career as a historian and with my overall intellectual development (as a historian of technology). Solomon Wank of Franklin and Marshall College, my alma mater, has been a mentor since a first-year course in modern European history. More than anyone else, he has been made me sensitive to the deeper meaning and significance of serious alternatives to existing values, institutions, and societies—even when, as with Henry Ford, one's own politics and ideology might well be at odds with the person or movement or practices being examined.

James Banner directed my doctoral dissertation at Princeton University on technological utopianism, a topic far removed from his principal area of expertise. Long after leaving Princeton for a variety of other positions, he remained a steadfast and sympathetic advocate of my work and my career as I sought a permanent academic appointment, not only writing endless letters on my behalf over several years but also providing exceptional guidance and reassurance amid seemingly unending disappointments. No less important, Jim Banner has demonstrated to the entire historical profession the value of connecting to the general public without for a moment compromising one's intellectual integrity. Among other accomplishments, his cofounding of the

History News Service and his efforts to establish a National History Center in Washington, D.C., exemplify the means by which professional historians young and old can be of service to the nation and, in the process, raise the general public's historical knowledge and sensitivity.

I deeply regret that Norman Smith and Melvin Kranzberg are not alive to enable me to thank them in person for their support and encouragement. Dean of the University of Maine's College of Engineering, Norman Smith was a specialist in agricultural engineering who had a lifelong interest in the history of technology. Beginning in 1988 and continuing until his untimely death a decade later, we team-taught courses on technology past and present to growing numbers of engineering and nonengineering students. In the process we learned much from each other and, despite repeated disagreements over the nature and extent of technological "progress" and over contemporary politics, had the highest mutual respect. As political correctness belatedly made its way to our semirural campus, we totally agreed on the need to reassert academic freedom, inside the classroom and out, and to reject intolerance of those with whom we disagreed. As Norman Smith routinely told our students, advice stemming from his boyhood in rural England and his grandfather's words, one should always leave the land better than one had found it. This he most assuredly did.

The late Melvin Kranzberg founded the field of the history of technology and welcomed into it numerous younger scholars like me whose graduate training had not been in the field. Among my earliest publications were book reviews in the journal he founded and long edited, *Technology and Culture*. From our initial conversations at the 1975 annual meeting of the Society for the History of Technology—the professional organization that he established—until shortly before his death in 1995, Kranzberg was unfailing not only in assisting my career but also in providing a model of academic achievement in the face of numerous obstacles. Throughout his own career he treated others—including his critics—with kindness and respect. He was a genuine hero to many historians of technology who ordinarily disavow the heroic theory of history in their field.

Amid a contemporary culture in which personal responsibility for one's actions often takes a back seat to accusations of victimization by other people or more impersonal forces, I nevertheless take full responsibility for the contents of this book.

Bangor, Maine
September 2004

Introduction

Henry Ford, Centralization, and Decentralization

"TECHNOLOGY SPURS DECENTRALIZATION ACROSS THE Country." So read a 1984 *New York Times* article on real estate trends in the United States.[1] Then in its early stage, the contemporary revolution in information processing and transmittal today allows large businesses and other institutions to disperse their offices and other facilities across the country and across the world without loss of the policy- and decision-making abilities that formerly required regular physical proximity. Thanks to computers, word processors, faxes, the Internet, and the World Wide Web, decentralization has become a fact of life in the United States and other highly technological societies.

Decentralization through technology is not, however, as recent a phenomenon as that 1984 *Times* article might suggest. In various forms, it is at least as old as the American Industrial Revolution itself—this despite the common association of assembly lines and mass production with centralization. The Jeffersonian ideal of decentralized production through small rural manufacture, as a means of preserving agrarian values while encouraging domestic industries, is an early example of this orientation.[2] Indeed, such an ideal was common to the early stages of the English as well as the American Industrial Revolution and in both countries often coexisted with the later centralized stages. Significantly, as the business historian Alfred Chandler has repeatedly demonstrated, many of the most successful of the large American corporations that emerged in the late nineteenth and early twentieth centuries—not least, General Motors under Alfred Sloan—combined centralized policy- and decision making in one headquarters unit with decentralized divisions

1

for the financing, manufacturing, and marketing of their various products.[3] In turn arose the branch assembly and production plants common to those corporations. This was the "visible hand" of corporate management revolutionizing American business and industry.[4]

Decentralization as such was nevertheless limited in scope. Not only did policies and decisions continue to be made in a central headquarters building—thanks in part to the absence of information-processing equipment and techniques—but the branch plants themselves were often quite large in size and quite centralized administratively. Moreover, the ideal for most of the major industries was, despite those branch plants, putting entirely under one roof all the processes needed to transform raw materials into finished products. This aim reflected a common strategy of vertical integration, of seeking to control most if not all the stages of manufacturing and marketing of products (as well as, of course, the more traditional strategy of horizontal integration, of seeking an ever larger market share of products and thus reducing competition).[5]

Nowhere were this ideal and this strategy realized more fully—and more literally—than in the Ford Motor Company: first in the Highland Park and then especially in the River Rouge complexes created by Henry Ford (1863–1947) and his associates in the 1910s and 1920s. Both became symbols of America's industrial might and technological prowess in the first half of the twentieth century.[6] As a self-described "experienced observer of industrial undertakings," journalist John Van Deventer, wrote in 1922 about the growing Rouge plant, "Each unit [is] . . . a carefully designed gear which meshes with other gears and operates in synchronism with them, the whole forming one huge, perfectly timed, smoothly operating industrial machine of almost unbelievable efficiency."[7] In the Rouge plant, raw materials such as coal, iron, limestone, timber, and silica—most of them derived from Ford-owned mines, quarries, plantations, and forests—were funneled by Ford-owned ships and trains into facilities—including a huge steel mill and the world's largest foundry—from which emerged finished automobiles. The result was one unceasing, moving process of gigantic dimensions. This was a fully centralized manufacturing and assembly process, as opposed to the only partially decentralized administrative process in Ford Motor Company and General Motors alike. (To be sure, however, even when the Rouge plant was at its peak in the 1930s, the company still relied on some 6,000 independent businesses for parts and materials.)[8]

Both Ford plants embodied the mechanical genius and administrative talents of one man: Henry Ford himself, folk hero to millions of Americans throughout most of five decades. No American, in fact, contributed more than Ford to the development of giant factories and assembly lines, with all that they imply about the specialization, degradation, and, yes, centralization of industrial work in modern technological societies. No American, for that matter, was more fervent about large-scale mass production as an instrument of social progress—for workers as well as for managers and owners. Few American businessmen, moreover, ever exercised firmer control over their enterprises than Ford did over his, and fewer still left a deeper imprint— positive and negative alike—on their enterprises than he did on the Ford Motor Company.

As Ford's biographers have amply detailed, he was a complex man whose cultural and social values frequently conflicted with and even undermined his business practices. The business historian David L. Lewis confessed in 1975, "I probably know more about Ford's life and work than any other writer. But I cannot say that I have completely sorted him out, nor am I sure that I shall fully understand him."[9] The farm boy whose mechanical skills led him into the manufacture of the very vehicles that threatened the agrarian way of life he cherished (despite his own aversion to farm work) never resolved his mixed feelings about modernity: above all, the congestion, heterogeneity, rootlessness, impersonality, inequality, and materialism of twentieth-century America's industrial cities.[10] "The modern city has done its work and a change is coming," Ford told the journalist Drew Pearson in a 1924 interview. "The city has taught us much, but the overhead expense of living in such places is becoming unbearable. . . . The cities are getting top-heavy and are about doomed."[11]

Ford did not, of course, ever completely renounce either large cities or the large industries that helped bring them about. Instead, he devised various means of coping with these alleged ills of contemporary life, means that went beyond his characteristic endorsement of the virtues of rural existence—its rootedness, wholesomeness, cleanliness, and so on. His strategies ranged from (1) periodic retreats to the countryside (annually from 1918 to 1924 with inventor Thomas Edison, tire magnate Harvey Firestone, and naturalist John Burroughs, traveling in the comfort of custom-made touring cars and surrounded by servants)[12] to (2) the lifelong embrace of farmers (particularly those who had purchased Ford cars and tractors)[13] to (3) revivals of old-fashioned harvesting, fiddling, and dancing[14] to (4) the collection of innumerable agricultural as well as industrial artifacts at his Dearborn museums beginning in the 1920s and, not least, to (5) the establishment of nineteen "village industries" in southern Michigan between 1918 and 1944 (see Appendix).

This book is the first systematic study of the Ford village industries. I initially came upon them in 1980, when David Lewis led an illuminating tour of most of those sites. The seeming incongruity between the small plants and the gigantic Rouge complex I had visited a bit earlier intrigued me then and intrigues me still. That the same man who embraced the one simultaneously embraced the other made no sense at first glance, and, like Lewis, I cannot say that Henry Ford makes complete sense to me now. But as I delved into the village industries' rich and largely neglected history, I became ever more convinced of both their historical and their contemporary significance.[15]

At the same time, I became ever more convinced that a purely technological explanation does not account for Henry Ford's prolonged commitment to, if not obsession with, the village industries. Here as throughout history, "technological determinism"—the notion that technology shapes any society and culture—is at best one-sided, at worst outright wrong. If, on the one hand, the technology that spurred decentralization in Ford's day was certainly critical to the village industries' establishment, on the other hand, their establishment was due to a variety of factors—such as Ford's aversion to cities—that predated the technology itself. Whatever Ford's motivations, the village industries were as much a vehicle (no pun intended) for his expression of lifelong values about the way life should be as they were an endorsement of decentralized technology.[16]

Yet Ford's own values and visions must always be placed in the broader national context between the late 1910s and the early 1940s; otherwise, one risks reducing the village industries and much else of Henry Ford's life, career, and outlook to that unique bundle of incongruities and outright contradictions that never go beyond the man himself. In this regard, it is important to note that "The Machine Age" was a term repeatedly applied to this period by public officials, corporate executives, journalists, popular writers, advertisers, engineers, inventors, scientists, artists, and, not least, historians. In two companion volumes edited by the distinguished historian Charles A. Beard—*Whither Mankind? A Panorama of Modern Civilization* (1928) and *Toward Civilization* (1930)—he and other prominent figures from the United States and elsewhere explored the dimensions of "The Machine Age" and came up with fundamentally optimistic assessments. Beard concluded in the first work:

Science and the machine have changed the face of the earth, the ways of men and women on it, and our knowledge of nature and mankind. They break down barriers before us and thrust us out into infinity. . . . Old rules of politics and law, religion and sex, art and letters—the whole domain of culture—must yield or break before the inexorable pressure of science and the machine. . . . [Yet] by understanding more clearly the processes of science and the machine mankind may subject the scattered and perplexing things of this world to a more ordered domain of the spirit. . . . [O]ur authors . . . are not oblivious to the evils of the modern order, but they do not concede that any other system, could it be freely chosen in place of machine civilization, would confer more dignity upon human nature, make life on the whole richer in satisfactions, widen the opportunity for exercising our noblest faculties, or give a sublimer meaning to the universe in which we labor.[17]

Similar sentiments were expressed by many other Americans and Europeans in these years.[18] In this, then, as in so much else, Ford was neither thinking nor operating in a cultural or intellectual vacuum.

As someone devoid of any personal or familial ties to Ford and his family or to the Ford Motor Company or to the village industries or to the state of Michigan, I have come to this project without conscious biases one way or the other. I have tried to maintain my professional detachment throughout the book's research and writing. I find much to praise in the village industries but also much to criticize. Early on, however, it became clear to me that it would likely be impossible to satisfy either those who still worship Henry Ford or those who still despise him—and the numbers in both camps surprised me. So I expect dissent from my mixed evaluation of him and his decentralization scheme. If Ford is not quite so controversial a figure as he was during his life, he remains highly controversial nonetheless. Reflecting on his achievement in a 1998 *Time* magazine special issue, *100 Builders and Titans of the Twentieth Century*, Lee Iacocca, former president of Ford Motor Company and later chairman of Chrysler Corporation, likens Ford to a "virtual dictator" whose power and methods would be simply unacceptable today, yet he praises Ford for innovations that (allegedly) created America's middle class.[19]

Let me state that I bring to this work a similarly detached view of decentralized technology—and society—in the past and the present alike. I believe that Ford had a very interesting and not impractical vision, but by no means do I embrace it as a panacea.

CHAPTER 1

Henry Ford's Village Industries

Origins, Contexts, Rationales

NOT FAR FROM THE SUPERHIGHWAYS, SKYSCRAPERS, AND huge auto plants of the greater Detroit area are the remnants of Henry Ford's surprisingly little-known but still significant experiments in decentralized technology. The "village industries," as Ford himself called them, were designed as small-scale, widely dispersed, frequently pastoral alternatives to the huge urban industrial systems characteristic of modern technological societies—the very systems Ford had helped to devise. They constituted a degree of decentralization considerably greater than that found in other large corporations of the day. "Everybody talks about industrial decentralization, the same as they do about the weather." So wrote Arthur Van Vlissingen in a 1938 issue of *Factory Management and Maintenance*, of which he was editor. "But there the analogy ends. Because somebody most decidedly is doing something about it. Several somebodies. Notably Ford Motor Company."[1] The village industries Van Vlissingen went on to describe made different parts for Ford cars and trucks and were an integral part of the Ford Motor Company. So intriguing was Van Vlissingen's analysis that no less a popular organ than the *Reader's Digest* reprinted it (condensed, of course).[2]

Set in communities along the often picturesque Rouge (seven sites), Raisin (five), Huron (four), Saline (two), and Clinton (one) Rivers in southeastern Michigan—none of them more than sixty miles from Ford world headquarters in Dearborn—these factories coupled rural settings and "traditional" values with the latest tools, machines, and assembly-line processes in a variety of interesting combinations. As such, they constituted twentieth-century versions of the "machine in the garden," to use Leo Marx's now classic phrase.[3] They were the successors to Lowell, Lawrence, Waltham, and other nineteenth-century pioneering industrial communities established in pastoral locales. Less directly, they were the successors as well to the hundreds of small colonial settlements built on rivers, each community with its saw, grist, paper, fulling, or other type of mill in the center.[4] As William Simonds, a Ford publicist, declared in 1927, "Industrialism does not necessarily mean hideous factories of dirty brick, belching smoke stacks and grimy workmen crowded into ramshackle hovels"; instead, "the little Ford plants are placed in leafy bowers and surrounded with flowering shrubs, green bushes and trees. The spots you would select for a picnic Henry Ford has picked for factory sites."[5] Addressing a national radio audience on the Ford Sunday Evening Hour in 1935, another Ford publicist, W. J. Cameron, observed that "some who felt as Ruskin and Wordsworth did about the invasion of the countryside by railroads, have found to their pleasant surprise that these country industries are really a native note in the landscape."[6] True, one would expect positive comments like these from Ford's publicists; but one would not necessarily expect the explicit refutation of the machine allegedly ruining the garden.

That all the village industries were established in locales long familiar to Ford was hardly an accident. As a child he had gone to one future site (Nankin Mills) to grind grain with his father; as a newlywed he had spent his honeymoon at another (Northville); and as an aspiring auto manufacturer he had sought funding for his fledgling company in a third (Plymouth). Moreover, he had been born and raised in then rural Dearborn and lived his entire life there. As a schoolboy he had made his first moving device, a small waterwheel with a dam and a mill that he constructed in a ditch near his schoolyard—to the delight of his friends. In 1909, as the Model T was becoming successful, Ford had bought property on both sides of the Rouge near his boyhood home. A year later he had built his first hydroelectric system. Five years after that, he at once built his permanent home on this site and enlarged that system, assisted in that enterprise by Thomas Edison. Some, in fact, see his estate, Fair Lane, now a National Historic Landmark, as "a partial prototype for the village industries that followed."[7] Although Ford's first factory, the Mack Avenue plant in Detroit (1903), was both small enough in size and workforce and flexible enough in management style to resemble the later village industries, its urban setting bore no relation to the latter enterprises or, for that matter, to Ford's own background.

Far from being simple retreats from modernity, however, the village industries were sophisticated *alternative* forms of emerging technological society, intended as models for others to emulate. This is their principal significance. As editor Van Vlissingen put it, decentralization "is not setting up branch assembly plants to save by hauling solidly packed carloads of parts

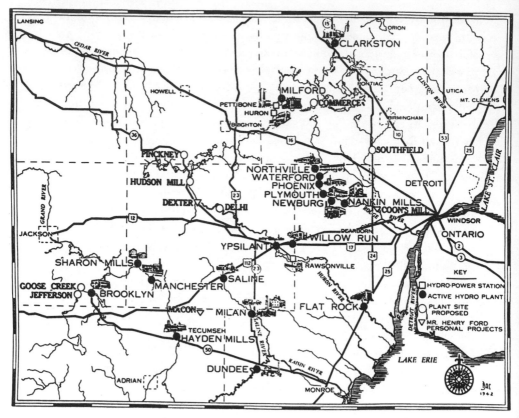

"Locations of Ford Village Industries" as of 1942, with names of existing plants between Detroit and Jackson. Cherry Hill, the last to open (in 1944), is not shown.

instead of less compact finished automobiles. Nor is it relocating plants from North to South or from city to country to tap a lower wage market." Rather, he explained, "What Ford means by decentralization is taking out of a main plant—which [by 1938] is almost invariably the huge Rouge plant—some units of output and having them thereafter made in small plants out in the country."[8]

The Ford Motor Company had, in fact, established its first combined dealership/distribution/service agency outside of Michigan in Kansas City, Missouri, in 1905—just two years after its founding—and opened its first branch assembly plant outside of Michigan in that same city in 1912. But this initial agency and initial branch plant, like their many company successors, were located in cities, not small towns, and were set up primarily to improve customer service and to reduce shipping costs. The same conditions and motivations eventually characterized the entire American automobile industry. The less quantitative, more social and cultural considerations that prompted the creation of the village industries generally did not apply to the company agencies or to the branch plants.[9]

Moreover, far from being the frivolous indulgences of one extremely rich but rather eccentric man, the village industries were serious efforts by thousands of his admirers as well to change the course of American history: to stem the tide of increasing urban concentration and industrial centralization.[10] As Ford predicted in a 1924 interview with the Progressive journalist Paul Kellogg, "Fifty years from now there will be a great many more small cities, rather than a few bigger ones. Instead of centralizing in one city there'll be ten cities." The village industries were only the logical extension of smaller cities. "Put up a nice dam and a factory," Ford told Kellogg, "and the first thing you know, everything and everybody will be better."[11]

In their own day, the village industries were hardly obscure. Both the Ford Motor Company and Ford's personal public relations staff publicized them extensively throughout the United States. Press releases, newspaper and magazine articles, radio talks, and films brought these experiments to the attention of millions of Americans.[12] And such professional partisans as Simonds and Cameron naturally made certain that all this publicity was ever more glowing in tone and content alike. At the very time (1924) that the Ford Motor Company was billing itself in a general publication as "one of the largest industrial institutions in the world, if . . . not actually the largest," its monthly *Ford News* (which Simonds edited) was beginning to run short articles about the initial village industries. "Small Ford Plants on River Rouge Become Efficient Production Units" read a typical headline. Each proposed new plant would be highlighted in a different issue, with other stories to follow as each one finally opened and, presumably, prospered. There was, of course, no seeming contradiction between these news items and those about the Highland Park and especially the growing River Rouge complexes. The Detroit newspapers themselves carried repeated stories about both developments and do not appear to have seen any conflict, or irony, in so doing.[13] Quite the opposite: these "Little Industries in the Country," as *Ford News* often called them, were one reason why that general publication could conclude in 1924: "The Ford organization is such an amazing thing that even the bald truth about it is apt to seem overcolored and exaggerated."[14]

Like so much else in the Ford Motor Company's early years, these experiments were invariably described as the reflections of Henry Ford's unique genius, as deriving from no one else's inspiration.[15] They were logical extensions of the "heroic theory of invention," which embraced Ford as much as it embraced any other American inventor, and more than most others.[16] According to Cameron, who was often Ford's chief spokesman, "The idea originally came to Mr. Ford in his frequent drives through the country, as he passed the places where the early settlers established their little mills run by water. He has a very high respect for the ability of those settlers to pick the right spot."[17] Ernest Liebold, Ford's longtime personal secretary, recalled that such drives repeatedly prompted Ford to dispatch him and a few others to seek options on the most appealing sites, usually with success (though by no means were village industries ultimately erected in every such location).[18]

Others, however, have suggested external influences on Ford, ranging from his dear friend Edison, who shared Ford's keen interest in water power, to the obscure visionary Edgar Chambless, whose *Roadtown* (1910) foresaw skyscrapers laid on their sides rather than extending vertically and spanning the entire American countryside.[19] (One can safely ignore the otherwise related and important writings of the Russian anarchist Peter Kropotkin as a likely source for Ford's scheme.)[20] Still others seeking external influences have pointed to England's "cottage industries," which flourished long before its Industrial Revolution began in the mid-eighteenth century. The cottage industries combined small-scale textile production in rural homes with traditional farming and in various ways anticipated the country's industrialization. Under the "putting-out system," these pioneering industrial workers processed materials provided to them by an entrepreneur. The textiles were usually exported, not sold locally, and these enterprises often became regional in scope. The workers gradually submitted to a degree of regimented labor that anticipated the harsher discipline of later factories and production lines. Yet most never became full-time industrial workers, instead remaining part-time farmers. The parallels with the village industries are striking, but the differences—for example, the cottage industries' lack of integration with larger-scale businesses remotely akin to the Ford Motor Company—outweigh the similarities. Moreover, there is no conclusive evidence that the cottage industries brought about the English Industrial Revolution, whereas the village industries were avowed responses by Ford to the alleged excesses of America's Industrial Revolution.[21] In any case, as Ford's admirers conceded, he had, characteristically, less a formal set of ideas about decentralized technology—and society—than a bundle of provocative notions that he left to others to sort out and refine.[22] As Charles Voorhess, a key Ford Motor

Company engineer, recalled, "I never thought he had a definite plan in regards to the village industries. He just went on and on. He saw how one
developed, and if it suited him, he developed another one."[23]

It is probably not a coincidence that Ford claimed credit for developing
the branch assembly plants which, following the first one in Kansas City in
1912, soon spread around the nation and, in due course, around the globe.
As James Rubenstein contends, however, the "principal credit for creating
and implementing the branch assembly plant concept [actually] goes to two
other Ford officials less well-known today, James Couzens and Norval Hawkins." Moreover, Rubenstein observes, once Couzens and Hawkins had left
the company because of conflicts with Ford over his growing insistence on
controlling company affairs, the "second generation" of those plants that
Ford *did* largely select reflected his "increasingly irrational behavior."[24] This
allegation does not in itself invalidate the separate enterprise of village industries, but it does reflect the sometimes ad hoc manner in which they, like
those later branch assembly plants, were selected and built. For instance, as
Liebold remembered about part of the construction in the early 1920s of the
Waterford site: "Mr. Ford undertook to look after that work himself. He had
a man working out there under his personal direction." But "there were no
particular drawings made or anything done about it. Every time Mr. Ford
would go out there he would see some change that had to be made. By the
time we got through, the capital investment in that plant was about $450,000.
. . . Not having any cohesive plan to carry out," the workers would "do what
they thought Mr. Ford wanted. The next day Mr. Ford would come out, and
if it wasn't what he'd wanted, he'd make them tear it out."[25]

Nevertheless, the village industries were usually described favorably by
outside observers—some of them, such as journalist Drew Pearson, after
taking up Ford's personal invitation to see for themselves[26]—and not surprisingly, insofar as the sites represented a measure of restored agrarian purity
and security amid the various social and moral impurities and insecurities of
twentieth-century America. Even an anonymous 1938 *Life* magazine article
devoted to the expansion of the Rouge plant concluded with a tribute to
Ford's ongoing experiments in the countryside: "Henry Ford would be less
than the man he is if, walking by the River Rouge, he did not thrill at the
sight of his huge plant growing huger and huger by the day. But the old man's
dearest dream is no longer of piling building on building in metropolitan
congestion. A farm boy who has kept his love of the land, Ford now visions
the 'little factory in a meadow' as the future shape of American industry."[27]

Back in 1924, Kellogg had accurately described these enterprises as social experiments: "A scientist will work for years on what goes on in a test tube. Ford's test tube is a small water shed. This is his laboratory. He is putting millions in it, against the advice of some of his shrewdest executives. He is experimenting on a scale which in some ways eclipses that of research institutions or governments. . . . The experiment is in its beginnings yet. It may fizzle out, a rich man's plaything. But it may be that Ford is working at the sort of spark that may yet explode cities and get people back into the country, an invention as far-reaching in its influence as Ford car and tractor."[28]

There was, however, a more practical reason for the popularity of the village industries, especially after the fall of 1929: they promised well-paying regular jobs to unemployed or underemployed farmers, craftsmen, and other rural folk while allowing them all to live and work in their native or nearby communities. That guaranteed a reduction in the number of workers seeking or already on relief. Although Ford's own once extraordinary popularity had in various sectors begun to wane by 1929, this part of his scheme could hardly be ignored—or criticized. For example, as the official (1982) history of Milford, whose plant opened in 1938, recounts, "The factory had a major monetary effect on Milford Township. It came during the latter years of the depression and provided employment for a number of young men who otherwise might have drifted away from home to find jobs elsewhere. It is a Milford tradition that almost every male graduate of the Milford High School Class of 1938 went to work at the carburetor plant."[29] The same positive sentiments applied to all the other village industries and, for that matter, to the entire state of Michigan—not only during the Great Depression but before and after, as rural Michigan was increasingly depopulated of especially its youth.

To take another example, the town of Dundee, whose plant opened in 1936, held a parade in honor of Ford weeks before the construction ended, and well before the particulars were known as to what would be made there or how many persons would eventually be employed. As a local newspaper reported at the time:

> Led by the high school band, 150 Ford workers will parade here Saturday afternoon at 4 o'clock to show the Dundee community what the Ford project here means in terms of employment. The present payroll for the Ford men is $3300 weekly, this being the total for men working on plant construction here and for the 50 or 60 who are employed in the River Rouge plant. The parade is being arranged by an Exchange Club committee which has undertaken to help in obtaining quit claims which Henry

Ford wants on River Raisin flowage rights. . . . Businessmen of Dundee helped in obtaining options on property which would have been overflowed, and they are aiding to present the quit claim requests to property owners. The parade Saturday will emphasize for the Dundee community the importance of the Ford payrolls to Dundee families. Some 400 persons, the Exchange Club committee says, secure their entire income from Ford employment.[30]

And another local newspaper elaborated: "At the present time 150 Dundee men are employed at the Ford project. This number of men and their families represent a total of over four hundred people, directly dependent on Ford work. The Ford payroll in Dundee amounts to slightly over $3300 per week. The majority of this is being spent right here in Dundee. . . . Given half an opportunity and a few months of steady employment, this payroll will make a difference to every resident of the community. Property values will be back to normal."[31]

In the lofty words of Ford's publicist Cameron in 1935, when the Great Depression still prevailed, "There may be no immediate *business reason* for decentralization" (though he elsewhere provided more than one) "but there may be a *human reason*" (by which he meant jobs for the needy), "and it would seem that our life is such that what is humanly desirable and morally right presently justifies itself as being also economically practical."[32] Cameron thus nicely combined morality and economics, and in a seemingly selfless manner. Yet it should not be overlooked that Ford's own business was suffering and that he and his associates needed to find buyers for their cars, trucks, and tractors as rural and urban Americans alike found it increasingly difficult to afford them.

Causes of declining sales of those vehicles included Ford's widely publicized description of the Depression as a "recovery" from the alleged "bad times" and "real panic" of the late 1920s.[33] Such comments were characteristic of his growing alienation from Americans who had once worshiped him—and had once purchased his products—and, no less important, from his own thousands of employees. The disillusioned included increasing numbers of rural Americans, the core of his admirers, who suffered as much as any other citizens throughout the economic crisis. Despite his retinue of publicists and ghostwriters, Ford's public image as a socially concerned and ever more successful businessman had, by 1935, been severely damaged not only by comments like these (which were well-intentioned anyway when amplified in longer interviews or articles) but also by other developments, not least the layoff of thousands of workers in Michigan and elsewhere and Ford's seeming indifference to their plight.[34] In 1928 the *New York Times* called Ford "an industrial fascist—the Mussolini of Detroit."[35] To be sure, the Depression sharpened class resentment against *all* capitalists, but none had previously enjoyed so high and so positive a profile as Ford's. The village industries projects were an excellent partial remedy for a public image needing immediate, extensive repair.

Those who had criticized Ford for such prior crusades as his *Peace Ship* folly to end World War I and his *Dearborn Independent* anti-Semitic diatribes could hardly condemn him for this seemingly humanitarian yet practical effort.[36] Similarly, those who had faulted Ford for the monotonous, dehumanizing work routines of the Highland Park, Rouge, and conventional branch plants could presumably only praise the varied and fulfilling work practices of the village industries. For that matter, those who had attacked Ford for the high turnover rates, the failure of wages for most employees to keep up with inflation, the repeated shutdowns in those larger facilities, and the consequent inability of employees to earn enough to purchase products of any kind in mass quantities—as Ford's mass production scheme required—could happily anticipate a much more stable and contented workforce at the various village sites, and so a positive contribution toward mass consumption and renewed prosperity.[37] Furthermore, those who had blamed Ford for recruiting, among others, rural workers who found large-scale factory work difficult could merely await the likely more positive attitudes on the part of these new rural workers.

Likewise, those who had condemned Ford for the heavily paternalistic and then ruthlessly dictatorial practices of his notorious Sociological and (successor) Service Departments and spy network could at least suspend judgment on the comparative freedom in both the small plants themselves and their surrounding communities. (The Sociological Department had been established in 1914 to Americanize potential company workers, especially those from central and eastern Europe and simultaneously to weed out those workers whose conduct outside the workplace did not meet Ford's own moral standards. Workers determined to be acceptable were then eligible for higher pay. Eventually deemed too benevolent toward its clients, the Sociological Department was replaced in the 1920s by the Service Department, which, contrary to its name, was set up to keep workers in line, particularly those who wished to organize unions.) And from the other side of the coin, those who had faulted these two departments for failing to control, much less to mold, an increasingly restless, heavily immigrant, often non-English-speaking workforce could hope that the new village efforts would prove more successful and perhaps less expensive.

Finally, those who had given up on Ford as a progressive businessman on the "cutting edge" of management and technology alike could only defer their dismissal as decentralization proceeded, especially once other business-men appeared to be moving, if more slowly, in the same direction. For that matter, those who had given up on American business overall as socially progressive could look to this experiment as a small yet significant step in the ongoing effort to defend capitalism from its critics.[38]

In short, the village industries could help offset the negative image of Ford eventually exemplified in 1930s fiction: John Dos Passos's "Tin Lizzie," a prose-poem sketch in *The Big Money* (1936) depicting Ford as a techno-logical pioneer and later ruthless capitalist who could not accept the social and cultural changes in modern America that he had helped to bring about; Upton Sinclair's *The Flivver King* (1937), a historical novel contrasting Henry Ford's fortunes over four decades with those of a loyal Ford employee and his family and concluding that "Henry remained what he had been born; a supermechanic with the mind of a stubborn peasant"; and Aldous Huxley's *Brave New World* (1932), where God is named Ford, where time is mea-sured as before or after the Model T, where the sign of the T has replaced the symbol of the cross, where all citizens are conceived in test tubes and trained by methods modeled after Ford's automobile assembly lines, and where the most reassuring words are "Ford's in his Flivver, all's right with the world."[39] ("Tin Lizzie" and "Flivver" were popular nicknames for the Model T.) More broadly, the village industries could help offset the negative image of assembly-line exploitation of workers by industrialists such as Ford, ex-emplified in Charlie Chaplin's classic film *Modern Times* (1936), where the literal entrapment of Chaplin's Little Tramp in the machinery itself is a logi-cal extension of the psychological as well as physical and economic enslave-ment endured by ordinary assembly-line workers.[40]

A 1944 *Saturday Evening Post* article by John Bird brought these various factors together in the uplifting story of one Albert Risch and his family of Milan, Michigan:

> Albert Risch looks like a professor of high-school physics. But when the electric alarm clock beside his bed goes off at five A.M., he's a farmer. He jumps into worn blue overalls and hastens into the early dawn to feed his pigs, poultry and cattle. An hour and a quarter later, he comes back into the kitchen carrying a brimming bucket of milk deftly extracted from the

Guernsey, and he finds his blond wife, Jane, and a stair-step arrangement of five blond little Risches waiting for him at a well-loaded breakfast table. . . .

Naturally and inescapably, Farmer Risch is a fuller man when he pushes back from the table at 6:45, exchanges his overalls for shop clothes, pins on his identification badge, hops into his car and drives five miles to town. Here, as Electrician Risch, he punches a time clock at seven A.M. and starts his day's work of maintaining the complex electrical equipment of an ignition-parts factory. At 3:25 P.M. he punches the clock again and heads home to a big dinner and evening chores, accomplished with at least two or three small Risches heeling him and telling him of the wonderful events that took place on the farm that day. In the evening, while Jane reads to the children and listens to the radio, he becomes Student Al Risch and bones up on electronics or dreams up electrical gadgets to make his well-organized farm-and-factory work even easier.

Bird went on to describe Risch's workplace:

The factory, where Al keeps his trained eyes on a control board rampant with dials, and the farm, where he uses an instinctive skill to make crops and livestock grow, are equally significant indicators of a hopeful, reassuring trend in American life. You wouldn't be apt to spot the factory as much if you happened to drive through Milan, Michigan, population 2340. The village is typical of backroads America, with quiet, tree-lined streets, small snug homes, and casual motor and foot traffic on the few blocks of Main Street. At the edge of town, where the meandering Saline River flows, is a place that strikes you as a village park of some kind, with a long low building in the foreground and an old-fashioned gristmill in the back under towering trees. However, the low building is the Ford Motor Company's Milan ignition-parts plant, and the old mill, which a century ago was grinding farmers' grain, now houses spotlessly modern soybean-oil-extraction machinery.

Bird's conclusion about his subject's life was inevitably inspiring: "Al Risch's life, and that of his family, is a completely full and contented one, for, at thirty-six, he has achieved his long ambition to follow the advice of his employer, Henry Ford—to have 'one foot in industry and another in the land.' It wasn't an easy goal to achieve, but he enthusiastically declares the results, in the form of a good job, a pleasant home and 100 productive acres, are well worth the struggle."[41]

Who would not be impressed?

CHAPTER 2

Decentralized Technology in the Village Industries

Scale, Scope, System, Vision

M ODERN TECHNOLOGY IS WHAT MADE THE VILLAGE IN-
dustries possible and—today—makes them more than antiquarian
specimens. As the experiments faded from public consciousness after Ford's
death in 1947 and as most were sold by the Ford Motor Company in the
following years, this point was soon forgotten along with the entire enterprise. Yet the concept of avowedly decentralized production that lay behind
these nineteen communities presumed certain transportation, communica-
tion, assembly, and production advances without which the experiments
would not have been practical. To be sure, some of the advances, such as
efficient generators, trucks, telephones, and radios, were already widely
available. (In fact, Ford established a radio hookup between the first village
industry, Northville, and his Dearborn tractor plant, only to have the Federal
Communications Commission close it down because of fierce competition
for wavelength space.)[1] But other advances, primarily smaller-scale tools and
machines within the plants themselves, were new. So, too, were sophisticated
assembly lines on a par with those at Highland Park and the Rouge. A Ford
Motor Company publication described a typical operation: "One of Northville's high points is the conveyor system that moves throughout the plant.
Stocked by hand with rough valve castings as they arrive in 400-pound capacity bins from the Rouge, the conveyors feed back and forth past grinding and
polishing machines. Mechanical hands tip the valves from the conveyors into
loading chutes. From the chutes the castings drop into place in the machines,
the operation is performed, and then they are ejected onto another conveyor
for transmission to another machining process."[2]

Roscoe Smith, appointed the first superintendent of all the village industries in 1937, deemed Ypsilanti the foremost of all the small plants just "because it had been tooled properly in the beginning." Its equipment included an "electronic tornado" carbon arc welder and a soldering machine, both specifically designed by Ford engineers to fit the facility. Smith deemed Ypsilanti—which, let me add, he himself managed prior to his 1937 promotion—"way, way ahead of all other electrical manufacturing organizations in the country."[3]

More generally, as Burnham Finney, then an editor of *The Iron Age*, noted in 1933, "The most modern machine tools are employed in the small plants, conveyors are installed wherever practicable, and every square foot of floor space is utilized in the best Ford manner."[4] Or as Charles Voorhess, the key Ford Motor Company engineer, recalled Ford's saying during visits to potential sites, "A machine that weighs a ton is [improperly and wastefully] used to make a part that weighs a few ounces." Hence the need, in Voorhess's own words, for smaller "machines [that] are built for [the] specific jobs for which they were intended."[5] Indeed, the scale of operations is what makes the village industries significant for our time. Although decentralization in itself need not entail a smaller scale of anything, usually it does, since it disperses what was formerly concentrated in one or a few places. Certainly "decentralization" today is invariably used in this fashion, especially in conjunction with the kind of "appropriate" or "intermediate" technology associated with the late E. F. Schumacher of *Small Is Beautiful* fame.[6]

Scale alone, though, is not the whole story. Voorhess observed that Ford had an additional reason for limiting the sites to those within easy driving distance of Dearborn and Detroit: the inadequate number and inferior quality of roads in the general area. The number of sites expanded as the number of roads increased and as their quality improved.[7] No less important was the integration of the nineteen plants with one another—some supplied others with either raw materials or parts to make their particular product—and, perhaps more surprising, with those huge Highland Park and River Rouge complexes. As with Northville's valve castings and completed valves, the raw materials brought to the village industries each morning (sometimes from conventional branch plants elsewhere) and the finished products taken away each evening to one of those two central facilities (or to a branch plant) naturally had to be small and light enough to be transported efficiently both ways. Hence the choice of such items as gauges, horns, valves, regulators, switches, and taps for manufacture and assembly. Moreover, these products had to meet Ford Motor Company standards of and controls over time, cost, and quality.

According to Roscoe Smith, "We got . . . our [monthly] production schedules from the Rouge. They would go to the various plants directly from the
Rouge. I'd get a copy of them all at the same time." As he recalled years later,
"The raw stocks necessities was [*sic*] all worked out by the Scheduling Department. It was broken down. You had your bill of material and all. . . . As
far as the accounting and production activities and so on, that was all handled
at the Rouge." Smith in turn "sent in a regular daily report of production"
and regularly visited each of the plants and each of their managers. To this
extent, the village industries were part of a system of more than local dimensions; they were part of Ford's own widely acclaimed system of producing
vehicles.[8]

In fact, the Rouge complex itself had begun as a partial effort in decentralization, a move away from Ford's original Detroit plants to a then remote
suburb of the big city.[9] Lindy Biggs contends that Ford chose Dearborn for
his grandest plant in part because he thought it "a place where he could
exercise more influence, politically and culturally, than he had in Highland
Park and perhaps better control the 'ills' of industrial urbanism." Although
the Highland Park plant had begun in an "undeveloped area" just beyond
Detroit's city limits, the enclave of Highland Park itself soon became "a dense
and thriving urban neighborhood," so that eventually the plant was no longer
physically separate from its immediate surroundings. By contrast, William B.
Mayo, one of Ford Motor Company's leading engineers, in his 1916 report,
envisioned the Rouge plant as a "new industrial village."[10] Where the Highland Park complex consisted of multistory buildings adjoining one another in
accordance with the foremost industrial engineering of the early twentieth
century, the Rouge complex consisted of single-story buildings separate from
one another in accordance with later industrial engineering expertise. In this
respect the physical layout of the Rouge was itself avowedly decentralized.[11]
As with the village industries, however, so with the Rouge, Ford had additional motives: more modern and more efficient working conditions for all in
what were each pioneering centralized assembly line operations; more at-
tractive living conditions near (but not next to) the plants for those skilled
workers and managers who, unlike the majority of employees, could afford
them; escape from Detroit's higher property taxes; and accommodation to
Detroit's population growth and expanding boundaries, themselves nonetheless spurred by the auto industry's own growth and dominance within the
city.[12]

Thomas Ticknor has pointed out that Detroit over the first four decades
of the twentieth century came to resemble the kind of depraved city that

Ford wanted to escape: "both a city of homes and a city of men's rooming houses," for its population explosion—a sixfold increase between 1900 and 1940, the greatest of any American metropolis of the period save Los Angeles—produced a population imbalance heavily in favor of single or (temporarily) separated men. "In many ways Detroit was like an army town—there was a high residual unattached male population with money to spend in search of excitement in local saloons, pool rooms, gambling clubs, betting parlors, burlesque theaters, and houses of prostitution" (more of the last than in any other contemporary American city). Such men had few if any community ties and were clearly not the sort of workers Ford wanted.[13]

General Motors and Chrysler, the other major automakers, also moved facilities and personnel beyond the city's limits once Ford paved the way. Yet the Big Three, who were frequently at odds over public policy as well as in fierce competition, still expected to retain collective political and economic power despite their increasing abandonment of Detroit. Their decreasing urban commitment proved costly, however, when in 1929 they promoted a bond issue to build a new subway system. That automakers would support a nonautomotive transportation scheme may seem puzzling, but their reasons were compelling: continued concern for reviving the declining original downtown commercial area; greater access to shops and offices in newer downtown districts, including the new General Motors headquarters; and, not least, easier access especially for unskilled and semiskilled autoworkers to their more distant plants. As Donald Davis notes, "Employers could expect neither punctuality nor alertness from factory hands dependent upon street cars, for the [street] railway system had failed to keep abreast of Detroit's outward sprawl. Yet only twenty-five percent of industrial workers commuted by automobile in 1929 and the rest needed improved public transportation."[14]

The proposed subway would connect the Rouge plant, where increasing numbers of Ford's employees now worked (fewer were still working at Highland Park), to nearly all of Detroit's streetcar lines. Yet despite the backing of Detroit's economic and political elite, the referendum drew merely 30 percent of the city's registered voters and was overwhelmingly defeated, primarily by small property owners fearing increased property taxes and further auto industry pay reductions and job layoffs. Ironically, Davis concludes, "the chief limits on the [auto] industry's power seem to have been largely self-generated."[15]

The referendum's defeat may have spurred discussion at Ford Motor

Company and elsewhere about the value of the village industries, which obviously required no subway system, as a practical means of advancing decentralization and of improving workers' attitudes and performance. But there is no evidence to confirm such discussion. What the defeat surely did, as Davis puts it, was to reduce the automakers' overall "obligations to Detroit, thereby freeing them to pursue more energetically their own self-interest"— in schemes such as Henry Ford's.[16]

Self-interest no doubt prompted Ford and his public relations staff to speculate frequently about establishing a series of village industries elsewhere in America. In 1938 the *Detroit News*, for example, carried a brief item about a proposed small plant in South Sudbury, Massachusetts (site of the historic Wayside Inn, which Ford had purchased in 1923 and had remodeled into colonial mills and a blacksmith shop) and quoted Ford as saying that "the industrial future of New England looked bright 'provided the manufacturers decentralize and make use of water power for smaller plants.'"[17] When interviewed in 1933 by the nation's most prestigious newspaper, the *New York Times*, Ford unhesitatingly outlined his vision in national terms: "I think we are through with the gathering of tens of thousands of families into greater industrial centers," he declared in introducing his scheme.[18]

Ford had been quoted by another publication in 1921: "Our plan is not to be confined to one portion of the United States, but will extend throughout the country," and in a 1921 interview he had declared that the plan would be extended to England and other countries.[19] Finney, now an editor of *American Machinist*, wrote in 1937 of Ford's plans for fifty village industries within the Detroit/Dearborn area alone.[20] At least ten Michigan sites beyond the nineteen discussed here were ultimately purchased, but only one of them, Macon, was ever developed, and it never opened because of Ford's declining health and power at the time of its completion in 1944.[21]

"Water power," Ford had proclaimed in 1924, "is the cheapest, the most efficient, and the least wasteful of all types of power," and the number of potential sites nationwide was therefore enormous.[22] (That Ford had two years earlier endured a coalminers' strike that forced him to close his major plants for five days was conveniently ignored here.) A preliminary list developed in 1938 by Ford's personal secretary, Ernest Liebold, numbered 212 possible locations.[23] As Harvey Firestone recalled about his periodic retreats with Ford, Edison, and Burroughs, "Mr. Edison and he [Ford] would dam every suitable stream in the country just to get the power. I doubt if, on our trips, we ever passed an abandoned mill without Mr. Edison and Mr. Ford getting out to measure the force of the stream, inspect the old wheel and talk about ways and means of putting the waste power to work."[24]

Once the village industries scheme became known to ordinary Americans, each time Ford visited a rural site in his extensive travels across America, local newspapers speculated about such possibilities. For example, when, in 1936, Henry and Edsel Ford and other company officials visited Milford, Michigan, which did become home to a village industry two years later, the town paper reported: "No announcement has yet been made as to what the Company proposes to do with its Milford holdings, but it is intimated that some announcement may be forthcoming in the near future. Unconfirmed reports are that there will be a factory for the manufacture of some part of the Ford automobile located here and that the visit . . . was for the purpose of selecting a site."[25]

Similarly, when officials of Dundee learned in 1931 that Ford had secretly acquired the local mill and dam (just condemned as a fire menace by the state fire marshal), speculation ran rampant in the local press:

> For several years Dundee has been endeavoring to get Henry Ford interested in the old mill and dam on the River Raisin near the M–50 bridge. Finally Mr. Ford did buy the property, unbeknown to Dundee, but the village inadvertently crossed Mr. Ford at the very point where they hoped to please him. The village council instituted a campaign last summer to clean up the unsightly spots along the river near the M-50 bridge. . . . But the old grist mill remained an eyesore and the village council was unable to get anything done. The state fire marshall was appealed to and in the course of time wrote a letter to the owner ordering him to remove the old grist mill. At least the marshall thought he was writing to the owner. . . . When Mr. Voorhess got the notice he promptly sent it back with the information that he had sold the property to Mr. Ford. The fire marshal then forwarded the notice to the Ford Motor Company in Detroit. Dundee first learned of the new ownership when a copy of the fire marshal's letter came to the chief of the village's fire department. Two weeks ago two men came into the village and opened the flood gates of the dam. That caused a lot of talk because no one knew them and they wouldn't talk to anyone. A few days later they came back and closed the gates. That started more talk. Gradually the rumor got around that Mr. Ford had bought the property but that rumor had been around so many times no one paid much attention to it. The letter from the fire marshall informed the chief of the fire department that Mr. Ford was really the owner. Now no one knows what will happen next. Mr. Ford has not been heard from.[26]

Because the plant did not finally open until 1936, there was ample time and opportunity for repeated speculation.

In these two cases as in many others, Ford apparently enjoyed keeping secrets about his intentions and, in effect, manipulating the hopes of local residents, none of whom could afford to be so bold as to demand more information from him and his associates lest he lose interest in their site.

As early as 1921, the *Elyria (Ohio) Telegram* observed, "For the past few years there have been more communities in the country which were supposed to be under the watchful and guardian eye of Henry Ford to upbuild and advance their interests than could comfortably be counted over on both hands several times."[27] Even though no real village industries were ever established outside of southeastern Michigan (not even in Sudbury), the level of interest aroused by such speculation invariably exceeded that aroused for a possible conventional branch plant.[28] In turn, the price of available land rose quickly, often to levels that Ford, despite his enormous wealth, refused to pay.

Going further, a number of persons wrote Ford about possible sites, just as others wrote him about countless other issues of the day. Usually the owner of the land initiated the correspondence, but even nonowners who lived near the site would frequently do so, presumably hoping to benefit their communities—if not themselves—if Ford became interested. Sometimes these were pristine locations adjacent to water power, but often they were existing mills (grist, saw, and cider) with machinery, generators, and turbines already in operation, albeit not necessarily in good condition. Most of the mills offered for Ford's consideration included the owners' homes. As the *New York Times* reported in 1922 about a typical inquiry from New York state, Ford responded that he needed details concerning the proposed site: the ownership; the speed, width, and depth of the stream; the proximity to railroads, highways, towns, and cities; and, not least, the purchase cost.[29]

All inquiries and proposals, as far as I can determine, received prompt and courteous responses from someone in Ford's office. Not surprisingly, however, those that came from persons in Michigan, especially in areas of Michigan where or near where village industries had been or were being developed, received somewhat greater attention. Yet there is no evidence that Ford jumped at the prospect of expanding his existing village industry sites simply because additional land and water—and mills and equipment—were available. The common response, it appears, was a polite decline of interest.[30] To the numerous farmers who wrote Ford about integrating their farms with his scheme and employing both themselves and their (often seasonal) help at existing or new small plants (some even asked for loans to start their own manufacturing enterprises), a company secretary replied in a form letter advising the writer to contact his county agent, since the organization did not do business with individual farmers save in extraordinary circumstances (as with village industry sites and factories).[31]

By contrast, in 1923 Ford pressured the Michigan state legislature to pass a bill allowing him, with the consent of the Michigan Public Utilities Commission, to expropriate up to 25 percent of the land next to the dam sites chosen for his factories. Thanks to Ford's enormous political and economic clout, the bill was passed, and he was thereby able to avoid further dealings, at least in Michigan, with either overly zealous or hostile site owners. To be sure, the bill was not restricted to Ford himself but rather applied to any private corporations in similar situations. The rationale for the bill, moreover, was not just the development of more water power sites but also, said the *New York Times*, the "winter employment at city wages of men from the farms."[32]

Ford did set up related industries and hydroelectric plants in Hamilton, Ohio; St. Paul, Minnesota, and Green Island, New York (near Troy), plus lumber camps and woodworking facilities in Michigan's Upper Peninsula (Alberta, Iron Mountain, L'Anse, and Pequaming). But none of these was intended as a genuine part of the village industry "system," and all were too distant from Detroit and Dearborn—and usually too large in size of operation—to be other than conventional branch plants.[33] As Voorhess recalled, Ford thought these sites "were a good source of preserving fuel supply by making good use of water power [and by providing, in some cases, abundant timber] and that they were good sites for manufacturing plants. They had no definite relation to these village industries."[34] What these other sites did reflect was, first, Ford's unceasing concern with ever greater vertical integration; second, his equivalent concern with using larger rivers and other bodies of water—not merely small rivers—as primary power sources; and third, the regional scope of his overall design.[35]

Regionalism was a popular topic between the world wars, and the prospect of a series of regional networks of village industries across rural, underdeveloped America naturally provoked much comment beyond the potentially affected communities. If, as many were then claiming, America was fundamentally a nation of regions, Ford's scheme could intensify regional identities as well as spur regional economic and social growth.[36] In addition, Ford's ill-fated attempt in the early 1920s to lease the Muscle Shoals, Alabama, nitrate plant, dam, and phosphate quarry from the federal government had already publicized him as a proponent of regional technological development—in that case, the Tennessee Valley. Muscle Shoals was a thirty-mile stretch of rapids in the Tennessee River—extremely difficult to navigate, as evidenced by two nineteenth-century canals that had proved inadequate to the task. Yet its potential for generating hydroelectric power—and so profits to either the public or the private sector—was enormous. Starting in 1899, the federal government had received repeated offers to build a hydroelectric power installation on the site, but none of the plans worked out. World War I "provided the trigger for action": the 1916 National Defense Act, passed before American entry into the conflict, authorized "selection of a site to produce nitrates for munitions in wartime and fertilizer in peacetime." The site ultimately selected was Muscle Shoals, and a dam was being built as a first step just when the war ended. Congress then suspended appropriations, and construction temporarily ceased.[37]

Ford's 1921 proposal to the federal government that he take over, finish, and operate Muscle Shoals did not exhaust his vision for the area. Of critical importance was his dream of a series of connecting small communities for the valley—akin to the later village industries and similarly integrating hydroelectric power (particularly in the Tennessee River)—for both agriculture (especially cheap fertilizers) and manufacturing (aluminum, steel, fertilizer, and, not least, car parts) to benefit the region's citizens (as well as, of course, the Ford Motor Company). These small communities would constitute a decentralized "Detroit of the South" and, like the later village industries, retain their autonomy yet be highly integrated with one another. Like them, too, those communities would provide the comforts of modern living in traditional, semirural settings. In case of wartime needs, the facilities could be diverted to nitrate production for explosives, which had been the original Muscle Shoals objective during World War I. Whatever their uses, the completed facilities, Ford proposed, would one day be turned over to either the area's citizens or the federal government for public benefit. "Ford Plans a City 75 Miles in Length," declared the *New York Times* in 1922 about his scheme.[38]

If, Ford predicted, Muscle Shoals "is developed along unselfish lines, it will work so splendidly and so simply that in no time hundreds of other waterpower developments will spring up all over the country." Going further, he declared that "in a sense the destiny of the American people for years to come lies here on the Tennessee Valley."[39] His suggestion that the Muscle Shoals project would be duplicated elsewhere in America naturally intensified interest, just as did similar speculation over the village industries later.

Only the fervent opposition of jealous potential competitors in the fertilizer, chemical, and electric power industries; of Pennsylvania's governor, Gifford Pinchot, and other avowed conservationists, who deemed Ford's scheme environmentally unsound; and of a liberal Nebraska senator, George Norris, who was suspicious of Ford's professed public interest and who favored governmental administration instead, halted these plans for Muscle Shoals, even though they did enjoy the support of many farmers and businessmen.[40] Five miles outside of Muscle Shoals are the ruins of a "Ford City" that never was, a square mile of streets and sidewalks deteriorating and overrun by foliage.[41]

Ironically, many of the foremost advocates of regionalism between the world wars might not have objected to such a Ford City, provided it either maintained existing small communities or established new ones (or did both) that did not become Ford company towns. Opposed though nearly all of the regionalists were to predominantly urban, large-scale, heavily industrialized America, some had visions complementary to Ford's of a more decentralized nation (see chapter 8). Far from insisting that regionalism be restricted to just one or two parts of the United States, most regionalists were, in fact, eager for it to triumph everywhere and might thus have welcomed the prospect of networks of village industries across rural, underdeveloped America. For if these regionalists naturally appreciated and wished to nurture cultural diversity between and among regions, they simultaneously embraced transcendent values based on regionalism's inherent "goodness" and "truth."[42]

Kellogg, among others, saw in the initial village industries the "springs of his [Ford's] offer for Muscle Shoals"—a point Ford repeatedly denied.[43] Once again, however, as Liebold later recalled, Ford had no concrete plans and, in retrospect, may have been better off in the long run without this potentially huge burden on his time and his company's finances. Yet Liebold conceded, "I don't know if Mr. Ford felt that way or not. I could never get much out of him about it."[44] A genuine visionary in many respects, Ford was clearly not in the tradition of visionaries who engage in rigorous philosophical discussion before trying to change the world.

CHAPTER 3

Farm and Factory United

SMALLER-SCALE TOOLS AND MACHINES AND NETWORKS OF communities were not the only important dimensions of Henry Ford's experiment. Equally significant was the prospect of healthier and happier living and working arrangements away from America's crowded, congested cities. Despite his initial predictions that "every man will be a farmer . . . and every man will work in a factory or office,"[1] Ford's eventual dream was to employ exclusively farmers, craftsmen, and other rural folk who could either walk or quickly drive (their Fords) to and from work. On the whole, this aspect of his vision was realized; relatively few urban dwellers, including city-bred workers in older Ford plants, were ever hired for the village industries. Ford usually insisted that all potential employees had to have been residents of their communities for at least six months and, to quell the fears of local businessmen of losing their best workers, that they be currently unemployed as well.[2] These aspects of his vision were also realized in most cases, though there were always exceptions.

All workers in the nineteen sites who lived in rural areas were strongly encouraged to retain or to acquire a plot of land on which to grow crops for personal consumption in their spare time: that is, before and after working hours and during their days off. Those workers who lacked either land or inclination for farming were nevertheless encouraged to set up small vegetable gardens near their homes in order to be more self-sufficient and healthier as well as more agrarian. As Ford was establishing the village industries, he also began promoting "Thrift Gardens" throughout his industrial empire, even among the most urbanized of his employees, who usually had less land available than their rural counterparts. Toward that end a company-sponsored Garden Education Service established four large garden areas in Dearborn that could be used by any Highland Park or Rouge plant employee.[3] For a small fee the company prepared the ground and assigned plots to individual workers. By contrast, many other large American corporations that provided space for employees' gardens did so only after the Great Depression had begun and those workers were desperate to supplement their incomes.[4]

"Rule 1 at all the small plants," journal editor Arthur Van Vlissingen noted, "is that any man may leave at any time to work on the farm, [and] may have his job back—barring shutdowns—when he gets through farming."[5] These full-time factory workers were, then, expected to be also part-time farmers to varying degrees. According to Ford, all were beneficiaries of the very modern technology at work and at home alike that allowed them the leisure to supplement their income. As Ford explained to journalist Drew Pearson in 1924, "It is nonsense to say that because the cities are overcrowded everybody ought to move to the farm. There must be a balance between the two. The farm has its dull season, when the farmer can come into the factory, and the factory has its dull season, when the workman can get out on the land and help produce food. Transportation is the connecting link."[6] In his 1922 book *My Life and Work* (written with—and largely by—his frequent collaborator Samuel Crowther) Ford had added that these arrangements "might take the slack out of work" (Ford hated "slack") and "restore the balance between the artificial and the natural" (i.e., the city and the farm).[7] Or as he put it more boldly in the *Ford News* of April 1937, "No unemployment insurance can be compared to an alliance between a man and a plot of land. With one foot in industry and another foot in the land, human society is firmly balanced against most economic uncertainties. . . . Stocks may fail, but seedtime and harvest do not fail."[8] (Actual farmers, of course, might not be so optimistic.)

The dedication of the cornerstone of the Henry Ford Museum in September 1928, with Ford, not surprisingly, presiding over the ceremony, symbolized his dual commitment to agriculture and industry. Thomas Edison not only inscribed his signature in the fresh cement but also pushed into it the spade of Luther Burbank, the famous American horticulturalist who had died two years earlier.[9]

Ford estimated that contemporary agricultural equipment and techniques had reduced the average farmer's planting and harvesting time to a mere twenty-four days a year, thus easily accommodating regular factory work.[10] "The most inefficient thing in the world," he told Kellogg in 1924, "is the farmer living on the farm. There's no reason a farmer couldn't work eighty acres and spend practically all his time in a factory."[11] As James Flink has noted, "Far from identifying with the Jeffersonian yeoman farmer glorified in populist rhetoric, Ford looked forward to the demise of the family farm."[12] For that matter, he believed, animals could be dispensed with and so liberate farmers from slavery to them. Tractors rather than horses could provide power; cattle and sheep could be raised by ranchers out west. The absence of animals could mean the elimination of fences and of most farm buildings save grain elevators. "We are in the opening years of power-farming," Ford declared in *My Life and Work*, "The motor car wrought a revolution in modern farm life, not because it was a vehicle, but because it had power." Ford's own farm in Dearborn, moreover, did "everything by machinery. . . . We are not farmers," he insisted, "we are industrialists on the farm."[13]

By the early 1920s, according to Robert C. Williams, part-time farming was already a growing trend and the subject of increasing discussion. If, on the one hand, many lamented the declining number of full-time farmers, on the other hand, others believed that it was better for those who could not survive economically as full-time farmers to become part-timers while also working in nonfarming enterprises. Tractors and additional farming machinery allowed some part-time farmers to grow and sell crops without much loss of income and, by combining farming with other jobs, to prosper more than they ever had as full-time farmers. Even though some part-time farmers "ceased any significant production and [their farms] became little more than rural residences," by 1945, part-time farmers were operating roughly one-fourth of American farms.[14]

So Ford's vision was steadily being fulfilled. Reflecting on his own youth, Ford observed:

> This is not theory with me for I was born and raised on a farm and have followed the plow many a weary mile. I have been both a farmer and a manufacturer. So I know what an advantage power and machinery have given to the latter.
>
> Can you imagine anything more wasteful or inefficient than for an intelligent man to be compelled to spend days and days following a slow-moving team without a chance in the world of using his brains or his initiative to speed up that work beyond the leisurely rate at which the horses choose to navigate?
>
> Imagine a modern manufacturing concern producing under such conditions.[15]

Yet here as elsewhere Ford preached the gospel of unceasing hard work—the counterpart to eliminating "slack"—not merely to acquire income and so the opportunity for eventual leisure but as virtually an end in itself, the way to build and maintain good character. Hard work, he repeatedly argued, was actually pleasurable, notwithstanding his own aversion to farmwork.[16] (To be sure, not every village industry employee agreed.)

What Ford did not preach was the gospel of farm cooperatives to give individual farmers more control over the sale of their products, reduced dependence on middlemen, and consequent higher prices and higher profits. "I don't believe in cooperation," Ford declared. "What can cooperation do for farmers? All it amounts to is an attempt to raise the price of farm products."[17] His persistent opposition to unions has its parallel here, for he saw both enterprises as clearly undermining his control of his own workforce and of the overall automobile production process.

Ironically, as a team of outside observers reported in 1945, it was the yearly style changes that the Ford Motor Company was forced to make after 1927 in order to stay competitive that undermined Ford's scheme for seasonal farming time. "In helping the worker," the report noted, Ford "planned that during the eight or nine colder months the products manufactured in these small factories would be overproduced sufficiently to create a surplus stock to last over May–August, the farm work months."[18] At the outset, workers did usually take leave in the summer and early fall, but this policy ended after just a few years. By 1928 there was no more summer leave time; instead, workers were thereafter often on full-time assignments, getting ready for the fall's new models. Any long-term leaves were then involuntary, the result of surplus parts or declining sales or both. Perhaps for this reason, among others, a 1948 Ford Motor Company press release listed only 15 percent of the village industry employees working on farms and only 11 percent more owning their own farms.[19]

Ironically as well, skilled workers at General Motors had faced seasonal unemployment, along with their counterparts at Ford Motor Company, exactly *because* of GM's earlier adoption of annual model changes. If, to be sure, their time involved in gearing up for the next year's vehicles was less than that under Ford's original scheme for his workers—that is, Ford's envisioned May to August—it still meant an annual absence of income. But GM's skilled workers did not turn to farming. Instead, many of them found useful employment in building the new machines that in turn would produce the new year's models, machines usually made in independent job shops where, as Douglas Reynolds describes it, highly trained workers "created the dies used to stamp a thousand fenders a day. They made the jigs and fixtures used to align and hold hundreds of engine blocks." They also "made the cutting tools and set production machinery capable of withstanding thousands of repetitive uses for the processing of parts." Starting in 1931, however, General Motors began "rehabilitating" existing machines rather than contracting for new ones, a change intended to save money as the Great Depression wore on. Thereafter, though some workers became year-round employees because their skills were needed to tend those older machines, overall, skilled General Motors workers—only about 15 percent of the company's workforce between 1925 and 1940—suffered considerable loss of income and, for 20 percent their number, the loss of their homes. Had these employees been encouraged to become part-time farmers, with or without formal company assistance, some might, most ironically, have fulfilled Ford's vision—which was by no means limited to his own workers.[20]

W. J. Rorabaugh mentions an interesting partial parallel in the case of the Springfield Armory in Massachusetts, operated by the federal government. In the early nineteenth century the armory hired skilled craftsmen to do various specific jobs. These "machinists, toolmakers, pattern makers, and shop tenders . . . enjoyed high wages and a ten-hour day, and, since government policy was to maintain a large work force even when military orders were low, the workers often had free time to care for their nearby garden plots."[21] This situation changed over time, thanks to the introduction of larger, more powerful machinery that led to the replacement of those skilled workers by semiskilled workers who had less time and less money to devote to garden plots. But the basic notion of otherwise full-time workers having garden plots anticipated Ford's scheme.

The other side of Ford's scheme, however, was the so-called Industrialized American Barn. His idea was to utilize empty or deteriorating barns (and other rural structures) for the purpose of supplying industry with semiprocessed materials grown on farms and, at the same time, either reduce or eliminate the crop surpluses created in part by Ford's own vehicles and other agricultural machinery and, after 1929, in part by the Depression.[22] Ford had already become prominent for processing the soybean to make plastic parts for his cars.[23] Not surprisingly, perhaps, given his concern for vertical integration, he had a large soybean-processing plant built at the Rouge complex in 1935. Its machinery produced a number of parts for Ford cars. But the Ford Motor Company also made extensive use of corn, cotton, wool, flax, rubber, sugarcane, wood, hogs, and cattle in producing other car parts. Ford told Van Vlissingen in 1936, "Any automobile necessarily contains a great deal of material which originated on the farms. Upholstery and other fabrics of wool, mohair, cotton; leather, glues, linseed and castor oils; solvents, anti-freeze, and shock absorber fluids from grain and from sugar-cane molasses."[24] The emerging field of plastics offered limitless prospects for the use of soybeans and other crops in the manufacture of car parts.

By 1940, Ford would be able to unveil a model handmade car with a plastic trunk. Then seventy-seven years old, Ford picked up an ax and hit the car's trunk lid as hard as he could; rather than crumple, the lid simply rebounded and looked brand new, thanks to its plastic composition. The incident provoked much humor but also a good deal of positive press coverage and temporarily restored Ford's image as a technological innovator. By the next year, Ford would unveil a car with an entirely plastic body. Its mass production would be halted only by the outbreak of World War II and not resumed until General Motors introduced the Chevrolet Corvette in 1953; nevertheless, Ford continued, "We have not in any instance adopted a material simply because it is of farm origin. It must in every case be better than the material it displaces, and almost always it must be cheaper."[25]

Ford wished not only to produce these raw materials on American farms but also to process them as close to their sources as possible. Thus the Ford Motor Company experimented for several years with small solvent-extraction units near the River Rouge plant and, later, at the Tecumseh/Hayden Mills, Milan, and Saline village industries. The latter efforts proved successful and, for Ford, helped justify the rural experiments overall.[26] (Ford employees outside the village industries were likewise also employed in these agricultural enterprises as the need arose.) Simultaneously, these units reinforced the network Ford was assembling between his largest and smallest factories. Together with Ford tractors, Ford grain elevators and flour mills, and Ford agents distributing wheat at cost to Ford employees in those and larger Ford facilities (which also had Ford stores), this constituted a form of vertical integration in itself.

Yet Ford conceded that the original experiments were insufficient to fulfill his complete objectives. In a full-page advertisement carried in many major American newspapers the week of May 30, 1932, he declared that "while this experiment has fully justified itself, . . . it is only a step in the right direction. Excellent as village industries are, they do not really bring industry and agriculture together."[27] One means of doing so was simply to expand the number of village industries, as Ford modestly did. Another was to add to the village industries and to many other rural sites the Industrialized American Barn, which Ford likewise did. A third means was to promote the emerging field of farm chemurgy, or the alliance of chemistry and other sciences with agriculture, as Ford also did.[28]

A model Industrialized American Barn was displayed in the Ford Exhibition Building at the 1934 Century of Progress Exposition in Chicago (Ford had boycotted the first year of the world's fair, 1933). Built originally in 1863, the year Ford was born, by Ford's own father, the barn had originally stood directly across from Ford's birthplace in Dearborn and for seventy years was used to store hay. Ford had it dismantled, transported to Chicago, reconstructed at the fair, and then filled not with hay but with various tools and machines to process the patch of soybeans surrounding the structure itself. Such equipment, Ford claimed, was inexpensive to purchase and easy to assemble. Similar exhibits were installed at other world's fairs and at several state and regional fairs throughout the 1930s.[29]

Just as those workers employed in the village industries would at once supplement their incomes and strengthen their rural roots by farming, so those farmers outside Ford's factories would by this means both supplement *their* incomes and strengthen their *industrial* roots. As Ford observed about the past, "The first farmer was the first tool maker."[30] An anonymous 1945 company paper, "The Song of the Water Wheel," boasted that the Industrialized American Barn "opens an entirely new phase of agro-industrial relations. It provides factories where factories are not now available"—that is, in individual farmers' own backyards—"and makes the farmer an independent agro-industrialist."[31] And Detroit newspaper writer (and Ford favorite) James Sweinhart proclaimed more bluntly in a 1936 Dallas newspaper article, "We are witnessing the beginning of THE AGRINDUSTRIAL AGE!"[32] In actuality, however, though the situation has since changed, few farmers in Ford's day ever engaged in this enterprise.[33]

Ford was also active in the chemurgy crusade. Industrial chemist William J. Hale had coined the term "chemurgy" in 1934, deriving it from the Greek words *chemi*, the art of transforming materials, and *ergon*, work. Ford, Hale, and other chemurgy proponents sought to blur traditional distinctions between agriculture and industry and to establish instead an industrial-agricultural continuum. Agriculture, they hoped, would become the predominant source of industrial chemicals.

In 1935 the National Farm Chemurgic Council was established by Hale and Carl B. Fritsche, a Detroit industrial engineer. They prevailed on Ford to sponsor a "Conference of Agriculture, Industry, and Science" to discuss chemurgy's prospects. Held in Ford's company headquarters at Dearborn, the meeting attracted three hundred participants. Most represented large industrial concerns or were academics with close industrial ties. Ford provided invaluable national publicity and legitimacy, yet neither the council nor chemurgy generally gained the massive public support that its proponents, including Ford, had anticipated. Farmers tended to be interested in more immediate forms of relief, and most processes to transform crops into industrial raw materials proved more costly than alternative means. Political factors also complicated the issue, for the movement's predominantly corporate, Republican leadership continually criticized New Deal programs, especially those taking land out of production or catering to small farmers. "In the midst of the chemical revolution we are chemically disorganized; in the depths of depression we are chemurgically incapacitated," complained Hale.[34] Unable to effect the changes deemed necessary to implement the new agricultural-industrial order, the council contented itself with reporting on chemurgic processes, objecting to government policies, and publicizing the chemurgic idea. Ford restricted his chemurgic enterprises once the United States entered the Second World War. Only in recent years has chemurgy truly expanded, and then largely in areas outside the automobile industry: food processing, livestock feed, and medicine.

Overall, then, Ford's dream of uniting farm and factory was only partly realized.

CHAPTER 4

Buildings and Workforce

T HE VILLAGE INDUSTRIES VARIED CONSIDERABLY, NOT JUST
in the automobile part manufactured or assembled on the premises
but also in building design and size of workforce. Some—like the first two,
Northville (which began operations in 1920) and Nankin Mills (1921)—were
reconstructed nineteenth-century mills, usually gristmills abandoned after
railroads leading to large milling centers made them obsolete and unprofitable. These reflected Ford's preference for preserving or restoring original
early American architecture whenever possible.[1] Others, however—like the
next two, Phoenix (1922) and Plymouth (1923)—had completely new, modern buildings, sometimes on the site if not the very foundation of former
gristmills "too generic in appearance, as at Plymouth," to justify rebuilding.[2]
Still others—like Dundee (1936) and Milan (1938)—had both old and new
structures. At Northville the original building was replaced in 1936 by a new
one twice its size.

All these efforts reflected Ford's preference for the kind of clean, efficient,
well-proportioned, well-heated, well-ventilated (including, as necessary, air-
conditioned), high-ceilinged, and naturally lighted structures found in his
conventional branch plants as well as (more important) in both the Highland
Park and River Rouge complexes. So, too, did the presence in most of the
nineteen village sites of woodblock floors, which Ford believed to be most
comfortable for workers. This style of industrial architecture is properly associated with Albert Kahn, whose firm designed not only those two huge
facilities but also the Plymouth, Phoenix, Flat Rock (1923), Ypsilanti (1932),
and Northville replacement buildings.[3] (He also designed the Ford Exhibition Building housing the Industrialized American Barn at the 1934 Chicago
Century of Progress Exposition). In all cases, though, the bulk of the
(re)construction was carried out by Ford Motor Company employees from
various departments.[4]

To varying degrees the village industries represent examples of what Lindy Biggs has called "the rational factory": a scientifically designed and efficiently operated "factory that runs like a machine."[5] It is no accident, moreover, that much of her book of that title focuses on Ford's major Detroit area plants, from his first on Mack Avenue and his second on Piquette Avenue to the Highland Park and, finally, Rouge complexes. In the name not only of increasing production speed, flow, and so quantity but also of controlling his employees' work routines, Ford "changed factories more often than anyone else during the dynamic period between 1904 and 1920."[6] Yet just as Ford's rationales for establishing the village industries are not reducible to one or two motivations, so the village industries' diversity of buildings and designs cannot reduce them to small-scale mirror images of Ford's larger factories. (See the Appendix for differences among the nineteen village industries.)

Nevertheless, the high standards of safety and maintenance associated with the Highland Park and Rouge complexes were carried over to the village industries. According to Roscoe Smith, their superintendent, "We always kept our plants clean. Those machines were always very highly polished. We always kept the floors scrubbed and everything shipshape."[7] Ford's surprise visits to the various sites also kept workers and foremen on their toes. Moreover, Ford prohibited smoking in these buildings as in his others. And in all cases the adjoining streams were themselves revitalized through either rebuilt or new dams and other equipment needed to provide sufficient hydroelectric power to operate the machinery. The lakes often created by these developments were carefully landscaped and made available to area residents for recreational purposes.[8]

The generators that Ford had installed were usually displayed in glass enclosures to demonstrate the utility of hydroelectric power to skeptical visitors. Northville, which, for lack of water power, did not use a hydroelectric system in either its older or newer buildings but instead relied on a steam generator, nevertheless had a waterwheel built purely for show. (Cherry Hill [1944], the last of the nineteen village industries, did not use water power either, relying instead on an oil-fired boiler, but lacked a waterwheel.) This practice of the public display of power systems by Ford Motor Company predated the village industries and was most visible in the Highland Park plant's powerhouse, which opened in 1910: "large, displaylike windows invited pedestrians on Woodward Avenue to stop and admire the powerful generators and gleaming brass fittings."[9] Naturally everything had to be kept spotless.

As Ford explained to journalist Paul Kellogg in 1924, "Our idea is to distribute plants around rather than distribute the power. Streams are better transmission lines than wires. There is a good deal more loss in wires. Water goes over a dam and is power still."[10] Ford had far less faith in windmills (too unreliable) and in steam power (too inefficient). Water power, moreover, was nature's own form of decentralization; Ford was rejecting the "large electrical grids or networks" that were increasingly common in the early twentieth century. Rivers, not transmission lines, would carry energy for his hydroelectric plants, and each plant along those rivers would be "independent of the others."[11]

Ford's commitment to water and hydroelectric power was a throwback to technological developments before 1870, when, as Louis Hunter has detailed, waterwheels and their successors, hydraulic turbines, were critical to the emergence of a predominantly industrialized nation. After 1870, however, steam engines became the most important source of America's industrial power; once made relatively inexpensive and generally safe to use, they provided far more mobility and reliability—and far more power for ever larger factories—than waterwheels and turbines, whose very locations were obviously governed by the availability of water itself and whose operations could be undermined by insufficient or excessive rainfall.[12]

Nevertheless, by 1924, Ford's faith in water and in hydroelectric power had begun to determine the placement also of his branch assembly plants. At his insistence, nearly all such plants of the 1920s and 1930s were established "adjacent to, or—in a number of cases—in a major body of water."[13] Dredging allowed for the construction of deep-water docks and for the use of barges and freighters in place of the railroads that Ford deemed too costly and too unreliable. Interestingly, though, Ford did not use the various rivers on which the village industries were located for transportation of either raw materials or finished products.

Still, so fervent was Ford's belief in hydroelectric power that the village industries were designed, at least initially, not to employ a given number of workers producing a given item but instead to fit the available water power, at the ratio of one worker for each unit of horsepower. As Liebold recalled, "The size of the plants was determined entirely by the amount of horsepower available."[14] Only then was it determined how many workers would be hired and, still more surprising, what automobile part they would produce. When Ford learned in a 1927 visit that the six-year-old Nankin Mills plant, then making screws, employed only a dozen workers despite its fifty available horsepower, he replaced that operation with engraving processes and machinery removed from the Rouge plant. The new operation happily required fifty workers and so satisfied his ratio. That the engraving of "Ford" on both parts and employee badges was a skilled process requiring the retraining of original workers as well as the moving in of many more was a secondary consideration.[15]

Ford did, however, reluctantly concede the need for modest steam plants and steam engines to supplement the water-powered generators, and several were installed. Moreover, according to John Tobin, "Ford used the old water wheel system at [only] some of his village industries but more often channeled water directly through a tunnel into modern hydroelectric turbines next to the plants."[16] As things turned out, the availability of water power and production needs did not necessarily coincide, and the larger facilities in particular could hardly arrange their schedules to meet varying water levels, much less to allow workers to return to farming simply because water levels were low, as Ford had planned.

As Hunter has shown, just as steam engines were beginning to replace waterwheels and turbines in the 1860s and 1870s there was "a temporary reversal of the trend toward centralization of power supply." In such industries as iron and steel, heavy machinery, petroleum, and chemical products the dispersing of plants and operations became "desirable, if not essential." This was because the growing number and size of buildings in these industrial complexes made it more efficient and less expensive to utilize smaller steam engines "supplied from their own boilers."[17] This trend continued until the early 1900s, just when the Ford Motor Company was getting established.

In his 1922 book *My Life and Work*, Ford had admitted that there was no one ideal power source. "It may be that generating electricity by a steam plant at the mine mouth will be the most economical method for one community. Hydro-electric power may be best for another community. But certainly in every community there ought to be a central station to furnish cheap power."[18] Yet, when, according to several sources, Clarence Avery, a key Ford associate, determined that one of the early village industries, Phoenix, still lacked sufficient power in summer and installed a backup generator for the steam engine, Ford became enraged. He ordered that both the generator and the engine be deposited on the front porch of Avery's home, allegedly declaring, "We built these plants to run on water power. When I want any other kind of power in, I'll let you know how to do it!" The generator and engine were immediately removed, though apparently not to Avery's residence.[19]

As this incident suggests, Ford kept close watch over the village industries, visiting them regularly during both their construction and their operation. Kenneth Truesdell, who worked at Northville from 1929 until 1967, recalled:

> Well I'd seen Mr. Ford come out there many a time, many a time. I'd seen him walk right by me—I could have reached out and touched him, but nobody dared touch Mr. Ford or even say a word to him. . . . When they moved from the old plant into the new plant [in 1936] they had a big machine there, it was about eight foot wide and about fifteen/sixteen foot long and they wanted it steam cleaned before it went into the new plant. I was steam cleanin' that machine on a weekend and who drove in the backyard, but a car and a man got out and shook his hand at me and I said I didn't know who it was. . . . And finally he shook his hand again and I shook my hand back—it was Henry Ford. I'd [later] see Henry many a time, and after the new plant was built he used to come through, he wanted to see the water wheel. He'd run right through the shop.[20]

Truesdell's reminiscences reflect the two sides of Ford—distant and folksy— reflected in so many of his enterprises.

Biggs notes that the owners and managers of the late nineteenth- and early twentieth-century "rational factory" were discouraged by industrial engineers and other technical experts from even attempting to know their employees. The paternalism routinely practiced by earlier generations of shop owners—albeit with far fewer employees to deal with—was at once impractical and self-defeating: "To know them might also mean to feel a personal responsibility for them," which in turn might hinder necessarily tough business decisions.[21] This, then, was another way in which the village industries differed from the very "rational factory" that Ford elsewhere had helped to conceptualize and to build.

Descriptions from both Ford Motor Company writers and outside observers of the actual workings of the village industries reveal the complexity of their operations and the number and variety of tasks performed there. At Northville, for example, the new one-story replacement building was air-conditioned and consisted primarily of conveyors and loading chutes carrying valves automatically "from one machine to another in the various stages of manufacture." The process—starting with the inspection of rough castings, continuing with grinding and finishing, and ending with the inspection of finished valves—involved twenty-seven operations but usually required only about two hours before the valves were put into heat-treating ovens for a four-hour roasting, followed by final inspection. Then the same trucks that had brought the rough castings from the Rouge took the finished valves back there.[22]

By contrast, Saline (1938) was a three-story, renovated old gristmill used for soybean processing and soybean water-paint manufacture. For the latter, oil, protein solution, and pigments were transported to Saline from Highland Park (oil) and outside suppliers (protein and pigments). As a company writer explained it: "On the third floor the ingredients are mixed in a secretly formulated ratio. A huge eggbeater-like arrangement stirs the paint in 100 gallon batches for two and a half hours. It is then gravity fed to the second floor where three large steel rollers grind the paint, making it of the same consistency. As the paint drains off the last roller it is caught in gallon-size tin containers, ready for labeling and distribution."[23] Unlike Northville, Saline appears not to have sent its output, the soybean water paint, to any one large plant.

To take a third example, Dundee consisted of both an extensively renovated old three-story gristmill and two new single-story annexes: one housed the turbogenerator and the steam engine; the other contained the boilers and the foundry. Dundee made copper welding tips. Copper was shipped there in the form of scrap from the Ypsilanti village industry. In Dundee's foundry the copper was converted into alloys capable of surviving the heat and pressure of welding. As the electrode castings left the foundry, they were checked for hardness. Then came the machining operation, which required great accuracy, performed by skilled workers. After machining the electrodes were checked again and then trucked to the Rouge plant, where they were either used directly on the main assembly line or boxed for shipment to other plants.[24]

Ypsilanti, the largest of the village industries, made starters and generators in a new air-conditioned, one-story structure with railroad spurs running alongside and into the building and with platforms for loading and unloading both trains and trucks. Two boilers used for heating the factory occupied an adjacent building. Many separate operations went into the manufacturing process, including stamping, welding, machining, soldering, baking, and testing. Frames for generators, for instance, derived from steel fed into a "giant press specially designed for the plant" which produced twenty frames per minute; no fewer than seven operations were involved, but all were done by this single machine. Other machines wound generators automatically. For the manufacture of starters, another machine specifically made for Ypsilanti cut slots at a pace of roughly 6,000 an hour, whereas previously the fastest worker could cut no more than 80 an hour. After each small individual part was assembled, it was "routed to the assembly line by conveyor, where all the component parts are put together." Testing of all parts as they came off the line was, of course, required before they could be transported to the Rouge plant or conventional branch plants. All told, it took about thirty minutes from raw materials to finished generators and starters—but composing those products involved approximately "350 steps in the manufacture and assembly of about 500 parts." Despite its being fully integrated with the other village industries, Ypsilanti featured "its own machine shops for repair and rebuilding work, its own electrical department, its own electrical experimental room, its own heat-treat furnaces, and its own tool room."[25]

Of all the village industries, Sharon Mills (1939) had the smallest workforce, only 17 to 19 employees; Ypsilanti had the largest, between 740 and 1,500. During the Depression, several of the sites lost employees just as new sites were being opened—an ironic consequence for plants intended in part to offset economic difficulties in their respective locales. Legitimate questions can be raised, however, about whether a factory with more than, say, 100 employees can achieve the informality and intimacy among them that Ford allegedly sought. For that matter, whether plants the size of Ypsilanti or Flat Rock—the second largest, with 1,200 workers at its peak—constitute genuine village industries in more than name only is also uncertain. Yet these larger facilities, which began as Ford expanded his sites from the Rouge to the Huron River, appear to have functioned with only modestly more impersonality and rigidity than the earlier (and later) smaller plants—and with an atmosphere still qualitatively different, for better or for worse, from that of the Highland Park or especially the Rouge complex.[26]

Most of these workers were men, but several locations had a few women; in 1947, Ypsilanti had 215 (plus 937 men).[27] But alone of all the village industries, Phoenix's workforce—which at its peak in 1946 comprised 184 employees—was overwhelmingly female, both married and single. Like their female counterparts at the other sites, these Phoenix women were chosen to perform "delicate" tasks not requiring heavy labor (yet they were given two daily rest periods, versus not even one at the other eighteen plants).[28] Married women could be hired at Phoenix and the other village industries only if their spouses were unemployed.[29] In most cases, their husbands were ill or disabled, but in at least one case the cause of unemployment was incarceration.[30] If single Phoenix employees got married, they had to quit. Some hid their marital status in order to continue working, but if their marriage was discovered, they were promptly discharged. Widowed and divorced women, of course, faced no such barriers.

The majority of Phoenix employees had previous work experience but usually nothing like their assembly line duties there. A company publication explained: "Phoenix women do practically all [the] production, assembling, inspection, and clerical work at the plant," for "making voltage regulators . . . is a job in which women excel. The few manufacturing processes are light, while assembly of [the many small] parts into the finished unit requires a series of twenty-eight fast-moving steps."[31] Besides assembly and inspection, specific tasks included calibrating, punch press operation, packing, power rivet operation, and soldering. As compared with most of the male-dominated village industries, Phoenix had "relatively little machinery per worker," and the production process involved comparatively "less technical sophistication."[32]

Phoenix workers' pay was generally lower than that of male workers in similar jobs elsewhere in the village industries system but higher than that of many other male employees throughout the automobile industry—and, for that matter, higher than that of many other male and female manufacturing employees alike. As that same company publication readily stated, "The men are employed in [better paying] supervisory, material handling, and mainte-nance roles."[33] Not by accident, the Phoenix plant manager was male, yet the female second-in-command, Frances Sullivan, personally hired, fired, and reinstated Phoenix's workers (though her male boss had the final say).[34] She remained at the plant for eighteen years. This was another example of Ford's paternalism trickling down to the village industries in a manner also akin to the operations of nineteenth-century New England textile mills.[35]

Despite her power, however, Sullivan did not indulge in a "completely ad hoc system of wage determination" that might, for example, have rewarded women who had never married versus those who were divorced or those whose husbands were unemployed, have paid more to women with depend-ents than to those without them. Instead, "pay was linked to tenure, produc-tivity and age." To be sure, as Bruce Pietrykowski suggests, this may well have been a subtle means of having older, veteran employees defuse poten-tial dissatisfaction on the part of younger, newer employees by demonstrating the virtues of deference to one's supervisor(s) and of acceptance of one's workplace conditions. As a practical matter of critical importance, because the more experienced workers would likely have a harder time than the inexperienced workers in finding comparable employment at comparable wages if they lost their jobs, the older employees generally accommodated themselves more readily to the work regime than the younger, newer ones. In addition, because jobs at Phoenix "were governed by the pace of the conveyor," those workers whose skills and dexterity had deteriorated over time had another reason to be more submissive than workers without these concerns.[36]

To her credit, Sullivan was "a lover of flowers" who, a newspaper reported, soon "transformed the grounds surrounding the building into a flower garden that would put to shame the Detroit flower show." Hills, factory windows, and walls were all "covered with flowers and vines that blossomed from early spring until late fall." However clean the other, male-dominated village industries buildings might be, none had anything like this.[37]

Yet a flower garden hardly compensated for the greater employment opportunities offered to men who worked or wished to work at the village industries. True, Ford established scholarships awarded annually to two female high school graduates from each of the communities with a village industry. These were for a six-month Home Arts Program at the Henry Ford Nursing School in Detroit. Graduates of the program were given a Practical Nurses rating, but few were then hired by the Ford Motor Company in any capacity. Some graduates did pursue careers in nursing and related fields, but most became homemakers. After all, according to one (quite grateful) graduate, the program's principal purpose was to teach "us how to be good housemakers [sic]. And our job was to go back home and be good mothers and wives . . . in these small towns."[38]

By contrast, most of the village industries employed a handful of young male apprentices from area schools or, in some cases, from the company's own Henry Ford Trade School, located near the Highland Park and, later, River Rouge complexes. Founded in 1916 as part of the company's overall welfare program, the trade school began as an enterprise to give poor boys an opportunity to learn a trade but was soon training skilled workers for the company, especially its tool and die shops. The school's combined classroom and shop curriculum required two years' attendance for the general course and two years more for specialized training. By making tools and repairing equipment, the trade school became "a profitable venture" for the company. And by emphasizing as well the familiar Ford virtues of thrift, cleanliness, and obedience to superiors, the institution simultaneously prepared its students to be model company workers.[39] Its paper, interestingly titled the *Craftsman*, regularly and proudly listed the names of alumni recently hired by or moved to the village industry plants.[40]

Meanwhile, older male skilled workers at each site were often expected to learn all aspects of their particular production process to make their operation more efficient.[41] Some enrolled in the Ford Apprentice School, an institution established in 1923 at the Rouge complex and restricted to trade school graduates and adult company employees seeking advanced training. The three-year course was connected to the Rouge's specialized fields. Neither the trade school nor the apprentice school allowed women to enroll.[42]

Simultaneously, younger and older male workers alike had opportunities for formal classroom instruction on the premises of their respective plants through company-sponsored free courses. Subjects included elementary shop mathematics, algebra, geometry, calculus, mechanical drawing, hydraulics, and business correspondence.[43] Moreover, the company sponsored free apprenticeship training after 1942, following the successful unionization campaign of the preceding several years (see chapter 7). Offered with the union's cooperation, the program supplemented the curriculum at the trade school, whose enrollment had declined, and replaced earlier, simpler courses. Those completing the four-year apprenticeship would be eligible for journeyman status in any one of six occupations: industrial machinist, toolmaker, diemaker, industrial hydraulic technician, stationary steam engineer, or industrial electrician.[44]

Of all the nineteen sites, the Waterford (1925) plant probably employed the workers most highly skilled. Here were produced all the precision gauges and other measuring instruments used by Ford Motor Company inspectors—instruments accurate to within four-millionths of an inch. Not surprisingly, perhaps, this was the company's only facility that had no inspectors; every worker was his own inspector. As one employee told a reporter, "Inspectors in this plant? Don't be silly. Where could you find anybody to inspect us?"[45] Significantly, the initial Waterford employees were almost entirely natives of Sweden, having come there when Ford bought and transported to Michigan what had been the Swedish Gauge Company of Sweden and then of Poughkeepsie, New York. Their new two-story building had heavy machinery, screw machines, shapers, furnaces, and a steam boiler on the first floor; lathes, grinders, and benches for finishing work on the second floor. This effort revived what had been a decaying Michigan community which had never recovered from a fire that had destroyed the state's largest gristmill.[46] (Interestingly, the Waterford workers' skills and the constant demand for their services prevented them from engaging in any farming, contrary to Ford's vision.)[47]

At Ford's insistence, aged, alcoholic, criminally rehabilitated, mentally handicapped, and especially physically handicapped workers (including many disabled veterans) were regularly employed at the village sites. Former employees recalled this policy. John Peters, for example, remembered about Flat Rock that "we had an armless fellow who just had stubs below his shoulder. He was a guard there in them days of 1936 up to the War years." And Fred Winstanley said of Milford, "If you could do the job, you worked. The Company had facilities for those who may have been disabled from work-related accidents." Winstanley's fellow worker Rodes Walters recalled "a few dwarfs, well accepted, no problem. Don't know about other plants." Nor do I, save for Willow Run (1941).[48]

The elderly and disabled were even hired in direct proportion to their numbers in each of the village industries, and the Cherry Hill site was devoted exclusively to the rehabilitation of disabled World War II veterans, the mentally as well as the physically disabled. Alone of the village industries, Cherry Hill employed no local farmers. Alone among them, too, most of the surrounding community knew little about who worked there (persons recruited from various military hospitals) or what was produced (ignition and door locks and keys and machined brass radiator petcocks). To his credit, Ford prohibited publicity in order to limit the pressure on those who had suffered enough and needed a comparatively relaxed work atmosphere. Most of the thirty or so employees lived in a residence hall adjacent to the plant, and nearly all eventually got good jobs at other Ford plants. In general, the Ford Motor Company was well ahead of most other large American businesses in these respects.[49]

Few of the village industries employed African Americans, however, and none employed Mexicans. A 1937 survey found no African Americans in ten of the then twelve sites and, at the larger Flat Rock and Ypsilanti plants, only one and nine respectively (or .18 percent and 1.12 percent of the workforce), hired for the most part as janitors.[50] A 1943 update, which did not analyze any other plants beyond these twelve, concluded that "the general picture does not appear to have changed since that time" and that nearly all the company's black employees worked in the Rouge complex: "In no other Ford establishment do Negroes comprise as much as 2 percent of the total labor force."[51]

Admittedly, few of the villages where these plants were located had any African Americans in their overall populations, and probably none had any Mexicans or persons of Mexican descent. Retired Flat Rock employee Charlie Oestrike recalls seeing "quite a few colored people," but they were employees of Stone and Webster, "who built the place," and they lived in "wagon houses, the forerunners of our present house trailer." Yet their temporary presence stirred the establishment of a Ku Klux Klan chapter in Flat Rock.[52] No former village industry employee remembers seeing any Mexicans in any capacity.

In the early twentieth century, tens of thousands of African Americans in the South, fleeing Jim Crow laws and other instances of post–Civil War racism, had come north in search of better living and working conditions. Between 1910 and 1920, for example, Detroit's black population grew sixfold.[53] And from about 4,000 African Americans in 1900, there were 120,000 by 1930. As it did for their southern white counterparts, Detroit's auto industry seemed a mecca for most of them: in 1930, when the proportion of African Americans in the auto industry nationwide had reached 7 percent, in Detroit it had reached 14 percent; no other American city came close. Moreover, in 1925, for example, the annual average pay for all wage earners in Detroit—not just, to be sure, autoworkers—was, at $1,701, considerably higher than that of any other eastern or midwestern city.[54] As the supply of eastern and southern European workers declined during and after World War I—thanks to severe restrictions imposed by the federal government on immigrants from those regions—southern whites and blacks alike found opportunities there. Many were actually recruited to come north.

So, too, were thousands of Mexicans, particularly those living in Texas. Far from coming directly from farms or small towns, as did many African Americans, most of the Mexicans who eventually gravitated to the automobile industry had already worked in other midwestern industries, including sugar refining, meatpacking, railroads, and steel. But the automobile industry paid higher wages than those others. Between the end of World War I and the early 1930s, over 58,000 Mexicans came to midwestern cities. In 1920, Detroit had about 3,000 Mexicans; by 1928, roughly 15,000 lived there.[55]

Awaiting a preponderance of the African Americans, however, were either no jobs or menial jobs, given both northern racism overall and the hostility of white autoworkers in particular. Because the total number of Mexicans was so much smaller and because Mexicans were often deemed superior to African Americans—if still inferior to whites—they generally fared better. Ford Motor Company, though, was unique within the automobile industry for its willingness to hire so many from both groups—and to pay them the same as their white fellow workers, regardless of their specific jobs.[56] As a result, Ford himself, having personally approved these employment policies, won the long-standing loyalty of numerous African Americans and Mexicans alike. In 1926, for instance, 10,000 of 100,000 Detroit-area Ford employees were black (reflecting Ford's de facto quota of no more than 10 percent of the local workforce, regardless of the racial composition of the local population), and by 1937, African Americans constituted 12 percent of the Rouge workforce.[57] Or, as Lloyd Bailer wrote in 1943 about the then largest American auto manufacturers, "Ford employed more than four times as many Negroes as any other concern, though it normally ranked third in the production of finished vehicles and second in volume of employment."[58]

Similarly, in 1928, Ford employed almost 4,000 Mexicans at its Highland Park, River Rouge, and Fordson plants, far more than any other Detroit-area carmaker. That Ford set no quota for the percentage of Mexicans who might be hired proved beneficial in some instances, harmful in others, depending upon the disposition of those doing the actual hiring. Some two hundred well-educated Mexicans, handpicked by their government, studied at the Henry Ford Service School in preparation for careers in dealerships either back home or in other Latin American countries. Of the less fortunate Mexicans seeking jobs at Ford Motor Company, Zaragosa Vargas observes that "to wear the silver Ford badge and short ('white-walled') haircuts, which were the distinctive trademarks of the Ford autoworker, became the ambition of Mexicans in the climb for status."[59] As he had repeatedly done before, Ford thus lured workers to the very urban center he simultaneously wanted depopulated, as through the village industries.

To be sure, working and living conditions for both African American and Mexican Ford employees were hardly idyllic. The overwhelming majority of both groups labored in unskilled or semiskilled manual positions that virtually no one else would take, such as in the foundries, the rolling mills, the paint shops, the stamping plants, and maintenance work.[60] (Outside Detroit virtually all black Ford employees, like their counterparts elsewhere in the industry, were janitors; too few Mexicans worked at Ford plants outside Detroit to make a comparison.) Often these jobs were dangerous as well as hard, filthy, and noisy. Opportunities akin to those at the village industries for planting gardens, much less for farming, in one's leisure time were painfully few. Personal confirmation of this situation comes from retired Ford employee John Peters, who worked at Flat Rock, where he saw no African American employees, and at the Rouge, where those he saw—in significant numbers—always had "bottom of the barrel" jobs.[61]

This arrangement was in accordance with Ford's belief, widely shared in his day, that African Americans were generally not fit for better, more intellectually challenging jobs. Interestingly, his very first black employee was one William Perry, whom Ford first met in 1888, when he hired Perry to help him clear timberland in the Dearborn woods. In the course of their time together the two twenty-five-year-olds became lifelong friends, and in 1914 Ford hired Perry to work at the Highland Park plant's powerhouse. He certainly respected Perry's physical prowess and good character but not his intellect.[62] (Ford somehow reconciled this attitude with his esteem for George Washington Carver, the famous Tuskegee Institute scientist whose research Ford supported and whose life he heralded.)[63]

Blacks' prospects for promotion, moreover, were limited both by their frequent lack of desirable skills and by a seniority system that gave only a small number of them any chance of moving up. To make matters worse, Ford used African American clergymen and other community leaders to screen all black job applicants in order to obtain a compliant and conservative workforce—just as he did by other means for white job seekers.[64] Not surprisingly, only a handful of African Americans at the company became skilled workers, foremen, and white-collar workers, and of these, a mere handful had been allowed to study at the trade school or the apprentice school.[65]

Joyce Shaw Peterson's summary of the living conditions of Detroit's African American autoworkers applies in some measure also to those of the city's Mexican autoworkers: "As far as the urban life of Detroit's black population is concerned, housing was probably the greatest drawback to enjoying city life. Often old, crowded, sometimes without plumbing or heat, urban housing did not provide an inviting place to which to retreat from the rigors of the factory. While most entertainment facilities were segregated, the city did offer its excitement and black Detroiters began to build a communal life, especially around their churches."[66] Meanwhile, Ford's hometown of Dearborn, the site of company's world headquarters, became notorious for its racial segregation policies and discriminatory practices. (At the same time, Ford, however paternalistically, spent thousands of dollars rehabilitating the nearby, overwhelmingly African American community of Inkster, Michigan, which had been devastated by the Great Depression.)[67]

The company's pre–World War II discrimination against African Americans in hiring and promotion continued after 1945, despite the rhetorical—and sometimes genuine—commitment of the United Auto Workers (UAW) to eradicating it. As Thomas Sugrue has detailed, decentralized hiring practices gave individual plant managers enormous power to select whomever they wished. The same conditions applied at General Motors and Chrysler. As a result, the racial composition of Big Three plants in the Detroit area was remarkably uneven, not reflecting the racial composition of the areas of the city or neighboring communities in which they were located. Because the

UAW was also heavily decentralized, its individual locals were no less arbitrary in supporting or not supporting these hiring practices. Decentralization thus had some ironic consequences.[68]

One can safely assume that Ford, like so many other whites of his day, deemed Mexicans inferior to himself but superior to African Americans. As Vargas notes, Ford was opening branch plants in Mexico and hoped that his American-trained Mexican workers would help to stem the revolutionary upheavals there upon their return home. He went so far as to contend that his production and management schemes, if applied to Mexico, would end the turmoil: revolutionary leader "Villa would become a foreman," while "Carranza might be trained to become a good time keeper."[69] Back in the United States, some Mexican workers, but hardly a majority, at Ford Motor Company *were* able to achieve modest managerial success. More often, Mexicans' very stereotypical reputation for working hard without complaint—above all in hot and humid work areas supposedly resembling their homeland—often led to their being put into those bottom-of-the-barrel jobs formerly restricted to African Americans (who, however, were usually segregated, whereas Mexicans, because of their smaller numbers and their relatively greater acceptance by whites, were usually scattered). Like thousands of other company employees—including some whites who had the opportunity to move to the village industries—not a few Mexican workers quit the largest plants because of their inability to keep up with the extraordinary pressure, pace, and monotony of the huge assembly lines; they did not enjoy such alternatives as the village industries.[70]

Thanks to periodic slowdowns, cutbacks, recessions, and, finally, the Great Depression, many more Mexicans were eventually laid off by Ford and other automakers. Some voluntarily left the Detroit area for their native land; others were forcibly repatriated, since unlike African Americans, most were not U.S. citizens. By the early 1930s, Detroit's entire Mexican population had dwindled to roughly 1,000.[71]

As the auto industry unionized in the late 1930s and early 1940s, African American and the remaining Mexican employees at Ford were frequently torn between loyalty to their paternalistic "master" and desire for union recognition with likely better job opportunities. This was a dilemma faced by the village industry workers, too (see chapter 7). For a time, most workers' traditional indifference, if not outright hostility, toward unionization no longer sufficed to quell any pro-union sentiments. Black and Mexican workers increasingly found themselves in no-win situations as strikes mounted and as they were simultaneously pressured to stay on the job and to go on strike. Many African Americans, in fact, were cynically used by the company as strikebreakers, thereby intensifying already strained racial relations. (Ironically, some of the initial Mexican workers had first been recruited from Texas by midwestern steel mills to be strikebreakers in that industry.)[72] This practice in turn prompted speculation about Ford's possible ulterior motives in hiring so many African Americans in the first place: to lessen unionization efforts through lack of cooperation between the races and to promote competition between the races and so greater efficiency for the company.[73]

Yet unionization had its own drawbacks, not least the fear of persisting racism with likely limited prospects for radical improvement in hiring and promotion. According to Bailer in 1943, as "late as April 1941," when unionization at Ford loomed, "probably a majority of the colored employees [there] were not particularly anxious that the Rouge plant be organized."[74] Gradually, however, the majority sided with the unionization movement, as did most of the Mexican workers. Indeed, once unionization took place, many African Americans at the Rouge became some of its most radical employees and frequently joined the Communist Party out of disillusionment with the Democratic Party.[75] At that point, Ford ended his moral and financial support of African American churches, charities, civic improvement projects, and civil rights groups. The company then became a more conventional discriminatory employer, along with General Motors and Chrysler.

Profoundly different though their overall circumstances were, white workers in the village industries and African American and Mexican workers at other Ford plants both enjoyed and resented Ford's paternalism. Whatever their feelings, they could not escape it.

An idyllic promotional illustration of the original Nankin Mills plant, the second plant to open, in 1921. A boy sits under a tree as workers enter the building, which was a renovated grist mill. Behind are acres of picturesque fields, and to the left is a stream that runs from the side of the plant to the Rouge River. Earlier versions of this illustration were published at least as early as 1932, but this one appeared ca. 1935.

Ford Motor Company executives on a 1937 tour of the village industries, stopping at Milan, which opened the next year. Henry Ford is on the far right; his son Edsel is third from the left.

Exterior of the original Northville plant, 1932. Opened in 1920, this was the first village industry. The building was a renovated saw mill and woodworking shop.

Interior of the Flat Rock plant not long after it opened in 1923. Designed by the prominent industrial architect Albert Kahn, the plant made all Ford Motor Company vehicle lamps.

Aerial view of the exterior of the Flat Rock plant, 1927.

Renovation of the old grist mill from which the Saline plant was built, 1936.

Exterior of the Saline plant, 1938, the year it opened.

Interior of the Saline plant showing its soybean processing machinery, 1946.

Interior of the Sharon Mills plant during renovation of the old grist mill from which it was built, 1933. The plant opened in 1939.

Exterior of the Sharon Mills plant, 1941.

Interior of the glass-enclosed hydroelectric powerhouse at Milan, 1939, a year after it opened. Nearly all of the village industries relied on hydroelectric power.

Exterior of the glass-enclosed hydroelectric powerhouse at Nankin Mills, 1937, the year an entire new plant replaced the original.

Exterior of the Waterford plant, 1945. For many years after its opening in 1925, the plant, as advertised, made all Ford Motor Company inspection precision gauges (and taps).

Exterior of the Phoenix plant, 1936. Designed by Kahn and opened in 1922, the plant advertised its original (but not its only) product. Beginning in 1936, the plant made half of all Ford Motor Company voltage regulators (and cutouts). Phoenix's workforce was almost exclusively female.

Surrounding area of the Phoenix plant, 1936. Phoenix had the prettiest landscaping of all of the village industries.

Exterior of the Ypsilanti plant hydroelectric powerhouse and waterfalls, 1932, the year it opened. Also designed by Kahn, this was the largest of the village industries in size of both structure and workforce.

Exterior of the Ypsilanti plant, 1936.

Exterior side view of the Ypsilanti plant, 1936.

INDUSTRIAL FARMING

"*I SEE the time soon coming when the farmer will not only raise raw materials for industry but will do the initial processing on his farm. He will stand on both his feet—one foot on the soil for his livelihood, and the other foot in industry for the cash he needs. He will have a double security. Agriculture suffers from a lack of market for its product, industry suffers from a lack of employment for its surplus men. Bringing them together heals the ailments of both. That is my conviction and that is what I am working for.*"

Henry Ford

"Industrial Farming" was one of several Ford Motor Company promotions of Henry Ford's vision of full-time factory workers also becoming part-time farmers. Published in Ford News, April 1936.

CHAPTER 5

Administration and Relationship to Local Communities

ONTRARY TO THE FORD MOTOR COMPANY'S PUBLICITY agents, the village industries never resembled the bastions of yeoman purity described in their various press releases. They were commercial enterprises as well as social experiments and, like nearly all else in the Ford empire, were under the constant scrutiny of Ford himself. "Anyone who knows Henry Ford's working principles knows that [they] are not primarily undertaken as a form of social uplift." So journal editor Arthur Van Vlissingen observed in 1938 about Ford's aversion to activities whose principal concern was not greater efficiency and greater profits. Ford "would never undertake to bring about any such condition as a company enterprise unless in so doing he could at the same time improve the job, do it more profitably. It just so happened," he concluded, "that what proves best industrially also turns out to be an improvement socially."[1] (That Ford admittedly had deep familial ties to the Dearborn area and to Michigan was conveniently overlooked here.)

A typical account for public consumption of these combined financial and social virtues appeared in a 1936 book, *Ford Production Methods*, whose author, Hartley Barclay, was also editor of the periodical *Mill and Factory*:

> Asked about production costs, superintendents replied invariably:
> "Our costs are lower because we are out in the country. The men work more efficiently. Most of the men have farms or houses with large gardens located within a few miles of the plant. They live more normal lives than they would if employed in a factory located in a congested industrial region. Even through the boom years we had virtually no labor turnover.
> "From a management point of view we can understand and deal with our men more satisfactorily because we not only know them personally but also know where they live and what are their personal problems.

"Bigness can often mean less rather than more efficiency. We know what every man and machine is doing all the time. We can route work through the small plants with a minimum of machine changes, handling of material and time waste."[2]

Despite this and many similar assertions, Ford repeatedly refused to divulge the operating costs of his experiments, claiming only that they were profitable. He may have destroyed—or perhaps have barely kept—their financial records; notwithstanding persistent searches, I have been unable to obtain such records.[3] Certainly he did not attempt to determine their costs and benefits to the same extent as for the Rouge or other large plants. An exception was his otherwise undocumented comment to journalist Drew Pearson in 1924 that it had taken 3.5 minutes and had cost 9.5 cents to make a Model T valve at Highland Park in 1920 versus 1.26 minutes and 4 cents at Northville in 1923.[4] As journalist Paul Kellogg confessed after their 1924 interview, "I was unable to learn what the total is that he has put into his . . . little factories up stream on the River Rouge; . . . but it was assumed as a matter of course by the people I talked with that the millions he has already laid out exceed anything on which he is likely to get a conventional return in anything like the immediate future."[5]

The reminiscences of Ford engineer Charles Voorhess are still more revealing: "As far as the actual running expense of these plants, there was no budget. No budget, he would say. Sometimes I would try to talk to him about jobs that I thought were going too high, and he'd say, 'Why worry about that?' You couldn't talk money to him in regards to these plants. Money was just a tool with him, and he wanted it to be used that way. Too much accounting practice, he didn't like, of course. These plants were built, in general, on work orders, so-called, to give a record of what they cost. They are the same work orders we use now [1952], same form."[6]

Kenneth Edwards, who was chief clerk of all the village industries from 1943 to 1946 after having worked at both the Rouge and the Milan plants, conceded in a 1988 interview that economically, the village industries "didn't make that much sense." The case of lawn maintenance, he said, "is just a humble example but it went through all these plants, with their grounds and their shrubbery and the lawns and the driveways that all had to be taken care of," where with one large plant "you just have the one. So that type of service was much more expensive per product than it would be in a bigger plant." Of course, initially "you never [actually] knew whether they were making money or not because the plants didn't have profit and loss statements. When we became centralized and a controller's office was established and the plants were put on a profit and loss basis, most of them, particularly the smaller ones, were not economically profitable." By that point, profit-and-loss statements were being required by the company and were "consolidated into the Company-wide statements."[7]

Even Ernest Liebold, Ford's longtime personal secretary, was skeptical of the alleged savings by the company in operating these sites: "I don't doubt that it was [actually] a matter of [imaginative] bookkeeping."[8] He suspected that changes in conventional company policies regarding overhead, capital investment, and other areas accounted for the supposed superiority of this manner of doing business. Historians Allan Nevins and Frank Hill summed up the situation: "Nobody had any financial authority over the village industries. . . . We can only guess at their gains and losses."[9]

In his 1926 book *Today and Tomorrow* (like his *My Life and Work*, written with—and largely by—his frequent collaborator Samuel Crowther), Ford boasted, "The bookkeeping and management of these plants is very simple. . . . None of the plants have offices or clerical staffs. There is no need for them—and that is a saving in expense."[10] (Yet there were managers, sometimes with assistants, at each facility.) And as Voorhess argued, "I think that regardless of what the books showed, he had the advertising value that he was doing a lot for the people."[11]

Such financial and administrative laxity was, of course, characteristic of the company under Ford's leadership, or lack thereof. His lifelong obsession with producing vehicles as cheaply as possible in his larger cutting-edge plants never translated into an accompanying desire to utilize modern accounting techniques that might have revealed possible further savings.[12] As *Fortune* reported in 1947, "Imagine a company that boasted of a higher order of integration than any similar organization in the country, with ownership of a steel mill, glass plant, timber stands, maritime fleet, etc., and no accurate knowledge of which individual operation was paying its way, or which was padding the cost of the company's end product by open-market standards."[13] And historian James Flink noted that the company's financial statements, including those that encompassed the village industries, had long been "closely guarded secrets even within the firm, because of fear that they might damage prestige or prompt an investigation."[14]

Interestingly, in their best-selling and influential book of two decades ago, *In Search of Excellence: Lessons from America's Best-Run Companies*, Thomas J. Peters and Robert H. Waterman lamented the excessive layers of management then at Ford Motor Company (seventeen) and praised contemporary corporations with modest-sized central offices and bureaucracies and with widespread decentralization of decision-making and administration: "The excellent companies are both centralized and decentralized. For the most part, . . . they have pushed autonomy down to the shop floor or product development team. On the other hand, they are fanatic centralists around the few core values they hold dear." Had Ford had better accounting procedures in place, his company might have won Peters and Waterman's praise. In fact, they cite the aversion of some model corporations of the 1980s, such as Motorola, to large-scale factories (over 1,000 workers) and preference for smaller ones. As they put it, "In theory to date, the small is effective idea is usually limited to discussions of innovativeness by small firms. In most of the excellent companies, however, we see various approaches to chunking [i.e., becoming smaller] as a main tenet of effective management practice."[15] In this context, Ford's village industries would surely have won their praise.

According to Roscoe Smith, the first superintendent of all the village industries, "The larger plants were very good after studying their production figures and their cost figures. The smaller plants just couldn't compete," for the latter "were all old grist or old flour mills. You just couldn't get enough people in there to warrant the thing." Smith tried to bring these matters to the attention of Ford, whom he saw irregularly, and of Ford's close associate Charles Sorensen, whom he saw more often. "I would come in and report to Mr. Sorensen once in a while," Smith remembered. "If I had anything of importance to take up with him or if he had anything he wanted to see me on, he called me in. Otherwise, I didn't come in at any stated period or regular interval." Regarding policy issues, Smith played no role: "I don't know what went on between Mr. Ford and Mr. Sorensen about those things." Similarly, he recalled, "Mr. Ford never talked to me about why he wanted an old [mill] instead of setting up new plants. I never asked him. I just assumed it was his desire."[16]

The village industries were never an official activity of the Ford Motor Company but one of Ford's personal projects. Smith's appointment in 1937 as their first superintendent—with responsibilities for the Upper Peninsula, Hamilton, and Green Island facilities as well—represented less a change in their status than a reflection of Ford's declining health and his interest in new projects. Smith recalled being both pleased and surprised. "I knew that there was a necessity for it and I had wished in my own mind that it could happen."[17] Yet various company and local documents and publications indicate that the parts manufactured and assembled at these nineteen sites were often produced nowhere else in the corporation, so the village industries presumably had to have been under the scrutiny of executives at Ford head-quarters apart from Ford himself. Thus, for example, by the 1930s *all* the company's inspection precision gauges and taps were produced at Waterford, *all* the lamps (front, tail, and interior) at Flat Rock, *all* the engravings (stencils, script dies, employee identification badges) at Nankin Mills, *all* the starters and generators at Ypsilanti, 95 *percent* of the taps for threads at Plymouth, 95 *percent* of the twist drills at Newburgh (1935), 50 *percent* of the horn buttons and starter switches at Brooklyn (1939), and 50 *percent* of the generator cut-outs and voltage regulators at Phoenix.[18]

The village industries' own company publication, the monthly *Hydro Plants News*, proudly proclaimed early in 1948, following the initial public showing of Ford's first postwar line:

> Every employee of the Parts and Equipment Manufacturing Division [the new name for those village industries that had survived company retrench-ment the year before] is a part of this achievement. From plants of this division came the following items: Brooklyn, distributors, starter switches, and cigar lighters; Flat Rock, lamps; Manchester, ammeters; Milan, ignition coils; Milford, carburetors; Northville, valves; Phoenix, voltage regu-lators; Ypsilanti, starters and generators. . . . In addition to these actual production items service parts were provided as follows: Dundee, welding machine parts and castings; Waterford, gages, signature dies, taps, drills, and special tools. Behind actual production is another story—the never ending battle for material and supplies waged by management to keep plants operating on schedule. This has been and continues to be a 24 hour a day, seven day week operation.[19]

A year before, in fact, another *Hydro Plants News* article had praised the Ford purchasing department for arranging air freight delivery to the nine-teen village industries of those items they needed to produce their particular parts, so critical were those parts to the company overall.[20] As a company press release stated later in 1948—just when, ironically, these experiments were beginning to be phased out—they "were very important cogs in the Ford Motor Company for they were the chief source of all those parts."[21]

Whether the village industries enjoyed the support of the company's top executives is another matter. Back in 1924, Kellogg had perceived opposition to the scheme from some of its "shrewdest executives," and Ford himself had then conceded, "I can't make anyone else around the place see that the small power plant and the village industry will pay."[22] Voorhess's reminiscences (1952) suggest the same—and, not surprisingly, especially on the part of those Rouge plant chief managers whose production and assembly lines were being transferred to the village industries set up in the 1930s. For that matter, Highland Park chief managers had felt similarly about losing production and assembly lines to the village industries established in the 1920s. "It took away control of things they had under their thumb. . . . In most instances," Voorhess recalled, "they felt they could have done a better job if left alone." Hence, "in some instances they were very cooperative and in some others, I don't think they were too cooperative."[23]

In addition, for several years Rouge plant managers engaged in bitter disputes with their counterparts at Highland Park about the increasing dominance of the newer complex over the older, and Ford might have seen the village industries as in part a means of transcending this feud (even if the bigger plants' collective resistance may account for the absence of any new small plants between 1926 and 1931).[24] Only with the change in 1927 from the Model T to the Model A, and the transfer of final assembly from Highland Park to the Rouge, did the latter finally dominate the former.[25]

Smith fondly remembered being comparatively free from excessive supervision while he was head of the new Ypsilanti plant from 1931 to 1937. "I don't think the fact that we were operating one of Mr. Ford's pet plants had anything to do with their keeping hands off. I don't know why we had relative freedom out there. At that time some of these other plants were running, and I don't think they bothered with those fellows either. They didn't come out because," he speculated, "it took time to get out there. As long as you operated the way you should and kept your place clean, there wasn't too much pressure put on you."[26]

The village industries, then, did enjoy a measure of freedom. Their communities were not conventional company towns; they were not owned by the Ford Motor Company; and they were comparatively free from the notorious, overtly paternalistic Ford Sociological Department and its still more notorious successor, the ruthlessly dictatorial Service Department and spy network (an interesting exception to this freedom being the questionnaires apparently sent to every Detroit-area employee by the latter asking about their interest in a Thrift Garden and the follow-up inquiries if they dared to decline the opportunity).[27] "Do you intend to build any model towns in conjunction with your village factories?" journalist Drew Pearson had asked Ford in 1924. "No, I am against that sort of thing," Ford had replied. "I believe that if people want to get things done, they can do them themselves. Cooperate with them, but don't hamper them. They get spoonfed."[28]

True to his word, Ford did not attempt to build housing for his workers, to set up company stores, to organize local farmers into cooperatives, or to exert political control over the villages.[29] Nor would he hire away from area businesses any workers already employed there. On the contrary, he extended the principle of decentralization to independent local merchants by allowing them to provide supplies to the Ford Motor Company. According to a 1938 *Life* article celebrating both the growing Rouge plant and the growing village industries, the company still relied on some 6,000 other businesses and manufacturers for parts and materials.[30] Only when the village industries themselves required new or rebuilt electrical, water, and sewage systems or bridges and roads did the company impose its will and undertake the task—and then usually free to the communities, which also benefited from the projects; often workers' homes were lighted with electricity furnished by the factories' power plants.[31] Not a few Michigan workers, businesses, and whole towns were thereby saved from financial ruin during the Depression. A 1938 company news release characterized the impact of the Ford factory on Dundee as "Village Makes Good: The Success Story of Dundee, the Town That Came Back."[32]

The restoration and renovation of existing buildings for several of the village industries and the construction of new buildings for the rest invariably enhanced each of the nineteen sites. So, too, did the other communal improvements spurred by Ford's presence. A local newspaper reported about changes under way in Dundee, for example: "The work at the old mill being carried on by the owner, Henry Ford, continues with thirty or more local men at work. Six trucks, steam shovel, etc., are being used in the work of cleaning out the old mill race in preparation for further construction work. . . . The village council is making arrangements for the cleaning of the north shore of the river. . . . Mr. Ford's efforts in cleaning the south bank of the river have been a great incentive in the urge for the same kind of work being done on the opposite shore. This improvement will certainly mean a great deal to every resident who for years have [sic] hated the sight of piles of tin cans at the approach to the main part of the village."[33]

In many of the communities, moreover, Ford assisted the local schools. In some cases he supplied financial aid to reopen closed schools or to renovate inadequate existing ones, but in other cases he intervened more directly, adding the schools to his own system of grade and high schools headquartered at Greenfield Village. In both cases Ford paid teachers' salaries when necessary. And in all instances he emphasized "traditional" education, often in a one-room schoolhouse and with a practical, vocational curriculum that included mechanics, agriculture, and home economics.[34] He thereby

achieved the farm and factory combination with youngsters that he pre-
scribed for adults. Beginning in 1932, he also funded small-scale gardens for
the children of his workers near several village industry locales, and he often
built or restored churches and community centers as further means of instill-
ing and preserving appropriate values for his workers and their families. In
the village industry communities, then, as well as in the plants themselves,
Ford's vision was pervasive.

CHAPTER 6

Workers' Experiences

A S NEAR AS ONE CAN TELL, IN THE ABSENCE OF MANY CON-
temporary inquiries of the village industry workers themselves, most
appear to have enjoyed their factory positions, their diversity of employment,
their comparatively lose authority structure (akin to Ford's own first plant on
Mack Avenue in Detroit), and the proximity of their residences to their
workplaces. In the words of Francis Michaels, one of several former village
industries workers whom I interviewed, "Working conditions in the Milford
plant were much better than at the Rouge plant where I was first employed
in 1935–38. I was transferred to the Milford plant in 1938," when it first
opened. "Life was more simple living in Brighton, Michigan, which was 12
miles from Milford. You became better acquainted with the employees in
the Milford plant and I would say the morale was quite high, you seemed to
feel more secure than at the Rouge plant." Moreover, the Milford plant "was
very modern and had up to date machinery for that period. There were a
variety of jobs, although any job can become monotonous," and there were
only "a plant manager, assistant plant manager, general foreman, and foreman" to deal with, unlike the Rouge, with its layers of management. Although
"a few of the workers came from farms in the surrounding area," a majority,
including Michaels, lived either in Milford or in nearby towns. Some, however, "still lived in Detroit, but there was no pressure on them to live in
Milford"—this contrary to Ford Motor Company publicity and, of course, to
Ford's own insistence.[1]

Fred Winstanley also worked at Milford, from 1939 until its merger in
1958 with a conventional branch plant in Rawsonville. Like Michaels, he had
transferred to Milford from the Rouge plant, where he had worked since
1931, following two years at the Highland Park plant. As Winstanley recalled
in 1988, "Those working in the small or outlying plants became like a large
and happy family, both in and out of the plant. . . . The equipment was equal

to and in some instances larger than what we began with while at the Rouge plant. There were, of course, regular routine jobs to be performed as in any automotive plant, but there was much more freedom in the small plants until the union came in, with the exception of smoking, a freedom we did not need and we find now being brought under control." In general, "over the years at Milford, both variety and specialized work was involved." Winstanley had graduated from the Ford Trade School at age sixteen in 1932 but had to remain in the apprentice program for two more years before he could become a full-fledged Ford Motor Company employee, given an age eighteen requirement. When he came to Milford, he was an aspiring tool and die maker.[2]

Winstanley continued: "There was a requirement that to work at an out-lying plant, one must live with a certain mile area of the plant. I'm not certain of the miles, but I think it was five or seven, [though] there might have been a case or cases where this requirement was being violated. There were farmers and others that worked at our plant, [but I do not] recall anyone ever referring to what they did after leaving the plant or as having two occupations." In order to meet this requirement, Winstanley himself "roomed with a die maker named George Zwiesler and his family on Grass Lake Road. He had been working at the Rouge and transferred to Milford. By the size of his property, he could have farmed at some time, but only raised chickens and had laying hens as a sideline. There was never any pressure put on anyone as to what they did or did not do outside of the plant duties. What one did after hours seemed to be treated as nobody's business."

About the actual operation at Milford, Winstanley remembered: "We did not have many, [but] we did have supervision at different levels and as need be for each department. . . . In looking back, it would seem to me that each of the plants were [sic] inter-connected with the other. Parts came to us and we shipped parts to others, and of course to the Rouge. The Ypsilanti plant had a crew that would service all the outlying plants on major repairs, retooling, improvements, etc. For the cast iron foundry I am certain the materials came from the Rouge foundry. Aluminum and zinc came in ingots from an outside source, as did gaskets, screws, and other items. Carburetors were packaged and shipped from Milford and orders were filled and sent to various other sources as required." Yet the Milford plant "was self-supporting with the exception of raw material, screws, nuts and bolts, gaskets, etc."

Regarding social life, Winstanley recollected that "there were many times that the Milford area people got together to socialize. There were many marriages consummated which might not have been had the Milford operation not been undertaken." Unlike all the other village industries (save Ypsilanti), the Ford Motor Company actually "wanted to expand the Milford plant in the early fifties, but there were those in local government who wanted to keep this a small town. That is how Rawsonville came into being. We were much better off, recognition was readily evident, promotions were easier to come by rather than through 'politics,' as what happened to me and others at Rawsonville between our moving to the new plant and my forced retirement on December 31, 1971. But the move to Rawsonville had other problems, it meant that personnel from other plants were now being integrated with ours, so that a good many people got left out in the cold." (Michaels, too, transferred to Rawsonville and retired from there in 1973 after nearly thirty-nine years with Ford Motor Company.) Winstanley concluded, despite his unhappy final year(s), "If I had the opportunity to relive those years at Ford's, I would do the same. It's not the Company, it's those who abuse authority, lie, play politics, and act in various self-serving manners that ruin situations in any organization."

The recollections of Rodes Walters, who worked at Milford from its 1938 opening until its 1958 merger with the Rawsonville plant, reinforce and extend those of Michaels and Winstanley. Like them, Walters had come to Milford from the Rouge plant, where he had worked since 1934 in conditions he described later as "pretty bad." Beyond the need to conform to Ford's overall village industries plan in founding Milford, overcrowding in the Rouge building where he worked prompted the removal of machinery for making carburetors to the new plant site. Walters helped move a "pilot assembly line" from the Rouge to Milford, which was a convenient thirteen miles from where he then lived in South Lyon. The company actively sought workers from the Milford area to go along with Ford's dictates, and Walters was among the first transferred there.[3]

For Walters, working conditions at Milford were "great; it was a challenge, a time of learning, hard but rewarding work. We had modern machinery. . . . We felt like one large family." He recalled more supervisors than did Michaels but not enough to diminish the sense of relative independence both they and Winstanley felt. Milford, moreover, "had air conditioning and this also helped make for a much more pleasant environment than most factories." He and his fellow workers understood that the company "wanted to produce 50% of each part of a Ford car, and we were producing that portion of the carburetor." The workers were knowingly competing with the independent Holley Carburetor Company "in order to keep the price of a carburetor competitive." The Milford plant's equipment, however, "was more

automated than Holley Carburetor's. We built a Holley engineered carburetor, and we had to incorporate any changes they [Holley] made into our
machinery. But where they used drill presses with fixtures and a lot of hand
labor, we used automatic machines with multiple heads and indexing fixtures
to complete an operation with much less labor." Milford's machinery included a complete small cast-iron foundry—the workers claimed that it was
the "smallest fully automated complete foundry in operation in the entire
United States"—plus a zinc die cast department, a screw machine department, and a shipping department. "In short, we took the raw materials
[which came primarily from the Rouge] and processed them, machined
them, assembled them, and then tested the final carburetor and packaged
and shipped them to the engine plants."

As for variety of opportunities at Milford, "jobs were pretty specialized,
but we did get some opportunity to change jobs or take on new assignments."
Walters, like Winstanley, remembered the "skeleton force of skilled trades
people" at the Ypsilanti plant headquarters that went as needed among the
village industries, but he also pointed out that Milford itself "had a small tool
room, a couple of electricians, and two millwrights."

Walters recalled that, "a few workers lived in Detroit. There was no pressure to live at Milford. A few remained at Milford after the plant moved to
Rawsonville." Some workers commuted in car pools. Similarly, there was "no
pressure to farm, though "several employees were from farms and worked
part time farming." Others "worked part time for their parents or for local
businessmen" or for themselves. Many workers "quit Ford when their side
line began to pay better than Ford. One fellow completed his tool and die
training at Ford; upon completing the four-year course, he quit Ford to join
a local company that manufactured hydraulic valves and ended up becoming
president of that company." Meanwhile, "social life was typical of that in a
small town. Bowling maybe once or twice a week in a Ford league," where
Walters met his wife, "or some softball games in the summer. There were
occasional picnics and dances, both usually sponsored by the union." There
were also fishing and hunting parties and card games. Walters retired in 1975
after forty-one years with the Ford Motor Company.

Tom Levandowski worked at the Plymouth plant for many years after
1937, when he transferred from the Rouge following three years there. Of
learning to use the machinery, he said: "I started out to be a thread grinder,
and [a fellow worker] explained everything about thread grinding. . . . And
then we went to Joe blocks and spring gauge to get the sizes—we had a lot
of trouble with sizes at first. . . . And then you had to set in the machine and

get your table to run a certain distance on the tap. . . . It first started out with a kind you had to stop by yourself, with a button. Then they did get automatic. When they got to the end of the line I'd just press a button and stop, see. But if it didn't, why you had to go right into the tail stock." Regarding Plymouth's cleanliness and friendliness, Levandowski recalled, "Honest, you could almost eat off the floor in the plant. That's how clean it was." And the people were so friendly that "I just felt like we were right at home."[4]

Similar sentiments regarding conditions at Newburgh were repeated by Louis Norman, who worked at that plant from its construction in 1933 until it closed in 1947. His father had already worked for Ford Motor Company for several years and knew the superintendent of the Newburgh plant, Jim Gallimore. "Dad came home one night and said, 'Mr. Gallimore wants to see you.'" He went with a friend whose father also worked for the company, and both were promptly hired for the Newburgh site, "although we hadn't even heard of it." Then eighteen years old, he was assigned the task of taking care of the construction tools. Few power tools were used, and much of the construction work was redone until it met Henry Ford's high standards. "They did it to create work, give people work," Norman said. Given the ongoing Great Depression, "there were a lot of people that were mighty appreciative of that." It was not that the work was or seemed makeshift, much less a form of welfare: "The workers were interested in what they were doing and took pride in it," he said. "Workers weren't interested just in making lots of money. . . . That wasn't the way people felt in those days. They took pride in what they made. . . . So anyway I spent fourteen years in there and then we was [*sic*] all transferred outa there and we all went down to Waterford [another village industry] and that's when I left Ford Motor Company and went into business for myself. But, like I say, that was the best years of my life."[5]

A father's influence, albeit more indirectly, also helped Kenneth Gates obtain his position at Nankin Mills, where he worked for many years:

As a small child I first heard of Mr. Ford through my father. Mr. Ford was on his way to the Northville plant. In front of the old Newburgh cemetery was a sand hill, and Mr. Ford got stuck in there with that Model T he was driving. Well he got out and waved to the farmer in the field, with a team of horses and, of course, that was my father. He unhooked the horses and went over and pulled him out, and of course, they stood and talked a little bit, and Mr. Ford says, "Thank you, Harmon," and away he went. Well that, at the time of my interview for the job with Mr. Cutler I told him this story and he said he would relate it to Mr. Ford, he was sure he would remember it. Well, two days later I was told to transfer from the Lincoln plant [i.e., the plant making Lincolns] to the Nankin Mills plant."[6]

Clyde Love's job at Nankin Mills came about without any paternal assistance. He was eighteen years old and was plowing on his father's farm across from the plant when two limousines drove by, and someone got out and asked him if he wanted to work there. When Love said no, the man told him he could have a job if he wanted it. "He gets in the car and takes off," Love recalled. But then Love's brother asked him if he knew who the man was. He didn't. "That was Henry Ford," his brother informed him. In due course Love went across the road and became a machinist at Nankin Mills, where he worked for many years.[7]

Another Nankin Mills worker, Warren Todd, remembered that appearance was very important: "If you worked on the main floor, you wore a white shirt," for the plant "was a showpiece." Children, moreover, were allowed to visit the facility "at any time" it was operating to see the engraving machines that printed Ford identification badges; this was Ford's own instruction to the superintendent. Todd, a tool-and-die apprentice, eventually left Nankin Mills for a job at the Rouge plant as an experimental parts fabricator. Any comparisons of the two experiences are unknown.[8]

Gates, like other Nankin Mills workers, had a garden:

> In the years that Nankin Mills was in operation, people had time off . . . [when Ford] would change models. Therefore the garden work came in handy, sometimes this could be two or three months long. It was about 1935 when the plant became the engraving department. Engravers, lay-out people, and machine personnel were moved from the Rouge plant. The employees who were already working at Nankin Mills at the change-over time were retrained to run machines that came with the engraving operation. At the change-over, approximately 1935, the inside of the mill was completely redone and they put down oak flooring, two inches thick, screwed 'em down and then put plugs on top of them, and highly polished, and we were supposed to keep it that way. In fact, they used rubber matting for the aisles where we walked and we were supposed to use that. The grounds surrounding the plant were improved with a new parking lot and landscaping.

As Gates concluded, "I really enjoyed working with these nice people [including his superintendent and foreman] the kind of work I did, and that was the start of thirty-six years with Ford Motor Company."[9]

Still another Nankin Mills worker, Ed Bauman, had similar positive sentiments. Bauman was a tool-and-die apprentice who had to quit his job and run the family farm after just a few years at the plant because of the sudden passing of both his father and his brother. "It was a nice group. We got along good, had a great foreman, and everybody cooperated." The village industries "put a lot of local people to work."[10]

By contrast, Bruce Richard, who worked at the comparatively large Ypsilanti plant from 1949 until 1979, found it somewhat more impersonal than the smaller sites. Many employees lived nearby, but others came from as far away as Toledo. Himself a native and resident of Plymouth Richard graduated from the Henry Ford Trade School in 1938 and, before serving in World War II, worked in Ford's soybean laboratory in Greenfield Village. He was an electromechanical engineer at Ypsilanti and, on the whole, had a positive experience there.[11]

Irene Shaw worked at the overwhelmingly female Phoenix plant from 1925, three years after it opened, until it closed in 1946 (after which she worked at Ypsilanti, where operations were moved in 1946, until her 1963 retirement). As she recollected, "The Highland Park girls came out to show them how to do the little [generator] cut out—what we were making then, and only single girls and widows were being hired. I was very fortunate to be hired in 1925. Mr. Ivor Evans was superintendent and Miss Sullivan was vice-president." Both had transferred from the Highland Park plant. It was characteristic of the gender disparities of the time that even at Phoenix, a man would ultimately be in charge—not that Shaw seemed either surprised or dissatisfied. Far from it: "We had a very unusual, clean plant. Hardwood floors—all polished, windows washed every week. Our wages started at four dollars a day. Then in 1925, I got five dollars a day. About 1927 it was seven dollars and forty cents a day." Here, however, Shaw was unhappy: "Ann Augustin was getting seven sixty—she was getting more production, they thought. I took the wire off my tally, which was covered, and had a wire attached to it. I found out I was doing more because I took the wire off and Mrs. Sullivan came over to me. She said, 'Why did you take the wire off the tally?' And I said, 'Because I wanted to know what I was doing. I knew Ann Augustin was getting seven sixty and I was only getting seven forty. And when I found out I [saw I] was doing more than I needed to do.' And she said, 'Well don't let this happen again.'"[12] Like the other village industries, the pace of work at Phoenix was demanding, with two three-minute relief periods and a twenty-minute lunch break (increased to thirty minutes with unionization).

Production of the voltage regulator began in 1935, Shaw continued, "when the eight cylinder car came out. Mister Ford [regularly] came through the plant, but he would just smile." One day, however, "he came through with the . . . first regulator that was made and he said, 'I want each part, I want the best operator to do the job. And they figured I—I being on nineteen years on soldering—I would probably be the one to do it. So they stood behind me and I soldered the first regulator. Was I ever nervous! And Mr. Ford looked at it and said, 'She's done a marvelous job and let's keep it up.'" Other Ford visits reflected his obsession with cleanliness and the consequent need to keep Phoenix spotless.

As Shaw concluded, "You work—you enjoy your work, if you enjoy it, it is wonderful, and I am so thankful that Henry Ford opened that shop to widows [and divorced women] because I was left with two children to support [through a recent divorce]—no alimony, and you can imagine how thankful I was when I started. And I give Henry Ford a world of credit for having that shop open to us."

Similar positive sentiments are found in the reminiscences of two other retired Phoenix workers: Grace Burley, who when hired was a widow with two children, and Carol Dodge, who when hired was a single woman trying to support her widowed mother. Burley worked at Phoenix from 1942 until it closed, then with Shaw at Ypsilanti until 1963, when she also retired. Dodge worked at Phoenix from 1934 until she married and left the company in 1945. All three characterized the work environment at Phoenix as "just one big, happy family," with regular observances of employee birthdays, weddings, and other special occasions, plus annual picnics for retired employees.[13]

Kenneth Edwards, later to be chief clerk of the entire village industries system, worked at Milan from 1938 to 1941 after having labored off and on at the Rouge since 1934. Following six months of making ignition coils at Milan, he moved into the plant's office as a clerk and then Milan's chief clerk. Having been part of both labor and management gave him a unique perspective on the entire enterprise. He found working conditions at Milan generally more pleasant than at the Rouge: "The place was so much smaller that everybody knew each other, . . . as compared to working at the Rouge where you were just another individual." A small labor force could mean a greater variety of tasks, but not necessarily so: "If you were a relief man on these jobs, we'll say on an assembly line, you would have to know several different jobs. But normally without the effect of absenteeism or changes in production schedules, you pretty much did the same job day after day." Relations between workers and managers were not automatically idyllic simply because there were fewer of both: "It gets back to human nature. If the superintendent of that particular plant was a person that tended to be obnoxious and a driver, he wasn't liked any better than he would be anywhere else. If he was a person that got along well with people, he was highly respected and well liked." Not surprisingly, "probably the workers knew the fellow that was in charge much better than they would in a lot bigger operation; whether they liked him or not just depended on his personality."[14]

Milan was, of course, integrated with the other village industries but would have formal contact with another plant "only in the event that there was some component we made that we shipped to another plant, or some service that we gave or received from another plant." Yet Milan was not just a lonely outpost: it communicated primarily with the Ypsilanti headquarters, but the parts that it—like the other eighteen plants—made "went directly to assembly plants across the country," not just the Rouge.

Edwards engaged in the same company-sponsored social activities at Milan and later at Ypsilanti as other village industry workers, such as sports and dances, but he didn't remember these company-sponsored events as having made a "dramatic impression" on the small towns themselves. As for the village industries overall, Edwards recalled that "there were instances, I would say probably not involving over ten percent of the workers, where they were from farms and would take time off in the summer to work on the farms and come back in the fall. But generally the personnel in the plants were citizens of the little villages themselves." Edwards himself was born in Michigan, was raised on a farm, and had purchased another farm five miles from Milan when he began working at that plant. He had intended to operate it part time and so practice what Ford preached. "I tried for a year or two [to] work both jobs but it was a matter of being up all night and getting very little sleep and because of that I was late getting crops in, they didn't do well, sometimes I'd lose a crop. So after a couple of years of that, I just rented the farm out" (though he lived in the farmhouse) and "concentrated on working at my job at Ford." Edwards's experience was clearly common.

As for hiring workers already employed by someone else in the area, a policy Ford disavowed, Edwards remembered just a few such instances throughout the village industries but didn't deny the likelihood of others. "It was like anything else, you know, in a small area like this it was the area politicians and community leaders and the Company would sometimes need things from the villages and people who were on the village councils or in the Ford sales organizations, particularly the Ford dealerships, they would have people that could come to them and say, 'Is there anything you can do to get us a job at Ford's?' And they would call and if people were being hired, they were very often given the preference." Edwards added that the very proximity of so many workers to their homes created "social pressure" to do a particularly good job, lest the local community learn through gossip of inefficiency or worse. Although the company's "quality standards were just the same" at the village industries as in conventional Ford plants, this peer pressure raised them. Edwards estimated that "probably 95% of the people that were working in the village industries preferred working there to working in the Rouge." Those who became discontented were usually those who were ambitious for other jobs and felt "stymied" in their small plants.

Such positive overall sentiments, however, were hardly unanimous even in my modest sample. Dale Noble spent one summer at Saline in the early 1930s while putting himself through college but never worked for the Ford Motor Company again. As he reflected over a half-century later, small-scale management did not necessarily mean greater democracy or better leadership: "Like everyone [I] had to have 'drag' to get what was nothing more than a common laborer's job. . . . [The] supervising hierarchy was composed of individuals that one simply could not respect. The foreman at the Saline project was a local 'dead beat.' He had a bunch of kids, never paid his doctor bills, or any other bills that he could possibly avoid."[15]

More significant, perhaps, because he was a lifelong Ford Motor Company employee, was the experience of John Peters. "I started at Flat Rock on November 17, 1936," he recalled more than four decades later. Before he got the job, "every morning, for about six weeks, you stood on the line outside the plant there, and they would come . . . and say no hiring. So I then wrote the plant manager there a letter that I graduated from Flat Rock High, and he sent me a card for a job at Ford that then was seventy-five cents an hour or six dollars a day. Six dollars a day was big wages then, and I was lucky to get a job them days, as them were the days of who you know, etc." (compare Norman's more positive recollections regarding his father's influence). At the Flat Rock plant "the better jobs were downstairs, and they belonged to the friends. Non-friends were expected to work there [only] three to four months a year. So I put in three months or four and then the mighty Rouge plant took a bunch of us as they needed more workers and that was the first time a transfer like that occurred. I jumped on that and asked to be transferred to the Rouge as the Rouge was recognized as more steady work, and more opportunity, as they had an apprentice school there also."[16]

Peters's employment route was thus the opposite of that of Michaels,

Winstanley, and Levandowski, who transferred from the Rouge to Milford and Plymouth. The Rouge plant was hardly free from the kind of favoritism Peters describes, but "being so vast, [it] was a more stable plant, with more opportunities," despite his having "to drive almost three times farther" from home than Flat Rock. Home, moreover, was a forty-acre farm he bought from his parents with income from his job, thereby representing a portion of Ford's scheme; most of his fellow Flat Rock workers either owned or worked on farms as well. But work at Flat Rock making headlights had been no picnic. Because "the new boys got the worst jobs and polishing [his job] was light but dusty from the polishing wheel that had dust flying from it, every hour or less you had to change it with your partner as two polishers were on one machine." In addition, Flat Rock "had no cafeteria, had a restroom and a coat room with just hangers, and we ate sitting on the floor spreading newspapers." After transferring, Peters worked at the Rouge for forty-five years, and thanks to the apprentice school courses he took there, he moved into a better position than the one he started with.

Another former Flat Rock employee, Ralph Cameron, who worked there for several years from 1939 on, remembered a hiring policy like the one described by Peters. "Someone would go out to the bridge and would pick men to go in—apparently if he liked their looks. He would point to as many men as he wanted, perhaps saying, 'You in the red jacket, follow me.'"[17]

Bill Carter, who worked at Flat Rock from 1934 to 1939, recalled the obsession with cleanliness. "If anyone wasn't working he was given a paint brush and told to start painting . . . they chipped paint off so they could repaint" and thus keep busy. More disturbing, "some men were paid five cents an hour more to spy on other workers." Yet Carter appreciated the high wages and the proximity to his Flat Rock residence.[18]

Charlie Oestrike, a Flat Rock employee from 1934 to 1941, also recalled that "it was a demanding place to work." Everyone "had to look busy all of the time, but then, business would be better today if this same principle was applied." And he, too, appreciated the high wages and the proximity to his Flat Rock home. "One advantage," he said, was that the plant "tried to hire people from the Flat Rock High School."[19]

The experiences of Noble, Peters, Cameron, Carter, Oestrike, and their fellow workers—or would-be workers—in the hiring process are strikingly similar to those of African Americans in the Detroit area after World War II, and not just at Ford but also at General Motors and Chrysler. As noted in chapter 4, Thomas Sugrue uncovered numerous examples of discriminatory hiring—or nonhiring—that reflected no discernible pattern, not even in terms of the racial composition of the communities in which various plants were located. Instead, he found arbitrary decisions, often but not always based on race. As with these village industry workers, the importance of personal or familial or other connections to those doing the hiring continued after unionization began and after the Second World War ended. The decentralization of hiring before and after the war hardly guaranteed fairness and, in some respects, allowed for discrimination that was not restricted to race.[20] Nor were such practices, of course, unique to either the Detroit area or the automobile industry but were fairly common throughout much of the nation in those days.

Still more disturbing, however, are the memories of Raymond Pflug, who, in order to earn money for college, worked at the Milford plant from its opening in 1938 until the early 1940s, thereby overlapping with Michaels. Like Michaels, Pflug lived in another town about fifteen miles away and drove to and from his job; likewise, he did not live on a farm. Pflug's criticisms pertain less to favoritism in hiring than to inefficiency in operation (if also to that obsession with cleanliness in the process). As Pflug wrote in 1988:

> Before the war I worked at the Milford plant, which was building carburetors. I was there from the beginning and it was a mess, with carburetors being shipped down to the Rouge plant one day and returned the next, rejected. (The plant employed, as I recall, between two and three hundred men.) The superintendent, whose name, I think, was Blacow, was under the gun, I suppose, and rode us to "get them out." My job was to get the top half of the carburetor on the belt, having checked it and inserted a flutter valve. The parts were cast, and the foundry, of course, was also new. I would remove the basket, dump the parts on the bench, and start. Often the parts, which had to be round in order for the flutter to seal, were oblong. I would take a mallet and try to pound them into shape, often to no avail. I recall one occasion when Blacow came up as I was pounding and the line was waiting for my parts. In his usual unpleasant tone he asked what was holding things up. I pointed out that the parts were deficient. He grabbed one, looked at it, threw it back on the bench, and red-faced, shouted, "I don't care; get them out." That was the pattern in the early days. When no parts appeared, one went to the toolroom for some rags and cleaned up. No standing around. Ford was a nut on cleanliness.

In these respects, conditions at Milford closely resembled those at the Rouge in its early days and, for that matter, at many other conventional plants—realities far removed from Ford Motor Company publicity. As Pflug concluded, "It was hard, dull work, as all assembly line work is. When I enlisted in the air force my days in the auto industry were over." Even so, all was not entirely unpleasant, for "there was some socializing—Ford paid in cash, in little brown envelopes on Friday, and some would repair to a local bar for beer, and when I left to go into the army, there was a fairly large gathering."[21]

Notwithstanding the pressure on all plant managers, from both Henry Ford and the company, to keep the village industries clean and efficient, those managers appear to have had considerable power not only in hiring workers but also in setting the tone for their respective workplaces. The positive and negative experiences reported here reflect to a considerable degree the varying personalities and styles of the managers. Gallimore, the head of both the Plymouth and the Newburgh site, resided in Plymouth for many years and became a highly respected local citizen after whom, in 1957, a new elementary school was named (some other plant managers, like some village industry workers, lived comparatively far from their places of employment).[22] Still, many of those supervised by even the kindest manager might, like Pflug, nevertheless wish to spend part of their pay at week's end on social activities.

Most village industries workers initially received a minimum of $6.00 per day from the company for their efforts—the same as their counterparts at the Rouge and conventional branch plants—but many steadily earned higher wages, including Shaw and other women at Phoenix. Those at Waterford, for example, started at $10.00 per day because of their skilled labor. In all cases, these wages had more purchasing power in the rural communities than in the large cities. As Peters, among other former workers, noted, however, "There was no such thing as anything over forty hours," for Henry Ford believed in an eight-hour day, five-day week.[23] Only unionization and World War II production needs (see chapters 7 and 10) brought overtime pay. To be sure, like Ford's $5.00-per-day minimum wage for all qualified (male) workers in 1914, his pay scale for later generations of workers, including those in the village industries, has been viewed by some as one of several means of satisfying potentially discontented employees and, simultaneously, restoring his public image.[24]

Many workers throughout the village industries participated in various recreational and social activities organized by the company that often brought together employees from several, if not all, of the nineteen plants. These included sports (baseball, bowling, fishing, golf, horseshoes, hunting, and volleyball), dancing, picnics, and photography. Michaels, for example, recalled participating in a bowling league in winter and a golf league in spring and summer, and Gates remembered playing ball during lunch hours in good weather. Team sports, moreover, created friendly competition among the different plants and so could raise individual and group morale while strengthening loyalty to the company.[25] They would also provide means for workers to get to know their counterparts at other plants and presumably to discuss administrative and operational matters in the process.

Despite some workers' negative experiences, the village industries did not, it appears, generate what the historian Wayne Lewchuk has characterized as the Ford Motor Company's overall "fraternalism as a managerial strategy." This strategy was gradually implemented as the number of skilled workers steadily declined, replaced by semiskilled or unskilled workers who, not surprisingly, generally disliked their specialized and monotonous tasks. In order to reduce the alienation of its overwhelmingly male workforce, the company not only provided comparatively high wages but also reconceptualized notions of masculinity to fit the new workplace. In place of the independence and decision-making power of earlier days under skilled workers' own considerable authority came fraternalism and hard work under managerial supervision and control. In place of skilled workers' various organizations came family activities under company scrutiny (such as that of the Sociological Department). Most important, "making useful products in the company of other men" became the revised masculine ideal.[26] At the village industries, by contrast, not just at the predominantly female Phoenix plant but at the other eighteen as well, the atmosphere was decidedly different: there were far fewer manifestations of this new masculine ideal.

Perhaps it is therefore not surprising that journalists such as Drew Pearson and Arthur Van Vlissingen gave their readers the false impression that the workers they met at the various sites were uniformly content and the perhaps more accurate impression that they were among the most dedicated and industrious workers in the entire Ford Motor Company. "Out here," reported Van Vlissingen in 1938, "the real importance of making top-quality precision gages has a chance to be felt. The men are not a sub-sub-department tucked off in a corner and almost forgotten. Talk with any of the men. You get a feeling of craft and personal pride which you thought had long since vanished from the factories of the earth." Individual accounts like that of John Bird about Albert Risch in the 1944 *Saturday Evening Post* only confirmed this rosy view.[27]

Yet Paul Kellogg, an otherwise favorably impressed journalist, did see limitations to the original scheme and was not awed by his conversation with Ford himself. He noticed that a number of workers had either insufficient time for large-scale farming or, given their comparatively high wages from Ford, declining interest in farming of any kind. Some had actually left their farms altogether for the local towns, either renting or selling their rural properties. "We'll quit farming and work with Henry Ford," Kellogg often heard them say—in an unintended and ironic rejection of Ford's plans. As Kellogg further reported in 1924, "I had not chanced on a tractor. It was a countryside seemingly unmindful of Ford and all his works."[28]

Those who did remain on the farm frequently had their families assisting them in daily chores, as did Albert Risch, who could himself work only before and after daily factory work and on his annual two-week vacation and who had been farming only briefly anyway. Or they engaged not in old-fashioned farming but in market gardening, in "single, cash crops to sell to commodities speculators" rather than various crops for general farming and self-sufficiency.[29] Similarly, those whose factory jobs varied with changes in production schedules and other economic conditions beyond their control had mixed feelings at best about farming and the work routines it required. Ford, however, as company engineer Charles Voorhess remembered, couldn't understand these reactions and so never deemed them fatal to his overall scheme.[30] Nor did he ever appreciate the irony of his own considerable contribution to large-scale power farming (in later terms, agribusiness) and the consequent decline of family farms.

Ironically, too, Kellogg perceived, some of the more ambitious factory workers felt limited in the variety and sophistication of their jobs. "What chance would it have offered Henry Ford," Kellogg asked, "had he been born fifty years later, and set off to Northville instead of Detroit to learn to be a mechanic? A slim chance compared with what a lad could pick up in the eighties at . . . the places where Ford himself learned his trade in Detroit."[31] Indeed, former Milford worker Michaels, generally pleased with his lengthy experience there, nevertheless conceded years later that though "there were a variety of jobs, you usually specialized in one and hoped you would get a better one." And as former Flat Rock worker Peters, who spent most of his career at the Rouge, reflected years later, although in both places work could be monotonous, the Rouge at least was more interesting in its diversity of specialized tasks, even if ordinary employees there too "did one job over and over, day after day."[32]

Ford, however, tried to answer this criticism in his *Today and Tomorrow* by making a virtue out of this kind of labor. "Of necessity," he conceded, "the work of an individual workman must be repetitive—not otherwise can he gain the effortless speed which makes low prices and earns high wages. Some of our tasks are exceedingly monotonous, . . . but then, many minds are very monotonous—many men want to earn a living without thinking, and for these men a task which demands no brains is a boon." Nevertheless, Ford continued, "we have jobs in plenty which [do] need brains . . . and men with brains do not long stay in repetitive work."[33]

Kellogg had confessed at the conclusion of his articles, "I have called Ford's . . . dams, and his handful of little power plants on the River Rouge a laboratory. The word conveys the wrong impression if that impression is one of the scientific approach of a research department." Rather, he continued, "It is more akin to his inventor's workshop. He is puttering in it as of old."[55] Ford's statement two years later (1926) that "business is a science and that all other sciences are contributing to it" would not, then, have won Kellogg's acceptance.[34]

Significantly, none of the former village industries workers whom I or others have interviewed, whatever their feelings about working conditions, thought of their plants as experiments. Nor, for that matter, did Superintendent Roscoe Smith and his chief clerk, Kenneth Edwards.[35] Even those who praised them always regarded them as conventional plants in both their production and organizational structures, notwithstanding Ford's stress on their alleged experimental qualities. Nor did these former workers have special ties to or sense of solidarity with the other village industries. First and foremost, they were part of the Ford Motor Company empire—as they were routinely reminded.

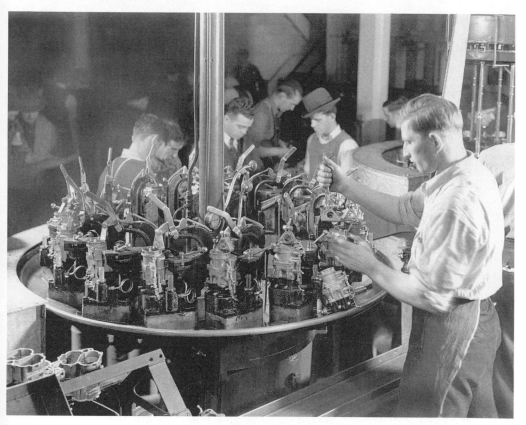

A worker testing carburetors at the Milford plant, 1938, the year it opened.

A Milford plant worker using a Morris drilling machine, 1945.

(OPPOSITE) *An engraver at the Waterford plant guiding the styllus of a Dedrich engraving machine in fashioning the contours of a tiny stamping die, ca. 1947. Waterford's workers were generally considered to be the most skilled of all the village industry employees.*

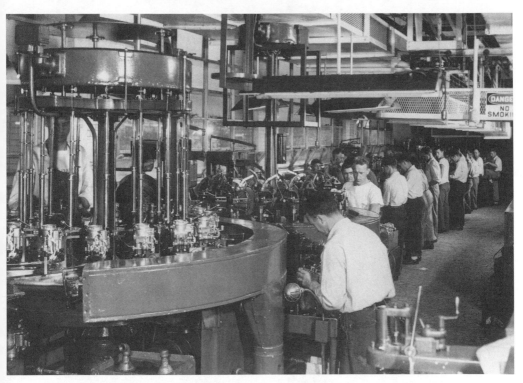

Workers at the carburetor final assembly line at Milford, 1946. Several of the village industries had assembly lines comparable in operation—though naturally not in size—to conventional Ford Motor Company plants.

Older workers at the Ypsilanti plant, 1937. All of the village industries employed older workers.

Women working on voltage regulators at the Phoenix plant during World War II, 1942.

A woman calibrating voltage regulators at the Phoenix plant during World War II, 1942.

A woman starting an engine at the Tecumseh plant (which opened in 1935), 1941. This was one of the relatively few women workers at the village industries apart from those at the Phoenix and Ypsilanti plants.

Workers at the Ypsilanti plant, including one of the few African Americans at any of the village industries, on an assembly line making small cylinders, 1947.

CHAPTER 7

Unionization

NEARLY ALL THE VILLAGE INDUSTRIES HAD COME INTO
being by 1941, when the Ford Motor Company allowed its workforce
finally to unionize—the last and most reluctant of the American automakers
to do so.[1] Ford's personal and in turn corporate hostility toward unions has
been well documented.[2] Suffice it here to quote the 1937 pamphlet *Fordism*
by Carl Raushenbush of the pro-union League for Industrial Democracy:

> On the industrial field in America, two formidable antagonists stand op-
> posed—the United Automobile Workers [UAW], backed by the CIO
> [Congress of Industrial Organizations], and the Ford Motor Company,
> backed by all the anti-union forces of America. The Company is fighting
> for a principle—*the principle of autocracy in industry*. The union men
> want better conditions on the job. They also want to have jobs made avail-
> able on the basis of equality, not dependent on political connections or
> subject to arbitrary firings. To them this is the matter of *principle*. Their
> method for restraining autocracy is the method of *collective bargaining*. In
> Detroit's first Labor Day parade in 20 years, the Ford employees who
> marched wore masks to show that they would be arbitrarily fired if the
> Company knew that they had taken part.[3]

Having repeatedly declared that his company would never recognize the
UAW or any other union—and that all his workers were loyal to him and
uninterested in organizing—Ford nevertheless reluctantly dealt with unions
in his foreign subsidiaries and in his domestic independent parts suppliers.
Several years before its 1941 agreement with the UAW, the company went
so far as to encourage a subservient union of its own, the Ford Brotherhood
of America, Inc., membership in which required signing a pledge of confidence in the company. Meanwhile, the notorious Ford Service Department
under Harry Bennett discouraged workers from joining the UAW by punish-

ing those who did and especially those who recruited new members. Punishment could take the form of demotion to lower-paid and less desirable jobs, outright discharge, blacklisting from other automobile company jobs, or physical violence. Such tactics led the *New York Times* to call the Service Department "the largest private quasi-military organization in existence."[4] In the absence (prior to the New Deal) of unemployment compensation, worker's compensation, and pensions, such reprisals kept many potential UAW members from even the consideration of joining.[5]

As David Gartman observes, the Depression fostered unexpected decentralization of a kind within the auto industry, above all in the Ford Motor Company. Just because of the scarcity of jobs there was greater opportunity for low-level foremen to exercise exceptional authority and to pressure their charges mercilessly to work harder lest they lose their jobs: "Formally, power over hiring, firing, and wages remained centralized and under the control of the employment departments. However, during the depression, top officials in the bureaucracy seemed to have allowed the de facto decentralization of power into the hands of foremen, because the centralized rule-governed structure was no longer necessary to ensure a stable and compliant labor force."[6]

If, on the one hand, the friction between labor and management that increasingly pervaded the Ford workforce in the 1920s and 1930s was largely absent from the village industries, on the other hand, the village industry workers certainly lacked the collective power of what became the UAW. Yet no doubt many of those workers, including some at the largest of the village industries, prided themselves on their very individuality and job flexibility. To suggest, as some have, that Ford established the village industries *solely* to stifle union activity in his company overall is to attribute to him singular motives that are without conclusive basis. The reliance on conventional branch plants in other states would probably have sufficed—and would surely have been much cheaper. This was the strategy of General Motors, especially after the sit-down strikes that led to its acceptance of unionization in 1937. As *Business Week* reported in that same year: "General Motors and Ford are on the move. Both companies are in the midst of major decentralization programs. In the case of General Motors, it represents mostly a trek out of Michigan; with Ford it is confined within Michigan's boundaries, but is aimed at getting away from the huge concentration of men at Dearborn. . . . Chevrolet will build immediately a plant at Buffalo to make 1,200 motors and axles daily. . . . Heretofore all motors were made at Flint, all axles at Detroit."[7] The article gave five reasons behind the move to Buffalo, but only two related to unionization efforts: GM's desire "to get away from labor-torn Flint," and the ability of union organizers there "to tie up production completely by shutting down the Flint engine factory." The other three reasons related to the cheaper costs and greater efficiency of operations made possible by spreading them outside of Michigan. Indeed, the article conceded that "the Buffalo plant is not an outgrowth of the G.M. strike, although the strike probably accelerated action. It has been under consideration for a year."[8]

Moreover, within the Ford Motor Company overall, the comparatively modest number of conservative rural workers hardly dented the growing ranks of union-oriented, militant urban laborers. Nor did their comparatively greater ethnic, religious, and racial homogeneity vis-à-vis the much larger urban Ford workforce eliminate the need for social control over, if not social uplift of, the latter; many of those in the foreign-born ranks no doubt resented Ford's Americanization crusades and sought unionization because of them, among other reasons. Even Thomas Sugrue, who contends that the entire automobile industry's decentralization efforts were avowedly antiunion, concedes that "the early decentralization experiments had little impact on Detroit." Sugrue does not discuss the village industries, but he acknowledges that "the city's share of national automobile production remained large throughout the first half of the twentieth century."[9] Only in post-1945 Detroit did decentralization, along with other factors, vastly reduce the UAW's ranks and its power.

What *can* be confirmed is the *perception* among union leaders that decentralization of any kind, by any of the automakers (not just Ford and not just the village industries projects), was antiunion in origin and design. The mere threat of decentralization, they claimed, was intended to scare workers into abandoning unionization efforts or, where unions already existed, either to force workers into compliance with management policies—not least, lower wages and longer hours—or to punish those who resisted them by moving their jobs to regions such as the South in search of cheaper overhead and labor costs. At the UAW's annual convention in 1937 a resolution was passed to examine more systematically all decentralization policies and practices by automobile and parts manufacturers. By the time of the 1939 convention the growth of unorganized small plants by unnamed manufacturers—including independent nonunion suppliers—was specified as a serious threat to unionization overall.[10] A 1939 cartoon crystallized labor's views.[11]

Certainly, organized labor was not unjustified in these fears, for Ford's hostility toward cities had been extended to other auto executives, concerned

KOKOMO EXPRESS

Such decentralization schemes are resisted by the UAW-CIO

Decentralization schemes were opposed by the unions, who saw all transfers of workers and plants to smaller towns and cities—represented here by Kokomo, Indiana—as undermining labor organizing and solidarity. From United Auto Workers Local #3 newsletter, August 23, 1939. (Walter Reuther Library, Wayne State University)

that the very industrial concentration they had achieved might lead to labor unrest. The sheer proximity of so many workers under so much pressure to produce so quickly might—and eventually did—prompt the kind of actions that shut down an entire industry just because of centralized production, as during the 1918–20 strikes in major body and parts plants and then in the 1936–37 sit-down strikes, in which workers stopped work but remained in the plant.[12]

Organized labor's cynicism and hostility toward the village industries can be summarized by the following article in a 1939 UAW publication:

START FORD SHOP IN MICHIGAN VILLAGE

A new Ford parts plant—another link to King Henry's chain of "strike-proof" decentralized factories—is rapidly nearing completion in Brooklyn, Michigan. Job applications were accepted only from workers who have lived within four and a half miles of the village at least a year.

Ford's motive in locating the plant there is to stem the rising tide of unionism by hiring rural workers whose minds have been poisoned against the UAW. About 100 men will be employed. The factory will manufacture headlights and horns.

Production is expected to begin within a month. Brooklyn merchants, visioning a steady stream of wages pouring into the community, are enthusiastic. The prospective workers are almost all farmers, unacquainted with Ford labor policies or factory discipline.[13]

In the same context, at the UAW's 1940 convention, one delegate lamented that Ford Motor Company's contract with an independent supplier of carburetors had been "taken away from the Detroit company who had it" and that "the carburetors were now being made in Milford." The wages paid Milford workers, the delegate claimed, were considerably lower than those of the UAW's "organized shops."[14]

Repeated assertions by Ford and others that the village industries were inspired by very different motives clearly made no difference to organized labor. Nor, for that matter, did the fact that the village industries had begun when the labor movement, at least in Michigan, was anything but powerful, much less growing.[15] Rather, the village industries (and conventional branch plants) were seen as critical to Ford's antiunion strategy: according to Raushenbush in 1937: "The Company has strenuously resisted labor disputes [i.e., union organizing] in its own outlying assembly plants, in contrast to Ford concessions in parts plants. When it has been compelled to recognize the union, it has done so indirectly"—though this was apparently not a major problem at the village industries themselves.[16]

Some Ford labor critics went so far as to attribute the establishment of the village industries to Ford's desire to avoid paying unemployment or retraining costs when the company was reluctantly forced into annual model changeovers. The opportunity for Ford employees to farm when production was halted so that machinery could be altered was thus seen as a way for the company to save money. The fact that this view ignores the increasing need for year-round production throughout the company and so an end to seasonal layoffs is revealing of labor's sometimes misplaced criticism of Ford. More important, such an argument ignores Ford's emphasis on hiring rural workers rather than the urban employees still affected by any seasonal layoffs and shutdowns.[17] A more persuasive rationale, one predating the changeover to annual models, is Ford's alleged desire to mitigate the discontent at least of rural workers, insofar as repeated overproduction of parts and cars between October and May left many out of work—and without unemployment compensation—for several months. Such workers would be less susceptible to unionization efforts if, as detailed earlier, they had farms or garden plots to supplement their factory income, which some former village industry employees recall as a benefit.[18]

Another UAW publication editorialized in 1939 that decentralization was actually "industrial feudalism." Ford, it went on, "has pioneered in this movement; General Motors is rapidly adopting the same policy; and Chrysler is following suit." The only solution, it concluded, "lies in the refusal of the union men to work with the products that come from these plants until they are organized and under contract to the UAW-CIO."[19] Lest the automobile manufacturers contend that, far from originating decentralization, they were merely following the strategies of other industries, the UAW declared in a 1937 publication:

> The textile, boot and shoe, knitgoods and other rulers of industries long ago attempted to kill unionism by decentralizing production. With what result? Unionism followed them to the ends of the country and today all these industries are being swiftly unionized despite the fact that plants are scattered throughout the nation. What is more: it is not as profitable or simple for automobile companies to decentralize production.
>
> We do not underestimate the decentralization policy of the auto corporations, but, gentlemen, is there not just the faintest suggestion of bluff in your publicity—the hope that workers will drop their union membership if threatened with plant removal? In conclusion, the UAW has become so fond of your companionship, it could not bear the thought of parting, and like an ardent lover would pursue you to the furthest and most remote corners of the earth.[20]

Union opposition to decentralization went still further, as evidenced in this 1938 UAW article regarding a new General Motors plant:

GM BUILDS PLANT TO THWART LABOR ORGANIZATIONS

The new Ternstedt plant, recently opened in Trenton, N.J., is one of the most efficient plants erected in the automobile industry. The plant has the most modern methods of production, a huge conveyor system, automatic machines which eliminate considerable man-power over older and obsolete methods used in other factories doing similar work. It is highly significant that the General Motors Corporation built this moulding plant in one of the backward sections of American industrial life. The General Motors officials and engineers designed the plant and took into consideration the possibilities of labor organization.

It is possible to store a full 18½ days production in the warehouse, or some 46,250 completed sets of body hardware, packed in cardboard containers ready for shipment to supply Fisher Body and General Motors assembly plants.

This is undoubtedly considered a bulwark against labor organization. It is readily seen that if the workers in this plant went on a strike to settle grievances, that the Company would be able to keep them out of the plant for at least 18½ days before they tied up the balance of the G.M. plants.

Another feature of the plant is its large storage rooms. It is finished products. Consequently, a feeder plant going on a strike could not expect to use a General Motors plant in Trenton, N.J., to pressure a management to settle a strike, because the General Motors plant would not be effected [*sic*] for a 30 day period.

This plant was built in New Jersey, because it is possible to pay lower wages in that district than is being paid in the Detroit area, for the same type of work.

The General Motors Corporation has again taken the lead in attempting to forestall labor organization, and consequently increase their profits.

The General Motors Organizing Committee, however, looks hopefully forward to organizing the workers in the Trenton, N.J., plant, and expect to give them the benefits of labor organization in the immediate future.[21]

What made this union critique of decentralization especially significant, but not unique, was its linkage of decentralization to technological advance as well as to hostility to organized labor. It reflected a pervasive fear, among autoworkers throughout the industry and workers overall throughout the country, of "technological unemployment": the loss of their jobs to ever more versatile and efficient machinery. Organized labor used the term explicitly, and in the same sense as those who, thinking themselves wholly original, use it today regarding the effects on employment of computers, robotics, and

other high-tech advances.[22] Moreover, the fledgling UAW fought technological unemployment along with more traditional antilabor obstacles and
viewed it, in the words of one union leader, as "inextricably bound up with
such other problems as seniority, shorter work-week, etc."[23] Although the
village industries barely made a dent in the overall number of displaced Ford
workers, and were clearly intended to provide jobs for at least a few thousand
new Ford employees, their own modern machinery made them suspect as
well.

To its credit, the UAW, at least in its public stance, did not oppose technological advances per se. As Emil Mazey, president of a Detroit UAW local,
and later UAW national secretary-treasurer, wrote in a union publication,
"Workers . . . know that the machine is not their enemy, that the ownership
of the machine is responsible for technological unemployment." In fact, "labor has a program for solving this displacement of labor by improved methods of production. We recognize the machine as our best friend if it is used
to build and advance the standard of living of society as a whole"—unlike, he
concluded, the then current state of exploitation for the sake of profits.[24]

Significantly, Mazey was responding to a *Detroit Free Press* editorial blam-
ing organized labor itself for technological unemployment on the grounds
that unions were allegedly forcing management to introduce machinery to
compensate for excessive union demands for higher wages and shorter hours.
Mazey found such blame misplaced: workers had been the victims of technological unemployment centuries before the formation of unions (such as
the craftsmen displaced by the English Industrial Revolution) and were seeking more pay and fewer hours precisely to offset the potential effects of
technological unemployment imposed by management upon them. Likewise, a 1939 resolution circulated throughout the UAW (and the entire CIO)
argued that "no [further] increase in unemployment shall result" if these
objectives were adequately fulfilled.[25] Exactly how improvements in wages
and hours would help workers who might still lose their jobs, much less those
who had already lost them—other than by providing greater savings for
emergency use—was not spelled out.

One General Motors employee declared that he and his fellow workers
"would not fight against the installation of automatic machinery. We welcome
it as a relief from the drudgery of monotonous labor." For workers, the basic
question was who would benefit from the use of labor-saving devices. Going
further, the increasingly militant—and creative—UAW asserted its own control over technology through its sit-down strikes especially at General Motors
plants and that company's acceptance of the union in 1937.[26]

Ford was aware of labor's stance on technological unemployment but was not, of course, convinced by the UAW's arguments. As he told the *New York Times* in 1933: "The machines are not driving men out of work. Quite the contrary. Our experience for thirty years is that every time we reduce[d] the number of men on a given job, and thus lowered costs, we had to hire even more men on account of increased business." He contended that "every efficient business creates many outside businesses" and so more jobs, including the work of building the additional machines.[27] That this argument did not convince workers that Ford lacked ulterior motives in promoting technological advances in his various facilities is hardly surprising. The real issue, as social critic Stuart Chase put it bluntly, was whether "the machine [was] destroying jobs FASTER than new jobs are opening up"—and he, at least, answered in the affirmative.[28] Consequently, Ford's defense did not lessen the UAW's reservations about either the village industries or decentralization overall.

Paradoxically, however, the extraordinary centralization and rigidity of the Rouge plant was also deemed antiunion and, more broadly, antiworker. As a UAW 1938 publication put it in its title, "Industrial Marvel of the Age Most Callous and Inhuman in Treatment of Its Workers." Acknowledging that "all in all, Rouge plant is [the] foremost in the world in size, science, and safety," the article nevertheless argued that "even the plant's [much acclaimed] cleanliness and safety devices are not motivated by humane considerations; they are instituted for purposes of more efficient production." Consequently, "there are even men who, driving out of Dearborn for a Sunday holiday, will go miles out of their way so as not to pass the factory, the place they hate— the hell on earth, as some of them call it." Not the factory itself, the article contended, but its management practices were the culprit.[29] Ironically, the UAW received one of its biggest boosts at the Rouge complex on May 26, 1937: thanks to the photos taken by Detroit newspapermen when future UAW president Walter Reuther and other union organizers were stopped from handing out literature and were severely beaten by company "goons," the event was promptly reported across the country, creating considerable sympathy for the union.[30] In these respects, the village industries would appear to have been appealing alternatives to management and workers alike.

By 1942, Bruce Pietrykowski notes, each of the village industries had its own UAW local in place and sent delegates to that year's annual convention. But the absence of a single local to represent the village industries as a totality not only limited their effectiveness within the UAW but also reinforced the sense of "separateness and isolation already experienced" by many village industry workers, even with unionization.[31] Moreover, as a team of outside observers concluded in 1945, "small plants in small communities don't necessarily all have good labor relations, no matter how pleasant the community life may be. In the end, relationships between management and workers depend upon how the two treat each other."[32] Once the overwhelming majority of Ford Motor Company employees accepted union representation by the UAW in 1941, those relationships had soured. Interestingly, Local 600, the bargaining unit for the entire Rouge complex and the largest UAW local, eventually challenged both the company *and* Reuther to be more responsive to workers' needs. But its radicalism and repeated work stoppages finally prompted the company to reduce the number of workers at Rouge precisely through "technological unemployment."[33]

The attitudes of the village industries workers toward unionization and toward the militant UAW—which had decisively defeated the more moderate American Federation of Labor (AFL) in a vote of all company workers—cannot be fully determined. The overall company vote was 70 percent for the UAW, 27 percent for the AFL, and 3 percent against both.[34] But as former village industries employee Francis Michaels wrote of his Milford plant, "I was one of the first to vote for the union. . . . Some of the . . . plant managers were like tyrants, so something had to be done." This was a common sentiment among the former workers I contacted. For similar reasons, Fred Winstanley did not "recall much, if any, objection" to unionization. According to Rodes Walters, although at the outset "there were no labor problems or thoughts of unions, we accepted the union when Ford was unionized and we welcomed its changes." And John Peters left Flat Rock for the Rouge plant primarily because of the absence of a union to protect him from abuses he experienced at the former (if to a lesser extent also at the latter).[35]

Kenneth Edwards, who at the time of the unionization vote was chief clerk of the Milan plant and so as a management employee ineligible to vote, confirmed these pro-union sentiments in his 1988 interview. If the balloting "had been set up as individual votes [rather than as nineteen collective voting entities], I think most of the [village industries] plants would have gone the same way as the rest of them [the conventional plants]."[36]

The experience of Raymond Pflug at Milford between 1938 and the early 1940s further revealed the conditions that likely led to a favorable vote for UAW representation by the village industries workers: "I was in a somewhat unique position. My father was a machinery salesman who sold quite a bit to Ford"—which was how he heard of the Milford opportunity. "This was known at the Milford plant. I had also joined the UAW while working at the General Motors plant in Pontiac, and retained my membership" after losing that job when the UAW went on strike.

> I also drove the only Chevrolet that was parked in the [Milford] plant lot. I did not get any static over this, I suppose because the National Labor Relations Board was getting closer and closer to Ford. As the election for representation approached, things became tense. There was what I recall as the Liberty League, which was a Company union, although the Company did not admit it, and men in the plant were stationed at the door to enroll members; they were also allowed to go about the plant on Company time; and they had their buttons. One day I wore my UAW button and was told by the Service man (Ford's euphemism for plant police) to take it off. But there was no violence that I recall. About an hour later men came around on Company time to try to get me to join the Company union. The election overwhelmingly went to the UAW, and things changed a bit."

Plfug went on to reflect: "I was at the time young and unmarried, and earlier times I would have been fired. For example, I would do or say something at Milford, and someone at River Rouge would tell my father to shut me up." And he concluded, "Yes, I suppose most Milford workers were pleased about the UAW victory, although it was a curious thing," for "once the UAW won at River Rouge, everything turned over, and the plants like Milford just went along with the head office—check-off, the whole bit. So in a sense the Milford workers never had much of a choice; they were just in."[37]

The changes adversely affected Winstanley, who had been not just a union supporter but a charter member of Milford's UAW local: "I went to Milford as a 'foreman,' but changes in management, combined with the union influx, many changes were the result. I finally became a full-fledged foreman in 1951, but had to fight for a journeyman's card as a diemaker because the union would only give you a card as a toolmaker or diemaker, not both, although I had graduated as tool and diemaker" from the Henry Ford Trade School years earlier.[38] Under the new contract the larger village industries were organized into separate UAW locals, while the smaller plants were combined. By the time the UAW held its first post–World War II national convention, in March 1946, there were twelve village industries locals for the eighteen remaining sites (though it is doubtful that Cherry Hill was ever organized, given its workforce of disabled veterans); Nankin Mills, Newburg, Phoenix, Saline, Sharon Mills, and Waterford together constituted the twelfth.[39] Such mixed blessings of unionization led retired Milford worker

Michaels to conclude, "The unionization of the plants . . . changed many things. I can see good and bad points."[40]

Whatever the views of these workers, their few thousand votes were insignificant beside those of the huge Rouge plant workforce, whose preferences they were obliged to accept as part of the new contract for all Ford employees nationwide (except for foremen and a few other ranks). Despite the acknowledged generosity of the contract, the workers at the village industries lost one critical measure of autonomy: their opportunity to learn to perform virtually all aspects of their particular production process—and implicit obligation to do so—gave way to rigid union rules assigning every worker to a specific task and preventing him or her from performing any other task unless the job classification was formally altered. These same rules prevented supervisors from wielding their pre-union-era power of giving workers a multiplicity of tasks in order to make their work more interesting and to increase their productivity. Such changes allegedly undermined the village industries' much-heralded efficiency (if not their always contested profitability).[41]

After World War II the Ford Motor Company and many other large corporations tried to undermine the UAW and other unions they had only recently accepted. The purpose was not to eliminate unions, since that was no longer politically or legally possible, but rather to discredit them and to reorient workers' loyalties away from organized labor and toward big business, away from a union ethos of community and solidarity and toward a corporate ethos of individualism and self-interest—all in the name of allegedly increasing everyone's productivity, which would naturally lead to increased prosperity. Part of this effort was the attempted replacement of such traditional union as well as plant-sponsored activities as recreation, parties, and picnics for workers and their families with exclusively corporate-sponsored programs. Another part was the attempted imposition of corporate-sponsored rewards to workers who made useful suggestions for bringing about greater plant safety—and, claimed union leaders, greater productivity for corporate benefit alone. Thus the relative autonomy of the village industries and their communities as generally pleasant places both to work and to live was steadily undermined by the UAW and the company alike in the years after 1945.[42]

CHAPTER 8

The Decentralists and Other Visionaries

H ENRY FORD'S VILLAGE INDUSTRIES DID NOT COME ABOUT
in a vacuum, as the realization of one very rich and powerful man's
unique fantasies. Rather, they were part of efforts in many parts of America
between the world wars to reverse the course of industrial urban life by
promoting decentralization through the depopulation of large cities and
through the adoption of smaller-scale but still modern technology useful for
farms, villages, and individual households. One historian has characterized
certain of these efforts as attempting to launch "the utopian reconstruction
of modern civilization."[1]

"Decentralization" became a buzzword of this period.[2] Visions of a decentralized America inevitably differed, but virtually all embraced cheap
electricity distributed to every citizen for domestic and business use alike,
regardless of the distance from power sources. What Henry Ford, through
the village industries, was trying to do in the private sector in Michigan,
the Franklin Roosevelt administration, through various rural electrification programs, was trying to do in the public sector across the country. In
both cases, cheap electricity was avowedly linked to social and industrial
decentralization.[3]

To be sure, this was not a vision peculiar to the 1930s. Carolyn Marvin
writes of the belief in late nineteenth-century America that "abundant, easily
distributed, versatile electricity would reverse the centralization of production in factories, lead to the rise of clean cottage industries, unify the home
and the workplace, and lower the divorce rate."[4] As in the 1930s, the large-
scale industrial centralization made necessary by steam power would no
longer apply. The difference with the New Deal, however, was the federal
government's pioneering and systematic effort to realize this vision throughout America.[5] (Although this same interwar period saw the rise and popular-
ization of various visions of skyscraper utopias centralizing huge populations

and institutions and heavily reliant on electricity, these otherwise antithetical schemes were both reactions against the overcrowding, congestion, crime, and related ills of American cities lamented by Ford, among others.)[6]

At least two prominent New Deal officials, Harry Hopkins, director of the Federal Emergency Relief Administration, and Rexford Tugwell, director of the Resettlement Administration, publicly praised the village industries, despite their considerable political and economic differences with Ford. Hopkins said that "it would be a good thing for America if large cities disappeared and their industries were scattered in a thousand smaller communities."[7] And Tugwell characterized these efforts as representing "Henry Ford at his best."[8] President Roosevelt himself, according to Reynold Wik, wrote Ford in 1934 of his own belief in the relocation of persons and smaller industries from cities to towns. He invited Mr. and Mrs. Ford to visit him in Warm Springs, Georgia, to pursue the matter, but apparently they never met, at least not about this.[9] The Roosevelt administration ultimately constructed approximately one hundred communities under various New Deal agencies, but most bore little resemblance to Ford's village industries. Many were predominantly agricultural; others combined farming with small crafts as opposed to actual factories.[10]

The community that probably came closest to the village industries was Jersey Homesteads, established in 1936 by the Farm Security Administration (FSA). Located five miles from Hightstown, New Jersey, Jersey Homesteads recruited two hundred garment workers primarily from New York City. They were hired to work nine months of the year in a government-sponsored garment factory and three months on a government-sponsored 600-acre farm. Because of the project's proximity to urban centers, the clothes manufactured there could be sold and shipped to those centers quite easily. This one experiment was to be the model for others elsewhere in the country.

These parallels to the village industries are striking, but so are the differences. To begin with, the workers did not own their own homes, unlike most of the village industries workers. Instead, the FSA rented the settlers some two hundred homes set amid 1,200 woodland acres. More important, the experiment failed after just a few years because the workers preferred to labor full time inside the modern, air-conditioned garment factory and as little as possible outside on the three often hot and humid farms. Consequently, the farm work was relegated to a few full-time farmers and some transient African Americans. Just as journalist Paul Kellogg had discovered in the 1920s that many farm workers would often readily give up their vocation to become full-time Ford Motor Company employees in the village industries, so the FSA learned in the 1930s that urbanized factory workers could easily resist the lure of the farm. For that matter, many of the homesteaders either never acquired or soon lost interest in the vegetable gardens that were also part of the project. Yet the factory itself initially lacked sufficient workers because delays in housing construction prevented many settlers from moving in as quickly as planned. Since each garment worker had contributed $500 to supplement federal government funding, this was especially irritating to them. Even once it was adequately staffed, the factory was poorly managed and lost money. Eventually many of the factory workers and, still more, their children drifted back to New York City or to Philadelphia.

That all these factory workers were poor immigrant Russian and East European Jews seeking refuge from the kind of anti-Semitism associated with Ford's *Dearborn Independent* diatribes is ironic. In fact, the Jersey Homesteads had begun earlier in the 1930s as a private initiative to resettle persecuted foreign Jews in America. Ironic, too, is the fact that the Jersey Homesteads were intended to be "the first triple co-operative in the new world, with co-operative stores, farm, and factory"[11]—unlike the obviously private village industries. Only after the federal government divested itself of the Jersey Homesteads were the remaining settlers given an opportunity to purchase their own homes. A final irony is that despite their deviations from the blueprints, those who stayed at Jersey Homesteads achieved a spirit of community at least as great as that found in any of the village industries. This result came about in part because of their similar backgrounds and religious beliefs but also because of their common experiences in trying to establish a model community based on both modern technology and older forms of cooperation. Once the enterprise had been liquidated, the community's name was changed to Roosevelt, New Jersey, in honor of the incumbent president its inhabitants generally adored.[12]

A team of outside observers reported in 1945 about Ford's projects, "The success of the village industries is particularly significant when compared to the failure of many of the U.S. Government's so-called subsistence homestead projects also designed to combine industrial with agricultural employment."[13] Nevertheless, for one of the first times in American history, numerous citizens were questioning the traditional, automatic American equation between technological progress and social progress. Just when the terms "machine age" and "industrial civilization" were being widely promoted as positive designations for the era, their flip sides kicked in, and technology—especially on a large scale and in big cities—was increasingly considered a problem as much as a solution to problems.[14] As Warren Susman has written about the 1930s, "Civilization itself—in its urban-industrial form—seemed increasingly the enemy," and "civilization meant technology" more than anything else.[15] It is hardly accidental that the term "technological unemployment"—the replacement of workers by machines—became popular during the Great Depression, when President Herbert Hoover and other engineers were in unprecedented fashion singled out by the American public for being as responsible as greedy industrialists for the very large-scale manufacturing machines that had been lauded as engines of prosperity and job creation.[16] Although there has never been an American counterpart to England's eighteenth-century Luddites, or "machine breakers," white-collar citizens in the 1930s, not just industrial workers, did make direct connections between automated machinery and job losses. Few Americans rejected technology outright, but Ford was hardly alone in pondering its overall direction.

Ford's alternative of decentralization had, to repeat, many other contemporary advocates, but none more prominent than Ralph Borsodi (1886–1977), Scott and Helen Nearing (1883–1983; 1904–1995), Arthur Morgan (1878–1975), and the southern writers collectively called the Agrarians. All were much like Ford in their intense desire to get away from cities and to establish or revive small communities and individual households throughout the country (and the world). Like Ford, all detested the crowding, congestion, noise, poverty, crime, and impersonality of early twentieth-century cities. Passages from their works might have been taken from Ford's own. Borsodi wrote in *This Ugly Civilization* (1929): "This is an ugly civilization. It is a civilization of noise, smoke, smells, and crowds—of people content to live amidst the throbbing of its machines; the smoke and smells of its factories; the crowds and discomforts of the cities of which it proudly boasts. . . . Above all, this civilization is ugly because of the subtle hypocrisy with which it persuades the people to engage in the factory production of creature comforts while imposing conditions which destroy their capacity for enjoying them. With one hand its gives comforts—and with the other hand it takes comfort itself away."[17]

Similarly, Scott Nearing explained in his autobiography, *The Making of a Radical* (1972): "No city or suburban life that I knew gave any real opportunity to contact and deal extensively with nature, with earth, water, sunshine, air, and the changing seasons. Above all, the linking of vocation and avocation that division of labor, specialization, and automation make all but impossible seemed to lie outside of cities. So it was outside of cities that I searched for a chance to live a good personal, social, and universal life."[18]

Likewise, Morgan contended in *The Small Community: Foundation of Democratic Life* (1942):

> A city is an aggregation of persons, families, communities, firms, congregations, and other associations for varied purposes, and with no necessary unity or harmony. The people do not undertake to know each other personally, and aside from a few elemental functions, do not feel personally responsible for each other and do not feel the necessity of working together in unison for common ends. What they do in common is to provide certain economic elements, such as water supply, fire protection, policing, and sanitation; and certain limited cultural advantages, such as schools and musical entertainments. Beyond this minimum basis for living, individuals are usually left to pursue their own courses.[19]

Like Ford, Borsodi and the Nearings and Morgan all eventually settled in rural or semirural settings: Borsodi, first in Suffern, Rockland County, New York, then in Exeter, New Hampshire; the Nearings, first in the southern Vermont hills and later in coastal Maine; Morgan in Yellow Springs, Ohio, site of Antioch College, of which he had been president before becoming the first chairman of the board of directors of the Tennessee Valley Authority (TVA). (One cannot so generalize about the Southern Agrarians: several settled in similar regions, but some remained in Nashville, whose Vanderbilt University first drew them together, while others moved to various urban areas.) By choice, none of these settings was as close to a big city as Ford's Dearborn home was to Detroit. But then, by choice as well, none of these persons aspired to live in the grandiose manner of Ford. Far from seeking wealth and status, all sought what David Shi has aptly called "the Simple Life."[20] Their specific versions of the simple life differed considerably, but their commitment was genuine, where Ford's was more rhetorical. That they had either grown up in or spent many years in or near cities only intensified that commitment.

Moreover, to varying degrees Borsodi, the Nearings, Morgan, and the Agrarians all despised the undermining of the so-called Protestant—or Republican—ethic by corporate capitalism, as epitomized by Ford and the Ford Motor Company: the steadily reduced importance of the family as the core of daily life; the growing loss of independent, self-sufficient labor by individuals and families alike; the increasingly crass materialism in an avowedly consumer culture; and the ever greater diminution of leisure time that could be devoted to family, community, and other noneconomic pursuits. They exaggerated some of these conditions, of course, and none could be blamed on just the Ford Motor Company or just the automobile (industry). Indeed, the anxiety over the fate of these values, and in turn over the fate of the nation, was hardly new, as John Kasson has shown in his *Civilizing the Machine*.[21] The respective critiques of twentieth-century corporate America offered by Borsodi, the Nearings, Morgan, and the southern Agrarians in effect extend Kasson's coverage by several decades.

For that matter, the anxiety over values shared by Borsodi, the Nearings, Morgan, and the Agrarians transcended their deep political differences. Borsodi was a Henry George single-taxer, progressive agrarian, and genteel anarchist; the Nearings were tough-minded socialists—and one-time apologists for Stalin and Communist totalitarianism; Morgan was a Hooverite Republican; and most of the southern Agrarians were conservative Democrats increasingly disillusioned with the New Deal. Moreover, the village industries were clearly a response to these same concerns, despite Ford's own contribution in other ways to creating such concerns. The vision of a decentralized America that was the centerpiece of the Ford project connects his efforts to those of Borsodi, the Nearings, Morgan, and the Agrarians for a geographically dispersed, smaller-scale society. And they all looked to modern technology to help to bring that about.

None was hostile to modern technology itself, a point that cannot be overemphasized. Borsodi, for example, thought modern technology could liberate rural individual households from the drudgery of housework and make them ever more self-sufficent. In particular, he advocated the use of electricity and of power tools: "saws, drills, and sanders; tillers in the garden, canners and an electric mill in the kitchen," plus pressure cookers, ranges, stoves, and sewing machines, among other items.[22] Nor was he opposed to all factories. Rather, he distinguished those necessary for modern society— factories producing useful goods that could realistically be made only in factories, such as wire, pipe, and sheet metal—from those he thought unnecessary: factories that produced either undesirable goods, such as weapons, or desirable goods, especially food and clothing, that could better be produced in individual homes or in small communities. Rural electrical lines and electric-powered domestic tools could enable these homes and communities to compete successfully with those unwanted factories:

> All civilizations have been ugly. They could not well avoid it. But this civilization is unique. Machines make it possible for this one to be beauti-

ful, and yet it is in many respects indescribably uglier than the civilizations that have preceded it. For this civilization, instead of using machines to free its finest spirits for the pursuit of beauty, uses machines mainly to produce factories—factories which only the more surely hinder quality-minded individuals in their warfare against ugliness, discomfort, and misunderstanding. . . . If mankind is not to be made into appendages to machines, then domestic machines must be invented capable of enabling the home to meet the competition of the factory [and factory machines]—the right kind of machinery must be used to free man from the tyranny of the wrong kind of machinery.[23]

Borsodi praised Mahatma Gandhi for his attempted revival of preindustrial spinning and weaving in India's villages. Here was "the right kind of machinery" for India. Yet Borsodi predicted "a pitched battle between individual production of yarn and fabrics and [the] factory production" introduced by the British colonists.[24] "Factory production" brought "the wrong kind of machinery" to India. But Borsodi's vision was as much forward-looking as backward-looking. His self-consciously promoted scientific management of the individual household and, in turn, the small community was akin to that recommended in *The American Woman's Home* (1869), a pioneering work by the famous sisters Catharine Beecher and Harriet Beecher Stowe which detailed an efficient home's organization and operation and analyzed virtually every component. Borsodi's writings continued that tradition.[25]

Like Ford, Borsodi at once lamented and called for the revival of "family dancing and folk singing," both of which had "gone the way of family and craft production . . . systematized out of existence."[26] Yet he advocated his own de facto management system, as did, in effect, the Nearings and Morgan as well as, of course, Ford. (The Agrarians were simply too diverse to qualify for inclusion here.)

The Nearings, in fact, "came to regard our valley in Vermont"—and, by extension, their successor Maine homestead—"as a laboratory in which we were testing out certain principles and procedures" for possible application elsewhere.[27] Unlike Borsodi, the Nearings were not interested in using the latest technology, but neither were they unalterably opposed to doing so. They drove cars, pickup trucks, and jeeps but drew the line at farm machines when human or animal power would suffice. They believed that machine tools, which they rarely used, undermined human skill and creativity. Only after Scott died did Helen get a telephone. Neither she nor Scott ever had a radio or television in their rural retreats, although they did allow themselves a phonograph for leisure enjoyment.

Though clearly differing with Borsodi about modern technology, the Nearings joined with him—and with Morgan, the Agrarians, and Ford—in their advocacy of what was later termed "appropriate technology." As they wrote in *The Maple Sugar Book* (1950), an account of their Vermont life and enterprises, "Much of the equipment used by our sugar-making neighbors was primitive and inadequate. We made various improvements and innovations and . . . cut money costs and paid the expenses out of our syrup income." "Improvements in capital equipment," they observed, "provide the economic foundations for broadening social equipment. We enjoy seeing our capital plant improving from year to year." In an afterword to a 1970 reprint they lamented some of the "improvements" in sugarmaking since they moved to Maine—such as the use of plastic bags and plastic pipes—and called themselves "conservative innovators."[28]

The Nearings nevertheless continued to link sugarmaking with decentralization. As they had contended in the initial edition of the book:

> The decentralist movement, which is being urged by theorists and is being pushed by the course of events, will find an ideal abiding place in the maple industry. The maple bush, because of its configuration, must be relatively small. The initial investment is moderate. Households or small co-operating units are the logical production units. The market is all but assured. The crop is sold for cash. The syrup market welcomes small containers. A mail-order business is easily built up. When syrup is converted into sugar and packed in fancy boxes, its market is greatly extended. Autos and improved roads have brought tourists who take packages of syrup and sugar back to town as souvenirs. Roadstands on the main highways handle the output of those who live on back roads.
>
> Sugar-country economy is, and apparently will remain, decentralized. Supplemented by a measure of co-operation and coupled with community integration and co-operation, it seems a logical area in which decentralists may test out their theories. Those who are looking to decentralism as a means of rehabilitating households and stabilizing community life have at least part of an economic basis for their efforts in the areas where maple production is commercially practicable.

The Nearings always believed that the maple industry would continue to operate as the province of "tens of thousands of households" and that "the manufacture and sale of sugar equipment" would remain on its traditional small scale. Thus the industry would always be decentralized.[29]

By coincidence, the New Deal official Rexford Tugwell had been Nearing's student and then his teaching assistant at the University of Pennsylvania. But Tugwell's admiration for Nearing's teaching abilities and character did not lead to any enthusiasm during the New Deal or after for the Vermont or later Maine enterprises and ethos. Whereas Tugwell could praise Ford for integrating modern manufacturing technology with modern agriculture, he found the Nearings anachronistic on both counts.[30]

Morgan had no qualms about using the latest technology, given his expertise and reputation as a leading hydraulic engineer even before his TVA service, but he did share with Borsodi and the Nearings a commitment to smaller-scale communities. One of Morgan's major achievements—and obsessions—as TVA board chairman was the town of Norris, Tennessee. Constructed under his supervision, located four miles from Norris Dam and not far from Knoxville, the town received much favorable publicity as a model residential site for workers. Its superior housing for both families and single workers, low rents, electrical appliances, all-electric school, community cafeteria, library, and other amenities complemented its natural footpaths and 2,000-acre greenbelt. Much as in Ford's village industries, each resident family or individual could use land on the outskirts of Norris for farming. Yet Norris's cooperative stores and service agencies were never profitable—partly because their workers' wages were relatively high—and in 1937 they were sold to private operators. Once Norris Dam and related projects had been constructed, the workers left town and were steadily replaced by commuters from Knoxville, who saw in Norris a comfortable de facto suburb. In 1948, TVA sold the entire town to out-of-state businessmen.[31]

Morgan had envisioned Norris as the first of a series of avowedly decentralized model communities spread across TVA's vast area, much like what Ford had envisioned for the region when he tried to lease the Muscle Shoals, Alabama, nitrate plant, dam, and phosphate quarry from the federal government in the early 1920s. Not surprisingly, hydroelectric power would be no less important to Morgan than it would have been to Ford. Like Ford, too, Morgan envisioned communities such as Norris that would offer opportunities for residents to farm as well as to pursue other occupations. And like Ford as well, Morgan envisioned commercial ties among communities that were not too far apart: not necessarily small manufacturing plants, as with Ford, but perhaps a regional "machine shop or

. . . a medical and health center, a printing plant, a large recreation center, or a local packing plant."[32]

For Morgan, moreover, small businesses more than small farms or domestic industries were the key to communal and regional success. Rigidly moralistic when it came to ethics, Morgan was far more flexible regarding centralization and decentralization. As he wrote in *A Business of My Own* (1945)—which, paradoxically, was not about his own business—"There is no universal tendency either toward centralization of business, or away from it. Some industries are steadily moving toward larger and larger units. Others are moving in the opposite direction." The objective, he argued, should be not "decentralization for its own sake, but escape from [that] centralization which is arbitrary, forced, and uneconomic." The result would be some increased centralization along with some increased decentralization. The example he provided from the automobile industry did not specify the village industries or the Ford Motor Company, but it surely included them: "In some instances, as in producing automobiles, there might be centralization of control and planning, but decentralization of operations. Parts could be made in decentralized plants in many parts of the country, and assembled at regional centers in all parts of the country, while yet under as centralized control and distribution as though the whole process should take place under one roof. Between such highly specialized and integrated decentralization on the one hand, and entirely separate and independent small industries on the other, there are occasions for many degrees and kinds of decentralization."[33]

In *The Small Community*, Morgan wrote that the properly organized and managed small community "can be the testing laboratory and the nursery for society."[34] By this he meant the opportunity for persons of different backgrounds and interests to learn to live and work together in cooperation and harmony. But one can also take "laboratory" and "nursery" literally, for Morgan worked diligently in Yellow Springs to encourage small businesses in science and engineering as well as in more traditional spheres. In *A Business of My Own* he described the opportunities for mechanics, engineers, scientists, and other technical experts as well as for farmers, storekeepers, accountants, clergymen, lawyers, doctors, and other occupations customarily found in small communities. And in *Industries for Small Communities: With Cases from Yellow Springs* (1953), Morgan detailed the transformation of a sleepy Ohio town with a virtually bankrupt small college at its core to a growing but still small community with a revitalized college and numerous small industries begun by Antioch College graduates as often as by outsiders. These industries produced thermostats, amplifiers, meters, granite surface plates, bookplates, industrial designs, bronze castings, stained glass, photographs, farm seeds, farm equipment, earth-moving equipment, brick supplies, and kennels, among other items. They employed from a handful to 250 people. They did not all prove successful, and some moved away just because they *were* successful and needed a larger community. But most of the Yellow Springs industries stayed put and flourished. The presence of a college or university, Morgan made clear, was not necessary for small industries. He gave the example of Berne, Indiana, a more traditional community of some 2,500, which developed numerous small industries that in turn stemmed long-term population decline.

Like Ford, Morgan did not provide a formula for the proper size of small communities or for the proper number of small industries or for the proper number of employees within each one; these were matters for the individual communities and industries to determine. Also like Ford, Morgan was concerned with optimum, not maximum size: "Size should be no greater than is necessary for the general good." As for technology, Morgan put it concisely: "Heretofore much of the promotion of small-community industry has been in the interest of old-time craftsmanship. Those of Yellow Springs accept modern technology as having come to stay, and seek to find a way to share in it, while maintaining the human values of the old community."[35] In *A Business of My Own* Morgan went so far as to paraphrase Ford (without citation and probably without knowledge) by using the words "One Foot on the Land" to recount how some part-time farmers around the country were simultaneously pursuing more modern occupations.[36] None of his examples included factory work, but Morgan would not have excluded it.

Defending himself against the common assumption that his advocacy of small communities and small industries automatically translated into opposition to modernity, Morgan offered a perspective that Ford could have readily applied to the village industries: "Quite frequently people who would promote small industry have thought of it as a going back to earlier and simpler ways of living. They fight against the inexorable trend of economic life toward greater complexity. They do not want to admit that we are moving from an economy based on smallpower generating units to power plants on a constantly larger scale; from natural materials to a world of synthetics; from an age of easy tolerance in our mechanical and chemical production to rigorous enforcement of exacting standards of manufacture; from relative independence of action in economic life to increasing interdependence."[37]

Morgan's perspective applies to the so-called Agrarians, who became famous for their 1930 collective work, *I'll Take My Stand: The South and the*

Agrarian Tradition. Such contributors to that controversial book as Donald Davidson, John Gould Fletcher, Henry Blue Kline, Herman Clarence Nixon, Frank Owsley, Allen Tate, and Robert Penn Warren were not, contrary to historical stereotypes, wholly opposed to the TVA or other "modernization" projects, much less to modern technology. On the contrary, as Edward Shapiro has shown, they generally favored both the TVA and the Rural Electrification Administration (begun in 1935) exactly because both promised to improve southern rural life and small-scale rural industries by providing cheap electricity to farms and villages hitherto lacking it.[38] That in turn would allow farmers and villagers to use the latest domestic and industrial technology to make their homes more comfortable and their farms and businesses more efficient and more profitable. Whereas steam, the traditional rural power mode, required proximity to coal sources, electricity could be used almost anywhere, and on virtually any scale. Because they also promised to revitalize and enhance rural life, such TVA projects as demonstration farms, cheap fertilizers, inexpensive farm machinery, and improved soil conservation also won favor with the southern Agrarians.

In an essay in *Who Owns America? A New Declaration of Independence* (1936)—a sequel of sorts to *I'll Take My Stand*, with many of the same contributors[39]—David Cushman Coyle, a civil engineer who had not contributed to the earlier volume, extended these arguments in ways quite compatible with the critiques of Ford, Borsodi, the Nearings, and Morgan. His essay "The Fallacy of Mass Production" distinguished between "automatic factory technique," which he accepted, and "mass production," which he rejected. The first meant the use of "electric instruments instead of men as machine tenders" and was both efficient and humane. But the second meant large-scale corporate structures and corrupt, exploitative business practices that, if not altered, would someday destroy capitalism from within. Coyle called on the federal government to break up monopolies in those industries where they existed, to convert the worst perpetrators into public service agencies like the post office, and to provide opportunities in remaining industries for small business competition. "High-technology production," as Coyle called modern technology in perhaps the first embodiment of the term "high tech," could be used in small-scale and large-scale industries alike. Like Ford, he contended that "small plants often are more efficient than large plants" and that they could be the salvation of rural areas overly dependent on traditional farming. In addition, as he put it, "the main virtue of small decentralized industry is that it will reduce the strain between unbalanced sections of the nation" and so make the South more nearly equal with the rest of the country without destroying its basic character and customs.[40]

Significantly, Coyle did not regard the automobile industry as a monopoly, despite the size of its major players. Conceding that the "optimum size of a factory varies for each kind of industry," he went on to acknowledge that "the automobile is on the borderline between large and small industry. There is some competition in automobiles" as long as "the market is apparently large enough to absorb twenty or thirty kinds of car." Standardization of "many small parts and of such things as screw threads and other connections" allowed for the decentralization of small automobile plants along with the centralization of others.[41] Ford could not have disagreed.

Whereas Ford, Borsodi, the Nearings, and Morgan wanted to depopulate northern and midwestern industrial cities, however, the southern Agrarians wanted to avoid enlarging southern cities that would otherwise attract and seduce farmers, small businessmen, and other vulnerable folk. In Atlanta, the booming commercial center of the New South, they saw these same tendencies now invading their region. For this reason they endorsed automobiles, whose flexibility allowed rural citizens to work and play in southern cities, if they so desired, but still to live outside of them and so have the proverbial best of both worlds. Ford could hardly have faulted this logic. What eventually soured some of the southern Agrarians on TVA was its growth into yet another huge, impersonal, and highly centralized government bureaucracy allegedly indifferent to the grassroots population it repeatedly claimed to serve, and allegedly intending to transform the South as much as possible into the industrial North and Midwest. These southern Agrarians thus came to despise the TVA no less than they already despised giant corporations like Ford Motor Company.[42] Presumably none of them knew that in its early days, TVA had compiled bibliographies on the decentralization of industry elsewhere in America which included several items by and about Ford's village industries. (Whether Morgan himself read any of these is unknown.)[43]

Borsodi, the Nearings, Morgan, and some of the southern Agrarians such as Davidson all became, like Ford, more dogmatic and more self-righteous as their influence grew but as mainstream America moved in other directions. Though differing on particulars, all sought to impose a moral code on those who would live in their communities and households if not in their regions. Indeed, Morgan's elaborate "Ethical Code for the Staff of the Tennessee Valley"—which grew out of similar codes for Antioch College and prior Morgan projects—was akin to Ford's Sociological Department and related efforts to mold his workforce and their families into his conception of good citizens. In fact, it went further: whereas the Sociological Department did not intrude in the village industries, Morgan fully intended to intrude in the lives of Norris workers and their families.

The respective failure of Borsodi, the Nearings, and Morgan to establish more than a handful of experimental communities and individual homesteads emulating their own—far fewer collectively than Ford's nineteen sites—did not seem to undermine their self-confidence in the appropriateness of their respective schemes. Furthermore, all four of these decentralists and several of the Agrarians as well lived long enough to see their major works reprinted and, in some cases, revised, as a new generation of Americans sought their wisdom. The Nearings became outright if somewhat reluctant celebrities in their later years, deluged with visitors and correspondents eager to learn how to live their own good lives.[44]

In short, the projects undertaken and works published by Borsodi, the Nearings, Morgan, and the southern Agrarians were not simple retreats from modernity, not superficial "back to the land" schemes.[45] Rather, like the nineteen Ford sites, they were characteristically American efforts to accommodate the latest technology to existing cultural values. As the Nearings put it, they—like the others in other realms—were "relating maple production to the livelihood problems of a technical, mechanized age."[46]

Lewis Mumford (1895–1990) was another advocate of decentralization in this era, but his perspective was considerably more historical, more sophisticated, and less dogmatic than those of his contemporaries. In such works as *Technics and Civilization* (1934) and *The Culture of Cities* (1938), Mumford connected smaller-scale, more geographically dispersed technology to regional communities and economies in both the past and the present. Generally refusing to impose any particular scheme, Mumford did favor a balance between agriculture and industry and between open and developed spaces.[47] His correspondence in the late 1930s with agrarian renewal proponent George Weller, however, illuminates his belief in a variety of work and leisure settings. He criticized Weller for "making the notion of domestic production and partial industrial and agricultural self-sufficiency the only possible pattern for future economic change or for urban planning. . . . [F]ar from denying it," Mumford continued, "I have followed it for three years, at least to the extent of running a garden that keeps us provided with vegetables the better part of the year" at his rural New York state residence. "But it does not seem to me that this pattern of life is necessarily the only valid one;

indeed, my own needs and those of my family are now sending me back to New York [City] again for the winter months."[48]

In *Technics and Civilization*, though he did not single out the village industries, Mumford praised Ford for his decentralization efforts. Thanks to rural electrification and (allegedly) efficient company central administration, "the size of the productive unit is no longer determined by the local require-ments of either the steam engine or the managerial staff: it is a function of the [overall] operation itself." Consequently, within "large-scale standardized industry, making products for a continental market, the small plant can now survive." Moreover, as the village industries had already demonstrated, prob-ably unknown to Mumford, "to be efficient, the small plant need not remain in continuous operation nor need it produce gigantic quantities . . . for a distant market: it can operate on an irregular basis, since the overhead for permanent staff and equipment is proportionately smaller."[49]

In *The Culture of Cities*, Mumford conceded that prior industrial decen-tralization schemes usually took the form of conventional branch plants far away from major ones and were invariably motivated by either the quest for higher profits or the desire to destroy unions or both (fairly or not, Ford escaped this condemnation). In that same work Mumford lamented the gen-eral absence of small-scale, decentralized industries—and, for that matter, of well-planned garden cities promoting and sustaining them—within the then emerging TVA project. Mumford described the model town of Norris as a "let-down: little of the order and imagination expressed in the Tennessee Valley Project itself or in the dams, reservoirs, construction works, and power plants."[50] He argued that industrial decentralization could now be as efficient and as profitable as traditional centralization. Thus "bigger no longer auto-matically means better," he wrote in *Technics and Civilization*. "Flexibility of the power unit, closer adaptation of means to ends, nicer timing of opera-tions, are the new marks of efficient industry."[51]

In *The Culture of Cities* and much later in *The Pentagon of Power* (1970), Mumford envisioned renewed and expanded decentralization as a practical alternative to the uniformity and conformity of the "machine age" and the "industrial civilization" that he increasingly condemned. Once again refusing to impose any particular scheme, Mumford continued to propose a variety of smaller-scale work and leisure settings which would all have in common the "organic" qualities that he found in small medieval communities and might well have found in the village industries. And all would stress qualita-tive rather than quantitative values and experiences.[52]

By contrast, the "Technocracy" crusade, which Ford criticized as misdirected, reflected the vision of those for whom quantitative measurements, along with centralized decision-making by technical elites, were paramount. Of the countless panaceas for America's Great Depression, few enjoyed so spectacular, if so spectacularly brief, a reign as Technocracy. Although the movement still persists, its heyday lasted only from June 16, 1932, when the *New York Times* became the first influential press organ to report its activities, until January 13, 1933, when its leader, Howard Scott, attempting to silence his critics, delivered a rambling, confusing, and most uninspiring address on a well-publicized national radio hookup. Before, during, and after those seven crucial months, Scott and other Technocrats preached ceaselessly about their "scientific" (and therefore presumably foolproof) scheme for not merely ending the economic crisis but also effecting unprecedented and permanent abundance for all Americans. The technical jargon and complex charts they employed invariably impressed and simultaneously perplexed their growing audiences. The great expectations thus raised were never met, and the present-day equation of a "technocracy" with a distinctly nonutopian society reflects the movement's dismal legacy.[53]

Technocracy's premise was that the ability to produce and utilize energy was the true measure of human progress, for energy was necessary to run the machinery that produced the goods that improved life. The Technocrats argued that progress had been limited until about 1700 by humans' almost total dependency upon their bodies for energy production (a misreading of history that conveniently ignored the many earlier technological advances that had greatly reduced such dependency); only with the Industrial Revolution of the eighteenth and nineteenth centuries did people become capable of increasing energy production significantly. Yet just when citizens were at last capable of producing enough energy to satisfy their basic needs, especially in the United States, greed and waste were undermining the efficient production of goods. Oddly, Technocracy proposed no solution to this dilemma, nor did the Technocrats ever provide a blueprint for their version of the good society, though one can safely assume that it would not have resembled the village industries or any other decentralized work and leisure settings. A nationwide system of huge plants, modeled after the River Rouge and located in a handful of giant cities, would have been far more likely.

On February 1, 1933, weeks after Howard Scott's ill-fated radio address, Ford commented on the Technocracy crusade in a *New York Times* interview. Questioning its actual technical expertise, he observed that although "its diagnosis of present conditions is partly correct, . . . when it assumes that present conditions are permanent, when it forgets the fluid and progressive elements in life, it simply goes on the rocks." For Ford, "the machine age is barely started."[54] To be sure, Technocracy never literally assumed the permanence of "present conditions," yet true to Ford's observations, it not only failed to take account of the possible resurgent national faith in technology—and in government—once the Great Depression finally ended in the early 1940s but also failed to anticipate such major later technological advances as computers and space travel.[55]

Ford was hardly alone in criticizing Technocracy for its naive extrapolation from the present to the future, but the subtext of his comments is more intriguing. For here, as throughout his later life, Ford was also seeking a "usable past," as were the other decentralists, Mumford above all. The search for a usable past has been a recurrent process in American history, but it intensified during the crisis of confidence in the present and the future inevitably brought on by the Great Depression. Though usually conducted by self-proclaimed intellectuals, to whom Ford was ordinarily anathema (and vice versa), this effort to illuminate the present and the future through the past was Ford's mission as well. That those writers and others engaged in this process manifested renewed, sometimes unprecedented, interest in common men and women—especially farmers, craftsmen, and workers, the same persons to whom Ford appealed—is not coincidental. For they, like Ford, "undertook to recover the traditional values and principles which the national experience had validated," wrote Alfred Jones, and to emphasize the allegedly "classless inclusive character of the national experience."[56]

Not surprisingly, the result for both Ford and those intellectuals was a frequent simplification and distortion of the past. But Ford was infinitely less tolerant of cultural and social diversity than they were. Indeed, his persistent effort to mold his foreign-born workers into respectable Americans, as through his Sociological Department and the Ford English School, was part of the same endeavor. Inculcating the virtues of efficiency, thrift, industry, and reliability was rationalized by Ford and other industrialists as patriotic as well as managerial, old-fashioned as well as modern—and without apparent contradiction. As Kenneth Ames observes about the so-called "colonial revival" in twentieth-century America (which included Ford's Dearborn museums and the Wayside Inn in Sudbury, Massachusetts—though not the village industries), "those whose livelihoods are based on industrialism are often those who most enthusiastically sing the praises of pre-industrial ways and who become most deeply committed to their preservation."[57] Or as Dona Brown demonstrates, the transformation for public consumption, especially tourism, of nineteenth-century New England from the nation's most industrialized and ethnically heterogeneous region into a rural, Anglo-Saxon bastion of small farms, villages, and seaports—a region allegedly holding out against industrial capitalism and urbanism—was accomplished by those who saw and achieved much financial profit in the process. In various ways these entrepreneurs managed to redesign the image of New England and to conceal from outsiders the region's actual contents.[58]

For that matter, as T. J. Jackson Lears concludes about the pre–World War I Arts and Crafts movement—whose generally affluent members romanticized the manual labor they themselves hardly practiced—it eventually embraced the very corporate system it once despised and gave up on its original vision "of a land dotted with villages, small farms, and cottage industries." Instead, for most Arts and Crafts advocates, "the critique of degraded labor and the vision of humane community slipped away; craftsmanship became a means of social control and self-fulfillment in a rationalizing capitalist society."[59] And Terry Smith specifies that the village industries and the Ford Museum/Greenfield Village, among other American phenomena, reflect a "driving contradiction of twentieth-century modernity [in] its tendency to project its future, to a significant extent, through what amounts to a cannibalizing of its own prehistory and by the consumption of any available, usable past."[60]

In Ford's case, however, the attempt to retain agrarian values and routines while establishing ultramodern manufacturing or assembly facilities is a significant difference. Far from concealing modern working or living arrangements behind colonial facades—as in his Dearborn and Sudbury buildings and as was the case with so many other colonial revival structures—the village industries readily displayed them in either reconstructed mills or completely new factorylike structures. More broadly, that Ford was linking older agrarian and newer manufacturing technologies to future national prosperity and so contributing concretely to a usable past—not merely extracting from it for ulterior purposes—further distinguished him from those contemporary intellectuals whose usable pasts rarely took material form. Robert Dorman has described many of the latter as "lulled by the precepts of cultural radicalism into equating understanding with action, criticism with program—to sketch their visions of aesthetic-traditionalist societies, garden cities, symphonic nations, and symphonious environments seemed enough."[61] Ford had no such illusions.

One can also distinguish him from those more recent advocates and practitioners of "living history" museums whose usable pasts do take material form, but more as escapes from the present than as guides to the future.[62] Ironically, when what became Colonial Williamsburg—probably America's foremost "living history" enterprise—solicited Ford's support in 1924, the effort was in part based on the ongoing "destruction" of that historic Virginia city then being caused by its proliferation of automobiles. The solicitation was made by Dr. William A. R. Goodwin, an Episcopalian clergyman and former Williamsburg church rector who had returned to the community the year before to become a professor and development director at William and Mary, the nation's second oldest college and Williamsburg's most prominent institution. Williamsburg, once the "cultural and political center" of the colony of Virginia, according to John D. Rockefeller Jr.'s biographer, had long declined into "a peaceful somnambulant town" of roughly one thousand citizens, many of them descendants of the original inhabitants and residing in colonial homes. But the prospect of American involvement in World War I prompted Du Pont and Company to open a munitions plant nearby in 1914 and, two years later, stirred speculation about a possible second Du Pont plant. Seemingly overnight, Williamsburg became a boom town, with outsiders overwhelming longtime residents and with unaesthetic temporary structures—not least, gasoline stations—threatening the already deteriorating historic buildings.[63] By 1924, although Williamsburg had largely resumed its quiet prewar ways, there remained endless remnants of its short-lived boom days.

Goodwin's solicitations to Henry, Edsel, and Henry's brother William Ford were met with polite indifference, perhaps because the letter to Edsel said that "unfortunately you and your father are at present the chief contributors to the destruction of this city." Moreover, in writing Edsel that "seriously, I want your father to buy Williamsburg," Goodwin noted that the town had been Virginia's capital "at a time when Virginia included the land on which the Ford factory [presumably the Highland Park and Rouge plants] is now located, as in those days the western boundary of Virginia was the Pacific ocean."[64] By 1928, however, Goodwin could finally make public the names of the donors who, having initially been solicited unsuccessfully *before* the Fords, eventually agreed to fund the restoration and reconstruction project *after* the Fords declined: Mr. and Mrs. John D. Rockefeller, Jr., of New York. The son of the legendary oil magnate funded the removal of unsightly and inappropriate gasoline stations, other contemporary structures, telephone and power wires, modern roads, and, of course, automobiles.[65]

Yet in 1956, Virginia's leading newspaper, the *Richmond Times-Dispatch*, editorialized about the ongoing and future industrialization of the James

River below Richmond, near Williamsburg, recognizing the need for some balance: "Factories in the proper places are greatly to be desired—are, in fact, indispensable. But the utmost care should exercised throughout Virginia lest the fumes, noise, and congestion which many of them cause turn out, in certain areas, to be liabilities rather than assets."[66] Still, this was not close to Ford's vision of Muscle Shoals, much less of the village industries.[67]

More broadly as well, Ford was linking older communitarian experiments to modern technology and so contributing further to a usable past. If one cannot equate the village industries with any of the dozens of avowedly utopian communities that sprang up throughout nineteenth- and early twentieth-century America, usually also outside of urban, industrial areas, it is nevertheless significant that many of the latter engaged in small crafts and other light industries, even in manufacturing, as well as in agriculture. They did so for practical as well as ideological reasons, and it is hardly accidental that the most successful and longest-lasting of such communities did not rely on an exclusively or predominantly agrarian base: the Shakers, for example, with their furniture, and the Oneida perfectionists, with their silverware. By contrast, few wholly agrarian utopian settlements lasted more than a generation. Like the village industries, the Shaker, Oneida, and other relatively successful utopian communities sought a form of mediation between technology and the pastoral, a version of the "machine in the garden."[68] However far apart in time, in objectives, and in operation, both sets of communities represent small-scale models of the "middle landscape" so pervasive and persistent in American history.[69]

Writing shortly after Ford's death in 1947, the management consultant Peter Drucker went further: "Though Henry Ford may never have heard of Brook Farm, of Robert Owen's New Lanarck, or of any of the many other utopian communities that had dotted the Midwest not so many years before his birth in 1863, they were his intellectual ancestors. He took up where they had left off; and he succeeded where they had failed." Citing the village industries themselves as exemplars of Ford's alleged utopian bent, Drucker argued that Ford, like the earlier visionaries, wanted "the full benefits of industrial productivity, but without . . . having to pay the price of subject[ion] . . . to the 'money power' or to 'monopoly,' or of having to work in the 'satanic mills' of Blake's great and bitter poem." [70]

For these reasons it is difficult to accept Smith's argument that the village industries represented the relocation of "the colossus of mass production into utterly antithetical settings." What disturbs Smith, among other things, is the Ford "dream of modernity as a seamless merging of industry and farming, a pastoral which plants machines in the garden as benign presences, powering away quietly, industriously, harmoniously, as if they had always been there."[71] In fact, they *had* long been there, if in different, simpler forms. It is likewise disappointing that the permanent exhibition "Michigan in the Twentieth Century," opened in 1995 at the Michigan Historical Museum in Lansing, reinforced the simplistic notion that farm and factory were antithetical in modern Michigan and, by implication, elsewhere in America. With a barn and silo facade built *opposite* the recreated exterior of Ford's pioneering Highland Park plant, and the state's agricultural products displayed *opposite* its industrial products, visitors likely never guess that Ford saw no such antithesis in the village industries or in the nation overall. Like Smith, these otherwise sophisticated exhibition designers miss the key point.[72]

In a still broader context, the village industries represent the desire for "both modernism *and* nostalgia" that Michael Kammen has described as permeating the years between the two world wars. Kammen's magisterial *Mystic Chords of Memory: The Transformation of Tradition in American Culture* discusses several Ford enterprises but not the village industries. Yet they, no less than anything else Ford ever did, epitomize the relationship between past and present in these decades which Kammen terms "perversely symbiotic. That is, each one flourished, in part, as a critical response to the other." Few who indulged in this "oxymoronic condition" of "nostalgic modernism," he continues, recognized the cultural and social tensions they were creating or reinforcing.[73] Yet the village industries did prompt such recognition on the part of not just Ford but also his associates, his employees at their nineteeen sites, and the communities in which those small plants were established. That recognition did not, of course, take highly intellectual forms, much less provoke extended soul-searching, but it did repeatedly occur.[74]

CHAPTER 9

American Industry
Also Preaches Decentralization

M ANY MAINSTREAM BUSINESSMEN AND ACADEMICS WERE
also preaching the decentralization of industry, as they usually called
it, between the wars. Admittedly, they did not have the missionary zeal of a
Henry Ford or a Ralph Borsodi or a Helen and Scott Nearing or an Arthur
Morgan or a southern Agrarian. Rather, they saw decentralization of industry
as primarily an economic strategy, a means of improving production, distribution, sales, and so profits.

In the pursuit of corporate decentralization, automobile manufacturers,
writes Sugrue, "were in the vanguard."[1] In 1936, for example, the Automobile Manufacturers Association itself announced that "despite the great concentration of automobile industry around Detroit and other Michigan cities,
more than one-fourth of the employment in automobile factories is outside
of Michigan, and is distributed over 28 states, from Coast to Coast," and that
there was still more decentralization—a term the association used—in separate automobile parts supply enterprises.[2] In large part, those numbers derived from the Chevrolet Division of General Motors, which, under the
leadership of William Knudsen—formerly a top Ford executive—had begun
an avowedly decentralized production system when he joined Chevrolet in
1922. By the time Knudsen became president of General Motors in 1937,
that system had been adopted by other divisions of the parent company.[3]
Meanwhile, in 1936 the *Los Angeles Times* proudly hailed that city as the
nation's "second largest center, both of automobiles and of rubber tires" and
likewise pointed to a deliberate policy of decentralization.[4]

Such factors as reduced manufacturing and transportation costs, cheaper
industrial water, and better climate were major reasons for this change, yet
businessmen and academics were not unaware of the social and cultural
implications of decentralization; they generally endorsed the return to

smaller cities and towns and the integration of modern technology with rural and agrarian values and institutions. As Joseph Geschelin, an editor of *Automotive Industries*, wrote in 1933, "Decentralization of industry—the shifting of industrial plants and industrial population to rural communities—has fired the imagination of many business leaders."[5] Geschelin did not automatically endorse decentralization and actually wondered about its alleged superiority to traditional centralization, but he definitely perceived a major trend within American society. He even mentioned the seven initial village industries and Ford's alleged intention to dismantle the Rouge complex someday.

Leading business and engineering journals between the wars were filled with articles that embraced the decentralization of industry—without Geschelin's reservations. For example, "Why We Moved to a Smaller Town," by the president of Royal Metal Manufacturing Company, formerly concentrated in Chicago, appeared in *Factory and Industrial Management*; "Electric Power Transforms Main Street: Utilities Play Important Role in Industrial Development of Small Communities," by the managing director of the National Electric Light Association, in the *Magazine of Wall Street*; "Modern Transportation and Power and Decentralization," by the chairman of the board of Westinghouse, in *Iron Age*; and "Engineering Progress: 1731–1831–1931: Predicts Further Industrial Decentralization as a Result of the Wide Availability of Electric Power," by the head of a large midwestern utility company, in *Electrical Engineering*. *Business Week* put out a special report for executives: "Industry on the Move: Why and Where Plants and Industries Are Migrating, What the Decentralization Trend Means, How New Competition Is Changing the Geography of Industry." Similarly, "Is the Big City Doomed as an Industrial Center?" by a prominent business writer, was published in *Industrial Management* and briefly cited Ford (but not the village industries specifically) as a major reason for its answer to the question: YES. Likewise, "Has the Small Plant a Future?" by another prominent business writer, published in *The Iron Age*, provided a resounding YES to *its* question.[6]

More general publications with probably larger readership also ran stories about these developments. *Current Opinion* published "Great Cities Are Declining in Population." In the *North American Review* the article "Wanted—Ten Million People" was subtitled "Decentralization of industry . . . will shift . . . many men and women to less populated communities within a few years." *Collier's Weekly* offered its readers "Let's Go Back to the Small Town"; "Factories in the Country" appeared in *World's Work*.[7]

Among the academics who were hardly oblivious to these issues was Carl

J. Friedrich, then (1929) a junior professor at Harvard who remained there to become a distinguished political scientist. "The change of industrial location" he wrote "is among the most generally discussed economic problems of today. In the nation-wide agitation for power development in the United States, for example, the argument is quite generally used that it will 'decentralize' industries."[8]

In a 1934 issue of the prestigious *Harvard Business Review*, Philip Cabot, professor of business administration at Harvard, put industrial decentralization in a context that Ford (whom he did not cite) would surely have appreciated: that of the future of farmers and farming as well as of factory workers and industrialization. On the one hand, he argued, "there are too many farmers now, and if we increase the number they will all starve." On the other hand, "subsistence farmers or farmers who are partly self-sufficient are a different breed of cats." Thanks to various technological advances, he continued, the time needed to produce various products would become ever smaller, so that farmers could easily work in factories and still have ample time—and income—to continue to operate their farms. Meanwhile, factory workers who left large cities for rural workplaces could supplement their income by becoming part-time farmers. This would be especially helpful if the predicted shorter hours for factory employees overall meant reduced income for these formerly full-time workers. Their adjustment, Cabot claimed, would be relatively easy, for "the human race has worked on the land for many thousand years. Such a way of life is bred into the bone of every man alive, and even the top executives of our industrial system would be better executives if they worked part of their time on the land." He concluded that the "development of relatively small industries in small communities is clearly indicated by the industrial evolution of recent years and it fits like a piece of a picture-puzzle into the plan . . . for adding ballast to our industrial ship" during the Great Depression.[9]

Ten years earlier (1924) the prominent American businessman and reformer Edward Filene had explicitly cited Ford in endorsing the decentralization of industry. In his book *The Way Out: A Forecast of Coming Changes in American Business and Industry,* he made clear that he disagreed with Ford in many respects: "He has, I think, made incredible mistakes in judgment when he has stepped outside his business"—as with Ford's ill-fated Peace Ship intended to end World War I, his blatant anti-Semitism, and his "autocratic control of his employees." Yet Filene greatly admired what he called a "Fordized America," by which he meant an America dominated not by Ford's "theories of public affairs" but by Ford's "theories of business affairs: specifically, his principles of mass production, mass distribution, and his primary emphasis upon service to the consumer." Whereas other business theorists feared that "a Fordized America would be a hell on earth," Filene believed that it would "give us a finer and fairer future than most of us have even dared to dream," for the decentralization of industry that Ford advocated and implemented would, if extended beyond the Ford Motor Company to other automobile companies and other industries, "mean better living conditions for the workers" in small towns and villages. Mass production and mass distribution, if likewise extended to other companies and industries, would mean lower prices, larger profits, and reduced unemployment. And these developments in turn would "greatly reduce the social and economic discontent that causes so much waste."[10]

Like Cabot, Filene implicitly embraced the basic notion of the village industries: "It does not seem to me any wild flight of fancy to assume that in years to come we shall be able, under a regime of mass production, to coordinate farming and other pursuits with industry in a manner that will greatly improve the health of vast masses of workmen, stabilize our seasonal industries, and eliminate many of the evils of concentration."[11] By "the evils of concentration" Filene meant not only the geographical and physical concentration of plants and offices but also—avowedly unlike Ford—the concentration of ownership in a relative handful of large corporations and powerful corporate executives. If, Filene argued, "the Ford idea of machine production, quantity output, standardization of product, and service to the consumer were general, the Henry Fords of the future would not necessarily own and operate a vast integrated industry; they could become simply the coordinators of smaller producers and of parts. Ownership could be widely spread" just like the plants (and perhaps the offices) themselves, bringing about "a new and modernized 'cottage industry,' . . . a regime of smaller factories scattered over the country." There would be decentralization at the administrative and financial as well as at the production and distribution levels. Yet Filene insisted that the "unified sort of business planning that has made the Ford success" must persist: "we can never allow a small factory in Indiana to hold up the assembling centre in Michigan."[12]

Toward the end of his book Filene cited but did not name the village industries experiment as a key component of what he termed a new Industrial Revolution: "Mr. Ford established a valve plant eighteen miles out in the country so that the men who worked in it could also be farmers. Once [you] bring the blessing of machinery to the farm . . . the work of the farm can be done in only a part of the time the farmer now gives to it, and they can have free a good part of their time for work in small factories which the coming decentralization of industry can establish in many farming communities. Such factories can produce parts that are not too bulky and that can be made almost anywhere."[13] Filene was optimistic that the fundamental negative trends of the earlier (i.e., originally British, then American) Industrial Revolution—above all, the centralization of industries in congested and unhealthy cities—would be reversed in its successor.

Another prominent businessman writing for a broader audience, Martin J. Insull, likewise endorsed the decentralization of industry and the revival of small towns. President of the Middle West Utilities Company—which, despite the name, was a holding company consisting of many gas and electric companies from Maine to Texas—Insull in 1929 envisioned "America's New Frontier as a world that Ford would likely find congenial: "The small towns comprise our new industrial frontier. The tendency of the early days of steam power development was towards centralization and congestion, but it has brought its own cure for this. The development of the steam turbine and of widespread electric transmission has permitted general distribution of electrical energy all over the country, even to the smallest hamlet and the farm. It is no longer necessary that manufacture should be centralized in crowded cities. With adequate transportation and power supply, the small towns are relieved of handicaps that formerly diverted industry to the larger centers. This is a promising sign of a simplified economic structure."[14] To be sure, Ford might well have preferred hydroelectric power over electric power from "manmade" sources. But Insull was, after all, including small towns and, in turn, power sources that were not necessarily near water. Moreover, he noted, "Electric power used in small communities goes directly into net gains of productivity and better living in a degree not equalled in the great cities where a large part of the power consumed is used in overcoming the handicaps of congested habitation." He added that the "vogue of mere size is past in manufacturing, as management has taken to heart the lesson that mere bigness is no longer assurance of real manufacturing economy."[15]

Ford would surely have found journalist Joseph Hart's position far harder to embrace than Insull's. In addition to having been a professor of education at several colleges and universities, Hart was associate editor of the *Survey Graphic*, the influential social scientific Progressive publication edited by Paul Kellogg. Published in the same 1924 issue with Kellogg's articles about Ford's village industries, Hart's "Power and Culture" blamed the steam engine and the automobile for the loss of "contact with nature," the loss of "that neighborliness which was characteristic of the older community," the loss of "practically all of the integrity of our old craftsmanship," and the loss of "practically all control of our destinies" to large-scale machinery. This indictment culminated in Hart's condemnation of the excessive centralization and mechanization of life, also allegedly brought about by the steam engine and the automobile.[16]

At first glance, Hart appears to be a typical romantic, nostalgic for an idyllic preindustrial world that never really existed. Yet his main audience was not naive "nature lovers" but hard-nosed businessmen and policymakers. Far from rejecting all modern technology, he readily embraced electric power in all forms as the principal means of reviving and enriching civilization in the United States and elsewhere, for electric power, "breaking away from its servitude to steam, is becoming independent. Electricity is a decentralizing form of power: it runs out over distributing lines and subdivides to all the minutiae of life and need." Electric power would allow its users to "feel the thrill of control and freedom once again." In the "reinvigorated small community, the free mind will become creative; and [genuine] schools, within which free minds may develop, will appear once more."[17]

It is Hart's conclusion, however, that elevates the debate over industrial centralization versus decentralization to a higher rhetorical—if not necessarily higher intellectual—plane: "This is the Day of Choosing: We stand, today, where the Greeks once stood: face to face with Fate. We have Power beyond their dreams of power: power that indisputably belongs in the realm of nature, the proper use of which need not degrade a single human being. . . . We can build communities upon the foundations of great but decentralized power, we can build small communities where life and culture can be rooted in normal relationships. . . . Or, we can surrender to the control of the greater machine, permit electricity to make permanent what the steam-engine began."[18] Why Hart did not allow for the integration of the automobile with his vision of a better future through industrial decentralization is hard to fathom. Because he did not specify his favored means of transporting goods and people to, from, and within revived small communities, one is left to wonder. Yet insofar as he passionately sought decentralization, his basic sentiments were akin to Ford's and to those of many others in the business, academic, and social scientific communities.

The foregoing books and articles are merely representative of a considerable early twentieth-century literature on decentralization which, like the village industries themselves, has been largely neglected by scholars.[19] The appeal of decentralization to so many tough-minded businessmen and academics precisely for business and economic reasons reinforces the need to remedy that neglect. Significantly, writing in 1939 about the New Deal and decentralization, Ralph Woods noted that the U.S. Department of Commerce, the cabinet unit usually most sympathetic toward business, had established a Committee on Decentralization within its existing Business Advisory and Planning Council. The committee issued several reports, one of which "stressed that industry was not being decentralized to keep pace with the population" and that "people in stranded communities were becoming demoralized." The report recommended that the federal government establish a separate agency to promote and partly fund the relocation of industries that would benefit those "stranded communities." But the report was never acted upon.[20]

The overall business trends identified above were, of course, directly and avowedly related to the impact of the automobile itself upon American society, economy, and culture—even when, as with Hart, it was blamed rather than praised for those trends—for the car (and the truck) clearly contributed significantly to the prospect of industrial decentralization throughout the country. As Insull declared, these connections were "obvious," for "the construction of highways and increasing use of motor trucks has served to equalize market conditions between large and small plants."[21] Moreover, policymakers and government officials between the wars placed ever more emphasis on cars and trucks and ever less on traditional mass transit such as trolleys, railroads, and subways as the principal means of transportation within, to, and from large cities. This was true not only of newer cities—Los Angeles above all—but also of older ones such as Detroit, where a majority of citizens grew frustrated with the cost, inefficiency, and outright corruption of existing mass transit systems and opposed their further expansion.[22] As Cabot put it in defending the practicality of small rural plants and in turn the reduction in workforce size of larger urban plants, "With modern roads and methods of transportation, factories of considerable size would not be handicapped by undue dispersion of their labor."[23]

The business and academic advocates of industrial decentralization were joined by growing numbers of suburban commuters—often well-to-do former urbanites—and in turn by newly professionalized city planners. Like Henry Ford, both commuters and planners viewed crowded, congested, crime-ridden central cities as America's foremost social problem, and the automobile and the superhighway as virtual panaceas. As Mark Foster has argued, "In the early years of the automobile, the planners' faith in the ability of technological . . . advances to solve problems appeared justified. . . . [B]etween 1900 and the 1940s the science and technology of safety and traffic control evolved rapidly," and such control invariably meant "diverting traffic away from densely settled areas."[24] The very precursors of the modern interstate highway system encouraged industrial decentralization by leading toward businesses on the urban periphery. Joining these efforts were experts in town planning and in rural life who advocated industrial decentralization to renew existing towns and to create new ones, including housing for urban slum dwellers.[25]

Paradoxically, however, as Joseph Interrante has shown, "while the distinguishing characteristic of urban metropolitanism was decentralization, the principal transformation of rural space was a centralization of institutions and activity." The very ability of farmers and other rural citizens to travel at unprecedented speed and in unprecedented comfort—if still within "a previously demarcated local area" rather than a vastly enlarged one—prompted the centralization of goods and services in the hinterland and the diminution of crossroads stores and mail order houses (which often became branches of department store chains). Those who still relied on horses and wagons found life increasingly difficult as the automobile "became a rural necessity."[26] Meanwhile rural towns and villages on or near highways grew larger as the farm population declined. Local institutions, from schools to banks to hospitals to post offices, were consequently relocated or expanded accordingly. For even supreme commercial pragmatists, then, decentralization meant a good deal more than creating branch plants or company towns.

The village industries were simultaneously beneficiaries of some of these broader trends and victims of certain others—not least, the increase in population of small towns at the expense of farms. The critical point, though, is the extent to which Ford's overall enterprise was a response to national trends widely and reasonably well understood by other tough-minded and unromantic businessmen and academics. In a 1938 article in *The Businessman-about-Town*, a Detroit publication, one Walter Cary went so far as to argue that Ford's scheme "must prove of first-rate annoyance to followers of Karl Marx. For the last seven or eight decades they have proclaimed the centralization of capitalism the final step toward the communistic state." Now "Mr. Ford cuts the ground from under the feet of the Marxist by putting it under the feet of the individual worker in industry." And "the decentralization of industry is certain to result also in the decentralization of government control"[27]—hence the further degree to which Ford, despite his personal eccentricities, was operating in the center, not the periphery, of both American industry and American culture in establishing his nineteen sites.

As if to confirm Cary's argument, the only two foreign governments known to have been influenced by Ford's scheme were avowedly anti-Marxist: those of Governor Erich Koch in Nazi East Prussia and of Marshal Henri Philippe Petain in Vichy France. Both right-wing leaders wished to scatter small industrial sites throughout their respective rural areas in order to reduce the size of their large cities, offset the urban social ills Ford described, and, in the case of Petain, minimize the impact of possible enemy attacks on those urban industrial centers. Both cited Ford's scheme as a source of inspiration.[28]

Cary was certainly correct that most Marxist leaders saw capitalist centralization as leading (eventually) to communism, but he missed the embrace of Ford's centralized manufacturing techniques and assembly lines by Lenin and other rulers of the Soviet Union. Hostile though they surely were to Ford in every other respect, they nevertheless admired his technological advances and wished to adopt them to their own ideological and material ends.[29]

Debates and policy decisions in interwar Britain focused on more traditional crafts and industries than auto manufacturing and did not envision anything akin to the technical modernity of the village industries. In the British context, decentralization was a matter of allowing rural workers and villages to make their own decisions about the future rather than granting the central government in London that authority.[30] Back in 1901, however, before either the Ford village industries or the Ford Motor Company itself had been established, a British journal, *The Engineering Magazine*, had published an article by one Charles Buxton Going outlining decentralization in a cross-cultural perspective. Concentrating on England and the United States but anticipating similar developments elsewhere, Going looked forward to what he called "the Second Summer of Village Communities." He meant the restoration of local community control and individual autonomy in modern industrialized workplaces, which increasingly precluded both when placed in large cities—and, no less important, when operated paternalistically if not autocratically. Going romanticized the village communities in the early days of the English and American Industrial Revolution, just he did some later ones in both countries, exaggerating the freedom from paternalism and the degree of worker autonomy save in the smallest workshops and factories. But he understood the value of smaller-scale industrial units within new or existing rural communities akin to the Ford village industries.[31]

Ford's own publicist and spokesman W. J. Cameron put these twentieth-century trends in perspective in provocative writings and speeches, particularly in a 1937 *Mechanical Engineering* article aptly titled "Decentralization of Industry." Decentralization, he conceded, "is not a new phenomenon. Something like it is continuous throughout life and history." Yet "it is not a meaningless shifting back and forth of constant elements. . . . The elements that are capable of being decentralized are not quite the same elements that were first conglomerated or that were first developed and differentiated in a mass process."[32] The new elements involved mass production and large–scale industrialization and urbanization: "What we have learned in mass production makes decentralization possible. Decentralization is not to be thought of as correcting a mistake that was made in developing mass production," for such a view would tarnish Ford's heroic image and perhaps call into question decentralization itself. Rather, "it is to be thought of as being made possible by our experience in mass production. . . . Both movements are justified." Moreover, "both movements must be looked upon as parts of one whole, a progressive whole."[33]

Cameron did not oppose centralization per se; he acknowledged that it would "always exist, in so far as the heavier operations of industry are concerned." In automobile production, for example, foundries had to remain intact; the making and casting of metal could not be carried out in small plants. But "in the contributory departments," he went on, "we may see decentralization proceed more rapidly than in the past. It is simply a matter of an industry that is large enough and has sufficient reasons for the step" to undertake the effort.[34] The importance of Cameron's—and Ford's—argument was confirmed by the coverage a year later (1938) in the *New York Times* of a slightly revised version of the article, which was delivered as a paper before the Seventh International Management Congress in Washington, D.C.[35]

Years before, Ford himself had made related arguments in order to justify both the then continuous growth of his company and the initial stages of his decentralization experiments. In the business magazine *System*, a 1923 article titled, interestingly enough, "If My Business Were Small"—which it most certainly was not—Ford had contended that size of operations should be quite secondary to cost of production and distribution and so to profitability. There was, he claimed, no fixed ideal size for any one company or industry; rather, proper size depended on conditions at any given time. Yet thriving companies in flourishing industries would surely continue to grow larger (and more profitable). "It is inevitable," Ford wrote, "that the business of the country shall be done by very large companies which reach back to the source and, taking the raw material, carry it through the necessary processes to the finished state"—as in the then expanding River Rouge complex.[36] Nevertheless, he continued, "The whole matter of size is apt to get out of perspective. A plant, for instance, may easily be too big." Or it could be too far away from either raw materials or cheap power sources or consumer markets—or all three—to be efficient. Ford also claimed that "nowadays there is no reason to locate a plant in a labor market. . . . [F]or labor markets usually mean masses of men living in cities under conditions which do not make for health and therefore do not make for work. If the production be planned, machinery can be devised which requires very little more than attendance upon the part of the operator."[37] Hence the logic of the village industries on the one hand and of their linkages to the Highland Park and River Rouge complexes on the other.

So confident was Ford of the correctness of his views that three years later, in *Today and Tomorrow*, he proclaimed, "We now know that business is a science and that all other sciences are contributing to it."[38] Moreover, in a 1930 article in the *Saturday Evening Post*, "Management and Size," Ford wrote that "there is nothing in our manner of making that need be peculiar to the automobile. Our methods will apply to any commodity, and these methods have by common consent been taken as fundamental to America's prosperity." Ford did concede that not every company or industry ought "to attempt to do everything with all materials from the source to the finished product." Even the Ford Motor Company, he admitted that same year, "never was committed to the policy of producing in its own plants everything that went into Ford cars and trucks."[39] More than 2,300 businesses throughout the nation, he readily acknowledged, were supplying the Ford Motor Company at that point. This situation, Ford went on, represented a further degree of decentralization, not least insofar as it reduced the number of workers who would otherwise flock to Detroit and other large manufacturing cities. By 1933 the number of outside American suppliers had risen to 5,300, and Ford declared that "there ought to be 50,000."[40] As he concluded in the *Post* article, the "eventual ideal" of, presumably, not just the Ford Motor Company alone "is a complete decentralization in which most plants will be small and so situated that the workers will be both farmers and industrialists."[41] Once again the village industries would be the model to be emulated nationally, if not internationally.[42]

That ideal, however, was hardly a reality outside the Ford Motor Company when Cameron wrote his 1937 article, despite the growing sentiment toward decentralization within the business and academic communities. As Arthur Kuhn has observed about the remarkable success of General Motors under

Alfred Sloan, "Though most writers note that the Sloan-Brown team insti-tuted tight financial controls, few acknowledge GM's *early* centralization in [hitherto decentralized] nonfinancial areas such as purchasing, engineering, styling, manufacturing, and marketing. Nevertheless, a careful reading of [Sloan's autobiographical] *My Years with General Motors* reveals abundant evidence to dismiss Sloan's decentralization thesis as a myth."[43] Cameron was thereby forced to admit that "we are discussing something that as yet hardly exists in practice; it seems rather to be just an idea floating around in the air."[44] Or as the journal *Commerce and Finance* had put it four years earlier, "Mr. Ford is not the first, of course, to predict the ultimate decentralization of industry. But he is the first great industrialist to stake his all on this vision and judgment."[45]

Traditional branch plants did not really count, for decentralization, as Cameron put it, is not a "mere change of location. Likewise, to move a factory to the South or anywhere else, to take advantage of lower wage conditions"—or, as in the case of General Motors in the 1930s, to curb union organizing and strikes—"is not to be confused with decentralization." It was Cameron's hope that other prominent American businessmen would shortly follow Henry Ford's leadership and pursue the decentralization of industry elsewhere. He boldly concluded, "No industrial advance of social importance has ever come from any source except industry itself. . . . Industry has been the greatest of reformers and liberators and leaders that civilization has had these 150 years."[46]

A little more than a year after Cameron's article appeared, he delivered a paper before a large international conference of business executives in which he declared that Ford's decentralization experiments had been "an unquali-fied success" and so perhaps a model for other countries as well as for the United States. In addition to the familiar reasons for decentralization, he noted more explicitly than before, reported the *Detroit News*, that each employee "lives in the 'best place on earth to live—an American village, or on land near that village.' He works in a small factory in beautiful surround-ings, where noise and strain are reduced to a minimum." (Presumably, the tone of American nationalism would not offend the foreigners in Cameron's audience and might instead inspire them.) Meanwhile, for the employee, such a plant "develops a pride and a skill seemingly impossible where that department is part of a vast central factory." No less important, for the em-ployer, "The men have more interest in their work, and there is almost no labor turnover because 'they are not part of the restless, constantly shifting population of a great industrial city.'"[47] Here was an appeal transcending national boundaries, if simultaneously confirming the worst suspicions of organized labor regarding Ford's ulterior motives.

Ford, however, had already demonstrated further dimensions of his scheme that might also appeal to fellow businessmen at home if not abroad. When, in 1933, two major Detroit banks failed, Ford agreed to take them over and so enable some 1,700,000 accounts to be available for otherwise deprived citizens. Contending that civic duty and concern for fellow Detroiters left him no alternative, Ford nevertheless emphasized an additional motive: to provide funds especially for small rural industries manufacturing automobile parts whose workers would also be farmers. Although the initial orientation would be Michigan projects, the eventual focus, Ford indicated, would be the entire country. These industries would be connected to but not part of the Ford Motor Company, in the manner of Ford's existing suppliers. In time, if properly managed, the new small industries would prosper, expand, and—not least—repay their Ford bank loans. In the meantime, Edsel Ford was to be in charge of this project, which his father labeled "'service stations' for industry."[48]

Here, then, was an offshoot of the village industries with national if not international potential, but one that did not entail the physical and social commitment of those nineteen experiments. It was therefore a more realistic scheme for large companies willing to go partway toward Ford's ideals, though not necessarily requiring them to take over banks; merely making loans to aspiring small rural businessmen in their respective industries would be sufficient. Like his Industrialized American Barn, Ford hoped this scheme would retain the autonomy and increase the self-sufficiency of the American farmer.

CHAPTER 10

Decline of the Village Industries during World War II and After

JUST AS SENTIMENTS IN FAVOR OF DECENTRALIZATION were finally beginning to influence American industry, World War II intervened, and the notion that bigger was not necessarily better and that decentralization might be more efficient seemed illogical, if not subversive. Nevertheless, months before the Japanese attack on Pearl Harbor, several of the village industries started gearing up for wartime production, and by the spring of 1942 all eighteen existing sites (Cherry Hill had not yet opened) had become integral parts of Ford Motor Company's war effort. In most cases, happily, the items manufactured or assembled in peacetime could readily be altered for wartime purposes. These included ignition coils; oil, fuel, temperature, and ammeter gauges; front, tail, and interior lamps and light switches; taps, generators, and starters; electrical cutouts and voltage regulators; drills, valves; tools and dies—even identification badges and soybean water paints. These items were used for military vehicles, primarily cars, trucks, tanks, and aircraft.[1] Soybean processing, however, was suspended at Tecumseh/Hayden Mills, Milan, and Saline during the war.

One of the last of the village industries, Willow Run (1941), quickly lost its rural character as the pastoral acres surrounding it were paved over with concrete airport runways and with what became at that time the largest factory under one roof in the world. This other Willow Run was a center for bomber manufacture. Although the Ford plant itself continued to operate for a short time, manufacturing locks and keys for civilian vehicles, it never had the opportunity to develop as a flourishing village industry site.[2] Despite a considerable increase in the number of workers at most of the village industries (a few actually lost workers) and in turn the usually unprecedented development of two or three daily shifts, no other sites lost their character

121

the way Willow Run did. Nor did the dependence on war production schedules to determine operations rather than on available water power undermine their integrity; as the need arose, they purchased electrical power from
area utility companies. As many of the predominantly male workers left for
the battlefront, those who remained or replaced them—many of them
women—retained the desired rural values and loyalties. Former Milford
employees Francis Michaels and Rodes Walters, for example, recalled that
no women worked in their plant until World War II; nor did former Milan
employee Kenneth Edwards recall any in his plant before the war. Those
women hired during the war were usually from the local area, supervised by
what Walters calls "mature women" or "matrons," and invariably replaced at
war's end by returning men.[3] Significantly, the wartime situation at the Manchester plant, as remembered by Edwards, by then chief clerk of all the
village industries, paralleled that before the war at Phoenix in hiring women
for certain skilled tasks: "One of the jobs they had was a rate-of-climb instrument. And this rate-of-climb instrument had a ceramic tube and it had to
have a 3/1000 inch hole drilled into it. Only women were able to do that job
because of the lightness of finger required. The drill press almost looked like
your hair, you know."[4]

Several of the village industries were cited by the federal government for
exceptional efficiency during the war. As John Tobin observes, "The village
industries played only a small role in that [overall Ford Motor Company]
effort, due to their size, but that bit part represented an almost total commitment of their resources." For that matter, "given Ford's abating interest
in their operations, the small plants might have been closed sooner but for
their war production capacity. But that [very] function" unexpectedly "transformed the country units into what amounted to standard, if small, production plants." Once the war ended, however, they "were no longer the unique
product of Ford's combination of novel and diverse elements." And that
helped to seal their fate.[5]

The Ford Motor Company sold nearly all the village industries in the years
after Ford's death, though a few are, under different ownership, currently
involved in high-tech enterprises. In 1952, Ford engineer Charles Voorhess
speculated that "if Mr. Ford had kept his health and had gone along the same
way, he would have continued these plants indefinitely as part of his own
policy. . . . He would have expanded them perhaps."[6] But Ford was not, of
course, able to keep either his health or his control over Ford Motor Company, and his successor and grandson, Henry Ford II, viewed the village
industries, like other "sideline activities" of his grandfather, as both periph-

eral and wasteful. (So, too, for that matter, had Ford's son, Edsel, and their top associates, Charles Sorensen and Harry Bennett.)[7]

Ford was to have visited Flat Rock on the day that he died (April 7, 1947) in order to see if the flooding that knocked out the lights in his home had damaged the small plant; it hadn't.[8] Given the overall condition of Ford Motor Company when the young Ford and his new team took charge in 1945—"an advanced state of disarray," as one scholar has put it, with administration so lax and bookkeeping so primitive that "only later did the company discover that it had lost $50 million in the first seven months of 1946"[9]—it is hardly surprising that many of the elder Ford's pet projects were negatively assessed. (The company still had many assets, however, including a generally positive reputation, and was hardly on the brink of bankruptcy.)[10] The very same 1948 press release that called the village industries "very important cogs in the Ford Motor Company" also conceded that "there were several . . . whose output was frankly of no commercial value and whose existence traced only to Mr. Ford's commonly known characteristic of extending the helping hand."[11] These naturally were the first to be closed down in 1947 and 1948. Eight that were "still deemed efficient" were incorporated, along with the Green Island and Hamilton plants, into a newly established Parts and Equipment Manufacturing Division also in 1947—just six days before Henry Ford died.[12]

The actual decision had been made on July 26, 1946, after the company's new Policy Committee reviewed data compiled on each of the eighteen remaining sites (Willow Run having unofficially closed down) plus the facilities at Green Island, Hamilton, and a few conventional branch plants also in Michigan. Ironically, the data used to eliminate eleven plants were probably more complete than for any other time in the village industries' history. They included the amount of land at each site, a brief description of the building(s), the product(s) then made there, the number of employees, the 1945 assessed valuation, the 1945 property taxes paid, the (presumably original) cost of each, and the current depreciation and book value of each (in most cases with the last two categories broken down into the cost, depreciation, and book value of each component, such as land, buildings, machinery, and vehicles). Left blank for each one was "Recommendation" for the plant's future.[13] The committee's decision came just five days after all the village industries had reopened, following a national coalminers' strike that affected the entire auto industry. (During the strike, which lasted a month and a half, rumors had spread that the village sites might not reopen. After World War II they had also often closed because of strikes in supplier industries.)

In several cases, machinery and workers alike were moved from the closed plants to the remaining ones, thereby reversing the process by which the original plants had begun: transferring equipment and employees to the then new sites from the Highland Park and Rouge facilities. Company reassurances that these "moves are being accomplished in all cases without layoffs" may have been true—it is impossible to determine their veracity—but hardly compensated for the social and psychic if not economic upheavals experienced by the displaced workers, their families, and their communities.[14] As the headline of a story in a local newspaper put it, "Another Ford Ideal to Help Mankind Crumbles to Earth with Closing of the Phoenix Plant."[15] Of course, the recurrent rumors of plant closings before the official announcements had hardly helped employee morale. Moreover, the schools that Ford had established at several village industries were soon either closed or turned over to public school districts; only Greenfield Village retained its schools (until they too were closed years later). Yet it is difficult to imagine that these local changes made much impression upon the company overall.

Having been the principal administrator for all the plants since 1937, Superintendent Roscoe Smith was the logical choice to become General Manager of the new unit, which had deputy administrators for each of its new eastern and western subdivisions.[16] Smith remained division head until 1952, when he retired and was succeeded by his assistant, Walter H. Simpson. That truly ended the elder Ford's influence. By then the company had regained its administrative and financial stability and had moved away from the economic problems it had faced a few years earlier.

At dedication ceremonies in 1948 of new buildings constructed for the division at its Ypsilanti headquarters, Ford's vice president, Del Harder, had tried to put a positive face on an increasingly uncertain situation: "It is true that the Ypsilanti plant is located almost within the shadow of one of the world's great manufacturing units—the Rouge—but that fact has never lessened our awareness of the importance of our decentralized operations." He conceded that "some time ago we decided it would be more efficient to decentralize some of our operations and to consolidate some others." He meant administrative as much as spatial decentralization, which differed significantly from Henry Ford's original scheme. The decentralization process, Harder continued, required moving certain (unspecified) "operations out of the heavily congested Rouge plant" but also closing down two (also unspecified) "smaller operations" and bringing them "into the Ypsilanti plant"— hence the need for larger and newer facilities in Ypsilanti. "I think," he contended, "you will find it one of the most modern and well equipped units in American industry."[17]

Moreover, the remodeling of Ypsilanti's old powerhouse had provided a modern administration building for all the remaining village industries and included facilities for conferences, for apprentice training, for medical care, and for maintenance for all the surviving small plants.[18] The contradiction between expansion and centralization in Ypsilanti, at least on a modest scale, and the ongoing reduction of genuine decentralization efforts elsewhere in the company, was apparently lost on Harder. Or perhaps he deliberately chose to ignore that contradiction. The fact that, a year earlier, Harder had established at Ford the world's first corporate Automation Department— and was thereafter hailed as "the father of automation"—was apparently overlooked as the various administrative changes were announced and digested.[19]

The Northville village industry, the first to begin operations, in 1920, was the last of the nineteen to cease operations, in 1981. Six of the other seven survivors of the 1947 administrative upheaval—Brooklyn (est. 1939), Dundee (1936), Flat Rock (1923), Manchester (1941), Milford (1938), and Waterford (1925)—were disposed of in the next several years; by then they had become fairly conventional branch plants. (Ironically, the *Hydro Plants News*, the company's monthly publication for the village industries, had in 1946 and 1947 run short articles about the ongoing improvements to and expansion of most of these later casualties.)[20] As the seventh, Ypsilanti, was absorbed into a much larger Ford manufacturing complex in the surrounding acres, it completely lost its character.

The company's glowing press release upon Northville's fiftieth anniversary in 1970, when it was the only site still in operation (making valves for the then latest models, just as it had done for the Model T) did not prevent a negative decision a decade later.[21] As had happened to most of the other village industries, Northville was deemed inefficient and unprofitable, however dedicated its workers. Yet "plants may shut down," a long-time Northville employee was quoted at the time, "but dreams never die."[22] And indeed, the plant was reopened by Ford a year later, in 1982, now making not engine valves but steel fuel tanks and shipping racks, and so was still the last functioning unit of the original nineteen.[23] The fact that in order to regain their jobs its fully unionized veteran workers had to renegotiate their contracts, help in the plant's conversion process, and accept special job classifications permitting multiple tasks rather than the usual single one is yet another irony of the village industries' fate: long before unionization, multiple tasks had, of course, been among the distinctive features of the village industries vis-à-vis conventional auto plants.

Yet Ford Motor Company hailed the new arrangement as "a model for the implementation of advanced 'people programs.'"[24] And the Northville Historical Society's administrator could write in 1986, "We still feel that this is a village industry even in the 1980s."[25] In fact, in 1972 the society had created the Mill Race Historical Village, a "living history" museum built on land donated by the Ford Motor Company (part of it plant property) and consisting of several structures, both originals and replicas, dating from the nineteenth century: church, school, blacksmith shop, gazebo, and homes—a kind of miniature Greenfield Village. The values celebrated here are hardly those of industrialization.[26]

In 1989 the plant closed once again, this time for good. The approximately forty employees remaining—far fewer than before 1981—were offered either transfers to a larger plant in Dearborn or early retirement. This did not satisfy the local UAW chapter, whose president charged various violations of prior agreements, but the dispute was resolved before the closing. As the Northville Historical Society's newsletter nevertheless put it, "The plant will long serve as a reminder of Henry Ford's tradition of quality and innovation, the qualities which won the 'village industries' their reputation generations ago."[27]

Interestingly, Henry Ford II and his new "Whiz Kids" associates embarked upon a policy of avowed decentralization in the late 1940s and early 1950s that entailed a dispersing not just of plants across America but also of decision-making across company lines. This was a major part of the overall administrative reorganization that moved the company away from the monolithic yet simultaneously informal structure characterizing the elder Ford's leadership: the kind of loose, top-down style applicable to a small plant or shop, as with the village industries themselves. In effect, the company adopted the corporate planning methods that had enabled General Motors, under Sloan, to surpass Ford in the late 1920s.[28] As the company declared in a 1952 pamphlet, *The Decentralization Story*, published in reaction to UAW fears of loss of jobs at the Rouge plant:

> Decentralization is NOT "runaway shops." It is NOT "runaway jobs." It is NOT a scheme to make a ghost town of the Rouge. . . . Ford's Decentralization Program has nothing to do with our plants or facilities or the *places* where we do our work. We *do* have a plant modernization and expansion

program, but that's not decentralization. . . . Decentralization means breaking down a large business into a number of smaller businesses by product or operation, and making each of them an independently managed "profit center."

Instead of being thinly spread over a wide area and a vast number of operations, [each] management team has pin-point control over a limited, specialized operation. It determines its own manufacturing processes, engineers its own plant layouts, schedules its own production, sells its own products, keeps its own books, and performs all the other functions of an independent business organization. All with the help at the planning and policy level of the Central Office, of course.[29]

Under this scheme, neither the village industries nor the new conventional branch plants constituted decentralization. The traditional paternalism, flexibility of job assignments, informal relations between management and labor, and appreciation of skilled workers were all fading away. For that matter, reports Bruce Pietrykowski, small-scale production itself had become "atavistic from the perspective of modern management and modern labor unions."[30] The original Henry Ford might have been puzzled by it all.

Yet the anti-urban sentiments of his grandfather were what Henry Ford II had invoked in an interview published several months after the former's death. Clarifying his conception of decentralization as primarily administrative rather than spatial, the young corporate executive nevertheless conceded, "It is generally recognized that many of the social problems of our time are made worse—and in part have been created—by concentrating vast numbers of people in crowded city areas such as Detroit. I sincerely believe that our heavy concentration in the Rouge plant makes our organization job and all phases of our human relations more difficult, in spite of the apparent advantage of such a concentration."[31] Moreover, the *Hydro Plants News* itself connected postwar expansion through decentralization to the elder Henry Ford's own policies of decades earlier. As a 1946 article explained: "Four new assembly plants, including two Lincoln and Mercury units, are important among the new projects. In assuring our continued ability to best competition in the years to come, they thus assure future job security with us. Lower costs of shipping parts rather than finished cars, made possible by branch assembly plants, greatly helped us in the past to give more transportation value and service for less money." (Before World War I, branch assembly plants had been a radical step, new to the automobile industry, undertaken to break a shipping bottleneck at Highland Park, where more cars were being made than the shipping docks could load into freight cars. Model T's had been designed to go crosswise in freight cars, four to a car. But each freight car could carry ten or twelve Model T's in the form of parts, so assembly plants were started at Long Island City and on San Francisco Bay.)[32]

Another 1946 issue of the *Hydro Plants News* announced "a new plan to decentralize purchasing in the Company's branch plants, so that hereafter their non-production needs can be met locally, without regard to Dearborn" world headquarters and, in effect, without centralized decision-making. The plan would allegedly not only save "up to two months' time on each branch plant purchase order" and cut the necessary paperwork in half but would also "strengthen relations between the branch plants and [the] thousands of local business men throughout the country who are, after all, among the company's best customers."[33] Far from being original, however, this scheme merely enlarged on Henry Ford's long-standing policy of utilizing local suppliers and so of promoting local smaller businesses, not least as with the village industries. Curiously, though, the comprehensive catalogue listing local sources for possible purchase by the branch plants was to be compiled at Dearborn central offices. And, in any case, these policies did not justify maintaining the village industries themselves.

Yet another article in the *Hydro Plants News* in 1947, largely quoting a *Fortune* magazine story, "The Rebirth of Ford," connected the new decentralization with the old, albeit with no assurances of the nineteen plants' continuation: "Ford needs more plant—away from the Rouge. It is building this plant as fast as it can; while simultaneously shucking off such deadwood as its soybean plants, Ford farms, rubber plantations, etc. It is, however, holding on to most of its small sub-manufacturing units in Michigan and elsewhere until improved control studies indicate whether or not they are carrying their weight."[34] To this extent, then, the two decentralization policies overlapped.

They also overlapped from the perspective of Detroit's post–World War II decline from America's leading manufacturing city—and its "arsenal of democracy"—to its most impoverished and most physically decayed urban center. As Thomas Sugrue has demonstrated, that decline was the result of many factors, including the automobile industry's accelerated movement of conventional plants to suburban Detroit locales and to other states and regions; the subsequent relocation to those areas of such auto-related industries as machine tool manufacturers, metalworking companies, and parts manufacturers; the introduction of automated machinery in both Detroit and other plants and the consequent reduction in the industry's workforce; the industry's return to making civilian vehicles while newer high-tech industries elsewhere were developing new technologies and new products, often for the military; the Defense Department's funding of those high-tech industries, especially in the West and the South; the UAW's growing conservatism if not indifference regarding the plight of its African American members and would-be members; and a steady movement by many previously liberal Democratic white voters in Detroit and elsewhere toward conservative Republican policies and candidates. These various changes, though not directly affecting the unhappy fate of the village industries under Henry Ford II and his associates, did implicitly endorse his grandfather's belief in corporate decentralization—and in decentralization as once again spatial as much as administrative. Everything that left so much of Detroit in ruins—both physically and psychologically—would only have reinforced Henry Ford's convictions and policies about it and other large traditional manufacturing cities.[35]

Nevertheless, as Sugrue rightly observes: "The assumption that companies in the postwar period had no choice but to move to sprawling suburban and rural sites, surrounded by acres of parking lots and manicured lawns, is wrongly based in an ahistorical argument about the inevitability and neutrality of technological decisions. Industrial location policy was not a neutral response to market forces or an inexorable consequence of economic progress. Corporations made decisions about plant location and employment policy in a specific political, cultural, and institutional context."[36]

The same argument applies, of course, to Ford's village industries.

CHAPTER 11

Contemporary Renewal of the Village Industries in High-Tech America

O F THE OTHER EIGHTEEN SITES BESIDES NORTHVILLE— the last of the village industries to cease operations—sixteen have become county or municipal government facilities—museums, offices, libraries, community and shopping centers, garages—or antique shops and, in six cases, plants or offices for other private businesses, some in high-tech areas. Willow Run has been abandoned and dismantled, and Ypsilanti was absorbed into the larger facility built in 1947, a Ford plant that remains in operation today. (See the Appendix for the contemporary status of all nineteen sites.) Historian David Lewis's 1972 description of most of the sites remains true today: "[They] remain astride their original dams, spillways, headraces, tailraces, and mill ponds. . . . Some plants also have retained their water wheels and generators, while others have kept two additional Ford plant hallmarks— pipe-filled tunnels (to facilitate pipe maintenance) and wooden block floors, which old Henry believed were easier on his workers' feet than concrete or other rigid surfaces."[1]

In the 1980s the town of Dundee—whose village industry had closed in 1954 and was sold to another car parts manufacturer, who in turn had sold it to the town for $1.00 in 1970—decided to restore the underutilized facility for village offices, a community center, and a museum celebrating Dundee's history. Despite the community's fond memories of the Ford plant, the local committee charged with the restoration chose to return the building to its nineteenth-century gristmill appearance, albeit with the hope of rebuilding the auto plant's water-powered generator to produce cheap electricity for the structure.[2] Such mixed feelings about modernity paralleled Henry Ford's own.

In this light, the appeal of decentralized technology in twentieth-century America would appear to have been rather modest, perhaps just a passing fad. That the village industries likely proved a financial drain on the Ford Motor Company, if not an outright disaster, only lessens the appeal. But such a judgment is premature, for decentralized technology in a variety of forms is more popular today—and more practical—than ever before, thanks to computers, word processors, e-mail, and the Internet. An estimated 15 percent of working Americans, or almost twenty-five million persons, are currently using those devices to work at home either full or part time, rather than commute long distances to work, and so ideally increasing their work or leisure time or both.[3] True, the so-called electronic cottage is fraught with potential problems, especially the possible exploitation of isolated and powerless workers, whose geographic separation from one another may leave them ignorant of their actual plight.[4] But it does offer interesting alternatives to the hitherto common separation of place of work from place of residence.[5] Other Americans, less willing or less able to stay at home and eager for some companionship on the job, are increasingly working in small neighborhood offices wired electronically to downtown central offices (in a manner akin to the village industries) or in "virtual offices" in either downtown office towers or suburban office parks that rent out furniture, computers and related electronic equipment, and secretarial services to aspiring individuals who cannot afford their own.[6] Still others—such as real estate agents, sales representatives, insurance claims adjusters, architects and construction supervisors, who spend most of their working hours in their cars—have put together high-tech offices in their vehicles.[7] In all these cases the conception of the office, says the *Boston Globe*, has become "a bundle of [technical and nontechnical] services rather than a physical place," though "the quality" of the decentralized workplace environment remains no less important than in traditional office settings.[8] These various high-tech work situations have given rise to the terms "telecommuter" and "boundaryless workforce."

Back in 1926, Ford envisioned a new industrialized household: "It is far from impossible that with automatic machinery and widespread power the manufacture of some articles may be carried on at home. The world has proceeded from hand work in the home to hand work in the shop, to power work in the shop, and now we may be around to power work in the home."[9] Indeed, Ford's own Industrialized American Barn scheme led directly, at least in his mind, to such an arrangement: in each designated household an individual farmer, using the most modern tools and machines, would make a particular item, perhaps an automobile part; the products of his labor would then be sold to others, including perhaps the Ford Motor Company. Ideally, the energy for operating his equipment would come from a small power station constructed alongside a stream or lake on his own property. Thus would new versions of traditional cottage industries be established throughout America.

Organized labor, however, saw this scheme very differently and vigorously opposed it. Despite the absence of any such industrialized households at the time, labor viewed Ford's proposal just as it viewed the complementary village industries (and Henry Ford II's different scheme), as a cynical means of either stifling or outright destroying unions. To organized labor, decentralization of this kind meant not progress but regress, above all the elimination of worker solidarity and the promotion of a self-defeating competition among individual workers. As one labor publication put it, "Henry Ford's attempt to institute a feudal relationship between worker and boss is rapidly gaining headway. His latest trick is to sell small machines to his slaves and then buy goods from them on a contract basis."[10] Such fears may have been exaggerated in the 1930s, but they have recently been revived, and with some justification. The Union of Needletrades, Industrial, and Textile Employees has repeatedly fought to outlaw "low-tech" homework in various industries, despite the keen desire on the part of the (would-be) workers to engage in making gloves, buttons, handkerchiefs, ski caps, jewelry, and apparel.[11] As Maxine Berg wrote about eighteenth-century England, so might these labor unionists write in a few years: "Though decentralized processes in cottage or workshop manufacture predominated, much of this manufacture was marked by poverty and insecurity."[12]

On the national and international levels, a growing number of American companies have created "global offices" to take advantage of lower pay scales and lower operational costs in rural areas of the nation, and in developing countries, without sacrificing the transmission and processing of information. The giant Citicorp, for instance, moved its entire billing operation to Sioux Falls, South Dakota, in 1981 and now has thousands of workers there, nearly all in data-processing or telephone-based positions—many of them from farming or small-town backgrounds.[13]

Even more reminiscent of Ford's farm and factory scheme was the creation in 1988 in drought-stricken and impoverished Linton, North Dakota, of a modest data-processing center for a large Philadelphia-based travel agency, which allowed some 165 farmers and their spouses and families to supplement their incomes and thus save their farms. Since then, other North Dakota towns have benefited from similar setups by Rosenbluth International. Similarly, and at approximately the same time, New York Life Insurance Company began processing claims from a rural village in Ireland—where job-seeking, well-educated young people abounded—to its operations center in New Jersey via a computer link.[14]

Not surprisingly, management consultants have been busy predicting new shapes of the increasingly multinational corporation. As one prophet has put it about such emerging network organizations, "The hub . . . will be small, centralized and local. At the same time, it will be connected to an extended network that is big, decentralized and global." The parallels to Ford's dream of a national network of village industries to remain nonetheless under his and his top associates' control from Dearborn are striking—though the author does recognize the inevitable tensions between centralization and decentralization and the need for flexibility in structure and decision-making.[15]

Equally important, microchips and transistors, among other post–World War II technological advances never prophesied in Ford's day, have brought new meaning to the notion of small scale and size. And fiber optics have revolutionized the digital transmission of data and made decentralized databases practical. Databases traditionally had been centralized because it was not possible to transmit data sufficiently fast to be of practical use to business; now it assuredly is. Meanwhile the decentralization of society—whether of government, industry, schools, or other institutions—has become public and corporate policy in many quarters, and not just in the United States alone.[16]

Given all these developments, management guru Peter Drucker asked in 1989 whether, in regard to business at least, the city's future as the traditional place of gathering and disseminating information and of decision-making was threatened: "The modern big city is the creation of the nineteenth century's ability to move people" through various transportation advances. Now, however, it is "infinitely easier, cheaper, and faster to do what the nineteenth century could not do: move information, and with it office work, to where the people are." And these people are increasingly outside the major cities or, if they had a choice, would be.[17] Like others who have periodically questioned the future importance of cities, Drucker has been shown to be unduly pessimistic. Even the introduction of the Internet and the World Wide Web for general use a few years after he wrote have hardly led to the death of cities as commercial centers, as some high-tech prophets have predicted. Nevertheless, an unprecedented decentralization of information gathering and dissemination, whether inside or outside cities, has certainly taken place.[18]

Furthermore, whereas the work of E. F. Schumacher and his disciples in "appropriate" or "intermediate" technology has primarily concerned less industrialized countries than the United States—countries that have not always experienced the large-scale developments that Ford came to question decades before Schumacher's *Small Is Beautiful* (1973) appeared[19]—the work of later critics has concerned "advanced" societies like our own. Phenomena ranging from solar energy units to smaller and more fuel-efficient automobiles represent a growing rejection, by many people, of the traditional American assumption that bigger is better and that centralization surpasses decentralization.

At the same time there has been a convergence of sorts between Ford's objectives and those of many contemporary Third World countries. As development expert Gavin Kitching has put it, the latter have increasingly sought "not to arrest industrialization but to direct it into new forms and channels, to maximize employment, increase equality, and stem the drift to the swollen cities." Most artisans in the Third World "are *not* preindustrial producers struggling to preserve an existence in the face of industrial competition (as in the early nineteenth century)" but are "often pursuing activities which depend for their very existence on modern mass production industry." Kitching's examples include providing "motor car or bicycle repair and maintenance" and manufacturing "rubber sandals and other goods from car tires." Nevertheless, despite this growing embrace of "modern mass production industry" and the steadily reduced embrace of the romanticized preindustrial world, one still finds a persistent vision of a "world of equality, of small property, a minimally urbanized world, an agricultural world"—and, not least, "a decentralized world."[20] Yet in India, which has long supported small-scale and traditional village industries (usually meaning artisans and handicrafts), efforts to integrate these with large urban industries often fail, thanks to the latter's frequent domination of the former in management and production alike. Still, the vision, if not the reality, of decentralized industry remains quite popular.[21]

Geographically and demographically, moreover, there are additional trends towards decentralization. As the *New York Times* reported in 1984 about North Carolina, then the nation's tenth (and now the eleventh) largest state in population, its growing industries, many of them high-tech, are "dispersed in rural areas and small towns," while none of its cities is especially large anyway. Notwithstanding the recent growth of Research Triangle Park, this remains the case. The state's evolution from rural to industrial society has skipped the traditional urban concentration stage, and this, according to experts, "is what urbanism is going to be like in the twenty-first century: decentralized, multinodal, multiconnective." It is exactly modern transportation and communications systems that make possible this pattern and a reversal of the nation's long-term rural depopulation. No less important, the state's central Piedmont area, where most of its small cities are located, is becoming increasingly regional in character and consciousness alike. Many citizens, in fact, keep or acquire farms (or suburban plots) while working at industrial or other nonagricultural full-time jobs within easy commuting distance of their homes. Where, says one expert, "the furniture worker once supplemented farm income with a salary, . . . now it's [often] the reverse." Yet "there's still a great attachment to the land, raising a little tobacco, maybe some livestock."[22] The parallels here to Ford's scheme are surely remarkable.

In a different sense of decentralization, the Ford Motor Company itself has been backing away from its founder's policy of vertical integration, of transforming raw materials into finished products primarily within the company alone. To be sure, as I noted at the outset, this policy was always more rhetoric than reality. The same 1938 *Life* article that illuminated the village industries even as it focused on the Rouge plant conceded that "Ford still buys parts and materials from 6,000 independent plants throughout the nation."[23] In recent decades, though, the company has gradually been divesting itself of far more phases of production and increasingly buys—or outsources—from others well over "half the components that go into a car, if not the entire car itself."[24] And after heated labor negotiations, Ford followed the General Motors precedent in spinning off its huge auto parts unit.[25] Moreover, Ford increasingly relies on small, independent companies to convert basic models into such variations as convertibles that do not have a large enough demand to justify their being completely produced by Ford but which enjoy sufficient popularity to justify these arrangements. Chrysler and General Motors have had similar decentralization schemes in a return to the custom coach-building enterprises that had disappeared in the 1920s.[26] And in what is potentially among the most significant examples of decentralization, Ford has pushed far ahead of its rivals in "offering built-to-order automobiles via the World Wide Web."[27]

Meanwhile, the last of the Ford Motor Company's freighters, the *Henry Ford II*, was sold for scrap in the late 1980s. Along with its sister ships, the *Benson Ford* and the *William Clay Ford*—both sold for scrap earlier in the 1980s—this once grand vessel had for decades transported iron ore, limestone, and coal to the Rouge plant via the Great Lakes. The three freighters epitomized the initial stage of vertical integration.[28]

Likewise, the Rouge plant's steel mill, the 500-acre heart of that huge complex, was threatened until its workers reluctantly agreed to accept reduced pay and other benefits that had been granted after earlier tough contract negotiations.[29] Yet even that did not stop Ford from finally selling it in 1989, after several years of trying, to an outside company established expressly to acquire what had been America's eighth largest steel producer, formally named Rouge Steel Company and since 1981 a wholly Ford-owned subsidiary, but without the Ford name. Operating as a separate entity within the huge Rouge complex, Rouge Steel eventually became quite profitable, but not in recent years. In 2003 Rouge Steel was purchased by Russia's second-largest steelmaker, OAO Severstal, which is presently hoping to replace its outdated blast furnaces with new and more efficient electric furnaces.[30] The Rouge plant's total employment, however, has fallen from more than 100,000 at its peak in the 1930s and 1940s to a mere 6,000 (roughly half of whom work for Rouge Steel); its thirty-four integrated factories have been reduced to six; its powerhouse has not resumed working since a deadly fire on February 1, 1999, and the powerhouse's eight giant stacks are being dismantled.

Meanwhile, the Rouge plant's once modern Guest Center, the starting point for free tours since 1974, has been altered for other uses; the tours were eliminated in 1980 for financial reasons and not resumed once Ford Motor Company became profitable again a few years later, for by then the Rouge was no longer the centerpiece of the Ford empire. Beginning in 2004, however, the Ford Rouge Center (formerly the River Rouge plant) opened and a new Rouge factory tour began. The center includes two multiscreen theaters, interactive cinema historical vehicle displays, and observation decks. Because the noise, smells, manpower, and sheer drama of the original Rouge complex have all been vastly reduced, the new special-effects show relegates the plant itself to secondary status—though visitors do experience heat, fog, and sparks while their seats spin. Later they can take a walking tour of the new Dearborn Truck Plant's final assembly area.[31]

Moreover, the company is improving the remaining Rouge facilities, which still constitute its largest single industrial complex. In fact, the cutting-edge Dearborn Truck Plant, replacing a 1917 factory, was built on a 550-acre Rouge site contaminated by earlier operations. The rebuilt plant constitutes the largest industrial redevelopment project in America history. Under the direction of the environmentally sensitive Ford Motor Company chairman and chief executive William Clay Ford, Jr., Henry's great-grandson, the huge plant was covered with a literally green roof, composed of soil and sedum— "a plant with thick, fleshy leaves." This roof can hold up to four million gallons of rainwater annually, "absorb pollutants that conventional roofs spill back into the environment," and help to regulate the building's temperature;

it more than pays for itself in replacing conventional chemical treatment facilities. The 10.4-acre garden roof was declared by Guinness World Records to be the "World's Largest Living Roof." The company is also committed to cleaning up both additional contaminated Rouge complex land and the unattractive Rouge River itself. Plans for the next decade or two include establishing a research park, converting the Rouge factory into an "industrial campus," and building nature paths, wetlands, fishing areas, a boat dock, and small parks with stores, restaurants, and entertainment facilities.[32] William Clay Ford intended to remake the Rouge complex into a twenty-first century model of industrial progress.

Ironically, the UAW leadership had long urged the company to transform the aging Rouge complex into a "complete modern manufacturing center to rival GM's Saturn and Buick City plants and Mazda's . . . Flat Rock plant."[33] As a UAW top official declared in 1988, "Our goal as a union is to save the Rouge complex. I don't know if we can, but we've been trying."[34] Over the next few years, the UAW and top Ford executives developed new strategies to downsize the workforce and increase its efficiency. In addition to the better quality and styling of its cars vis-à-vis General Motors, these changes in labor's attitude about plant size and management were partly responsible for Ford's remarkable reemergence in 1986 as America's most profitable automobile company—for the first time since 1924. The Detroit papers ran cartoons of Henry Ford gloating over this sweet triumph.[35] The triumph was short-lived, as General Motors soon regained greater profitability, but Ford's vastly superior relationship with its workers and with the UAW in the 1990s helped it financially and in other ways—until that relationship subsequently deteriorated.[36] Indeed, some even predicted that Ford would eventually overtake General Motors as the world's biggest automaker in terms of sales. Curently, however, Toyota threatens to surpass Ford, GM, and Daimler-Chrysler collectively.[37]

The Mazda Flat Rock plant praised by the UAW is not on the same site as the former village industry plant, but it is in the same small community, and there are additional pertinent connections between the past and the present. The present site had been the home of the Ford Motor Company's Michigan Casting Center, which closed in 1982. The company sold the land to the Mazda Motor Manufacturing (USA) Corporation, which opened it in 1987 as Mazda's foremost decentralization effort to date. The facility is heavily automated and computerized, with hundreds of robots, but it also has a restful Japanese garden. It is one of the few Japanese production subsidiaries in America to have embraced the UAW and the only one located near the

Detroit area with its rich pool of automotive technology and labor.[38] In 1999 the Mazda complex employed some 3,200 area workers, far more than in any of the village industries, yet the original goal of establishing and maintaining "harmony between people and technology" not only remained intact but also recalled the spirit if not the literal rhetoric of the village industries.[39] Moreover, the cooperative working arrangements negotiated between Mazda and the UAW for the plant—including job rotation, advanced on-the-job training, and reduced concern for seniority and job classification in return for a less confrontational atmosphere between management and labor—hark back to the conditions at the village industries prior to unionization and subsequent job specialization. No less important, Mazda has avowedly sought to create social and cultural as well as economic bonds between the corporation and its community—again in a manner akin to that of the village industries. Yet some of these objectives have fallen far short of fulfillment because of the inability to integrate the very different Japanese and American cultures.[40] Ironically, because of mounting losses by Mazda and the need to avoid total collapse, Ford Motor Company now owns a controlling 33.4 percent of Mazda overall and 50 percent of Mazda Motor Manufacturing, which in 1992 was renamed AutoAlliance International.[41]

As the Japanese auto industry threatened traditional American supremacy in the late 1970s and 1980s, much was made of the Japanese *kanban* or "just-in-time" (JIT) inventory system: keeping only enough parts on hand to fulfill orders, thereby saving considerable money, space, and labor. Ford and other American automakers had traditionally kept vastly larger inventories that were quite useful during strikes but generally not otherwise. (It was, of course, the existence of such huge inventories that, for a time, allowed the village industries' workers to remain or become farmers and not upset the manufacturing timetables.)[42]

Ford and Crowther's *Today and Tomorrow* was reprinted in 1988 by Productivity Press, a small publisher that generally puts out newer books on successful corporate leadership, organizational renewal, Japanese cost accounting, and, not least, *kanban*. The reprint, however, was no accident; nor was it done to demonstrate the outdatedness of that 1926 book. Far from it: the publisher, Norman Bodek, cites the official creator of just-in-time, Taiichi Ohno, as having "learned it all from Henry Ford's book." Ohno applied these ideas to Toyota's pioneering JIT production techniques (and recent further pleas by Rouge plant employees and the UAW to remodel the aging complex have in part been based on trying to emulate Toyota's Toyota City JIT production techniques). "How we in America deviated from Ford's teaching is a mystery," Bodek laments, for despite its 1926 publication date, the book's basic ideas "are appropriate still"—and not just JIT but such related concepts as raising workers' wages, reducing the cost of cars, keeping work environments clean, implementing hands-on management and supervision, upgrading training for interested workers, and continually changing and improving throughout.[43] In fact, a promotional notice for the book quotes a magazine as saying that because "Ford expected only a 33-hour lapse between the mining of iron ore and the production of a car from the metal from that ore, he might rightly be called the Father of Just-in-Time."[44]

The JIT inventory system is part of the larger enterprise called "lean production," which also includes highly flexible as opposed to single-purpose machines, multiskilled as opposed to barely skilled workers, tasks that involve greater intellectual challenges than in traditional assembly line processes, tasks that involve teamwork and decision-making rather than individualized monotonous operations devoid of worker input, and, consequently, decentralized rather than centralized exercises of authority. Visions of a new era of more humane, more democratic, and more decentralized workplaces with more highly educated workforces have followed, all of them founded on computer-based technologies that were not, of course, in existence in Ford's day.[45] In this context, however, Ford is hardly held up for praise; in fact, his overall production system has been given the negative term Fordism: "a single, standard model [car], special-purpose machines, . . . a mechanized materials handling system," as epitomized by the moving assembly line, de-skilled jobs, and high wages to try to alleviate workers' miseries.[46] The high-tech "lean production" alternative has been termed "post-Fordism."

How can Ford—and his production methods—be lauded in some quarters of high-tech America (and Japan) and be condemned in others? The reasons are, on the one hand, the failure of Ford's admirers to recognize the limitations of Fordism in terms of the prices paid by ordinary workers in the conventional plants (but not necessarily in the village industries), and, on the other hand, the failure of Ford's critics to recognize the modest successes to date of post-Fordism and the repeated inability to institute changes in the workplace that are truly permanent and pervasive. Both admirers and critics have been seduced by rhetoric that, for various reasons, does not always match reality. And as Ruth Milkman has shown convincingly in her study of 1980s and 1990s technological and management changes at the General Motors assembly plant in Linden, New Jersey, workers' own views and experiences are frequently ignored by scholars who pontificate on the basis of modest information and insight.[47] Significantly, Steve Babson's examination of the Mazda/AutoAlliance Flat Rock plant has revealed similar gaps between promise and fulfillment: "Where the productive system is lean, many [workers] see it as mean."[48]

For that matter, a 1992 study of working conditions for nonmanagerial employees in seven "advanced capitalist societies" (Australia, Britain, Canada, Germany, Japan, Sweden, and the United States), titled "The Myth of Post-Fordist Management," concluded that in every country, "flexible production techniques and organizational forms do not appear to have usurped the Fordist organization of the labor process." There was "little evidence in the data . . . to suggest that participative organizational practices have made any significant incursion into traditional managerial prerogatives in the workplace in any of the countries studied."[49] A complementary 1997 study of workers throughout the industrialized world came to the similarly negative conclusion that there is nothing "particularly 'post-Fordist' about lean production other than the tendency to decentralize the production chain" (without any benefits to the workers themselves).[50]

No less important, Philip Scranton has demonstrated that Fordism itself hardly characterized the bulk of American industrialization in the early twentieth century. Instead, smaller companies with customized and modest batch production were as crucial to the growth of the American economy as large corporations with standardized mass production such as Ford, Du Pont, and Standard Oil. Companies producing precision instruments, furniture, textiles, jewelry, books and magazines, elevators, turbines, and switchboards often remained as either family-owned businesses or closely held corporations. Far from engaging in deskilled and monotonous work routines, these often quite successful firms required both flexibility and skilled labor in order to accommodate customers with varied needs and, more broadly, the nation's booming consumer culture. For that matter, such industrial giants as Baldwin Locomotives and Pullman Sleeping Cars had followed a similar strategy of specialty production rather than of mass production.[51] If, as Scranton and others have recently concluded, there was no single "best" or "correct" route toward industrialization in the United States, much less in the West overall, then the village industries—however integrated they may have been with the conventional Ford plants and with the Highland Park and Rouge complexes—constituted partial exceptions to Fordism in this respect as well.[52] The Waterford plant, for example, exemplified the use of skilled labor engaged in multiple tasks with little supervision and producing small batches of high-quality precision gauges vital to the overall manufacture of Ford automobiles.[53]

Moreover, Scranton and others emphasize that even those smaller companies that did not follow Fordism were anything but helpless servants of the marketplace and that their often shrewd and savvy owners and managers understood quite well how to compete against giant Fordist corporations. All these contemporary scholars stress choice, and one can legitimately argue that Ford himself exercised choice by establishing the village industries in the first place and by funding them for so long. True, Scranton's *Endless Novelty* (1997) hardly characterizes the whole of the village industries' operations, subservient as they were to Ford and Ford Motor Company dictates. But it does apply to the variety of settings and of procedures that made the village industries very different from the rest of the Ford empire.

As Bruce Pietrykowski has put it, Fordism as practiced in the village industries reveals that "mass production itself contained contradictory logics of centralization and decentralization, deskilling and skilling, craft, technical, and bureaucratic control within specific geographical locales." The nineteen sites represented efforts to "combine elements of mass production with flexibility." Specifically, "spatial decentralization" managed to coexist with "the vertically integrated business organization" reflective of large-scale mass production.[54] Consequently, debate goes on over what constitutes Fordism and, in turn, post-Fordism. The village industries may not be at the heart of that debate, but their very existence illuminates the complexities of—and the continuities and discontinuities between—those two stages of technological development. Moreover, that very debate indicates that, in the twenty-first century, as in the past, there will continue to be "many [different] future worlds of work."[55]

By contrast, no one denies that the Renaissance Center, Detroit's foremost commercial effort to date to revive its declining downtown, has "become emblematic" of the city's "inability to sustain a thriving retail district."[56] Established by a business-government coalition headed by none other than Henry Ford II, the glass and steel complex of six office towers surrounding a skyscraper hotel opened in 1977 on the banks of the Detroit River. The site was a one-time flour mill—much like that of the village industries. The project was expected to lure shoppers if not businessmen away from the area's many suburban malls, several of which were among the nation's first (and all, of course, heavily dependent upon the auto). Instead, however, the $357 million enterprise lost over $200 million in its initial decade, continued to lose money, and spent $25 million more to correct design problems that turned off those who ventured inside its interior maze. Its moatlike exterior and two-story surrounding wall, intended to provide a sense of security from the crime-ridden downtown core, hurt the latter area's remaining shops and offices by draining off ever more commercial traffic while relegating the Renaissance Center itself to the status of a virtual island—a painful example of urban (re)centralization. In 1996 the General Motors Corporation, of all businesses, purchased the entire complex for (a mere) $73 million and, after a $500 million renovation, made the Renaissance Center its new world headquarters. A brief General Motors video running continuously in the center's buildings proclaims that, once completely renovated, the major plaza formerly closed to the public will be a "friendly, inviting plaza" open to all. Atop the tallest structure is to be a 250-foot-high "hood ornament" visible from Ford Motor Company's own Dearborn world headquarters. Displaced Renaissance Center tenants included some 2,500 Ford employees, who moved back to Dearborn in 1997, thereby ending Henry Ford II's dream of having Ford Motor Company lead Detroit's revival. The simultaneous dismantling of the company's large World of Ford exhibit in the Renaissance Center— and its replacement by an even larger GM World exhibit celebrating GM's first 100 years—symbolized that unfulfilled vision and the intense corporate rivalry.[57]

Within the rest of the city, as newspapers have pointed out, "patches of Eden" in individuals' home gardens still appear "amid Detroit's ruins." Reminiscent of Henry Ford's Thrift Gardens, albeit without corporate sponsorship, such patches glitter "in the most improbable downtown lots, near the grayest stretches of brewery and factory" and from the "rooftops of abandoned skyscrapers, warehouses, and hotels." Indeed, in recent years larger areas have been reclaimed as "community gardens and microfarms—some consuming entire blocks."[58] The prospect of contemporary Detroit as "an urban core giving way to an urban prairie" would certainly have pleased Ford. Still, as one scholar has put it, "metropolitan decentralization," including the loss of both population and auto plants, "has left Detroit with a declining economy and a tenuous future."[59] This situation was confirmed by the 2000 census, which determined that the city's population had fallen below one million for the first time in eighty years, while its suburbs' population surged.[60]

The contrast between downtown Detroit (including the Renaissance Center) and its weathy suburbs—some of them among the richest suburban communities in the entire nation—reflects Drucker's observation in 1947, following Henry Ford's death: "The central problem of our age is defined in the contrast between the functional grandeur of the River Rouge plant, with its spotless mechanical perfection, and the formlessness and tension of the social jungle that is Detroit. And the two together comprise Henry Ford's legacy."[61] Even the shrunken Rouge plant compares favorably with today's Detroit, the nation's poorest and most rundown big city, still recovering from the urban riots of two decades after Drucker wrote.[62]

By contrast, Dearborn area land acquired decades ago by Ford for both his estate, Fair Lane, and the company's wholly owned subsidiary Ford Land Development Corporation, has become Michigan's biggest planned real estate community and one of the country's largest. The development is so large that it may overshadow nearby Ford World Headquarters—now called the Henry Ford II World Center—with its planned hotel, office building, office park, condominiums, and shops. This is, in effect, suburban centralization and would likely have upset Ford, though Fair Lane itself has been preserved intact.[63] Ironically, until the Ford Land Development Corporation took over, some four hundred acres near the Henry Ford II World Center, already surrounded by high-rise developments, were devoted to soybean cultivation. This working farm would surely have delighted Ford.[64]

So, too, would the persistent popularity of healthy soybean-based products such as tofu and the snack Tofuti. A Japanese parent company has established a plant in, of all places, Saline, in the town's industrial park. Like the earlier Ford project, this one uses soybeans grown by local farmers and sold to the company.[65] Meanwhile the Ford Motor Company itself has switched, for environmental reasons, from petroleum-based ink to soy ink for most of its printing projects.[66]

Also in Saline, "the town where Ford first moved into plastics," Ford Motor Company built in the late 1960s the world's largest "injection moulding plastic plant," which prospers as "car design calls for more and more lightweight, corrosion immune building materials" with greater fuel efficiency.[67] Employing 2,400 workers, the plant is located at the other end of Saline from the village industry plant, which has become a combined antique shop and social center. (Sadly, though, the construction of this facility made obsolete the much smaller Brooklyn facility, which had also been making plastic parts.)[68]

The present Saline Ford plant is also part of a trend identified by geographer James Rubenstein: "After a fifty-year period of *decentralization* [roughly 1914–1964], the Midwest again is the preferred location for most . . . new [auto assembly] plants. Between 1965 and 1986 all fifteen sites for new automobile assembly plants were in the Midwest in contrast with a figure of four of fifteen erected there during the preceding twenty-year period." Rubenstein's 1987, 1992, and 2001 updates, which analyzed plant closings as well as openings and also considered new Japanese and Japanese-American plants, only confirmed this trend.[69] Whereas for most of the twentieth century, "most of the components that go into motor vehicles were built in southeastern Michigan" (because the most important component, steel, was increasingly made in or near southeastern Michigan), "most final assembly plants, where components are attached to vehicles, were located elsewhere in the country, especially near population concentrations in the northeast, south, and west coast" (because the components were relatively inexpensive to transport but the finished automobiles quite expensive to transport from Michigan).[70]

The reasons for renewed centralization are various, but a desire to reduce overall costs either by hiring nonunionized workers or by hiring unionized workers agreeable to greater flexibility than in older plants is a crucial factor that has led to the location of midwestern plants in rural areas with less militantly demanding workforces than in those close to large cities. Even so, all the new plants are near interstate highways and major airports: hence the connections, despite the general centralization, to Ford's scheme for rural sites with local workers who would likely be more docile than their urban counterparts.

All these contemporary developments suggest that the village industries are, if anything, more relevant to our postindustrial era than to Ford's. As John R. Mullin, a landscape architect and sympathetic student of Ford's scheme has noted, today it is exactly "incubator industries that seem to locate in villages," and "this small, self-started but [sometimes] underfinanced group of risk takers provide a large share of American jobs," not least those in high-tech areas.[71]

In 2000, a financial services company called Village Ventures, Inc., was established in Williamstown, Massachusetts. Although its name was not spurred by an identification with Ford's "village" industries, the company's founders *were* aware of Ford's project and sought intellectual connections between his enterprise and theirs: Village Ventures focuses on venture capital investments in "emerging technology markets that have been ignored by established" venture capitalists and frequently finds them in relatively rural, relatively inexpensive areas such as Williamstown. Just as Ford appealed to potential village industry workers to leave cities for small towns, so the Village Ventures organizers appeal to potential investors to recognize the "higher quality of life" available in their proposed sites as compared with that of contemporary American cities.[72]

Even where—as on Route 128 in Massachusetts or in California's Silicon

Valley or in emerging high-tech cities throughout the United States and around the globe, from Austin, Texas, to Boise, Idaho, to Cambridge, England, to Tel Aviv, Israel[73]—high-tech firms are geographically concentrated, sometimes with the entire company in one site, there is an ethos of flexibility missing from their older, larger, more urban industrial counterparts. This flexibility avowedly encourages innovation, such as the greater opportunity of skilled, educated workers to move from one job to another nearby as the occasion or need arises. Precisely such a situation characterized the American auto industry in its early years in Michigan. And the Ford Motor Company itself, lest we forget, began operations in 1903 on a single site and on a small scale, with a workforce of only eight, including Henry Ford himself, as part of another "incubator industry."[74]

Paradoxically, high tech has at once helped to save and helped to undermine the small Israeli communal societies, the kibbutzim, that have long had some interesting similarities to—and differences from—Ford's village industries. Originating in 1910, the early kibbutzim were both predominantly agricultural and avowedly socialist, and in these two respects were clearly unlike the village industries. The kibbutzim long concentrated on draining swamps, on transforming deserts into fertile farmland, and on introducing new crops and modern methods of cattle and poultry breeding. Yet achieving these goals eventually required the development of agricultural machinery, which led to the establishment of many small businesses. In turn came other industrial enterprises with some parallels to the village industries—for example, small assembly lines making laminated windshields for cars—and, in recent decades, various small high-tech plants in these still largely rural sites. Today, only about 30 percent of total kibbutz production is agricultural; the rest is industrial, yet the kibbutzim still grow 40 percent of Israel's agricultural produce, as well as making 10 percent of the country's industrial output and 7 percent of its exports.

Kibbutz membership size ranges from under 100 to over 1,000, comparable to that of the village industries. Comparable also, to a certain extent, are the growing numbers of members who live in towns and cities and commute to and from their work on the kibbutz (likewise, numerous other members work outside of the kibbutz and commute daily from and to their kibbutz residences). Today there are 270 kibbutzim scattered throughout Israel with varying degrees of economic, political, and ideological integration but nothing akin to the village industries' tight integration with the rest of the Ford Motor Company. Still, just as Ford envisioned the village industries not as mere escapist retreats from urban civilization but as alternatives to it that should be emulated throughout the United States, so the kibbutzim traditionally saw themselves as doing likewise for Israeli society, even as Israel became ever more urbanized. If the kibbutzim have never represented more than 7 percent of the Israeli population and have usually been closer to their current less than 3 percent, that small percentage, writes Daniel Gavron, has routinely "played a role in the nation's life out of all proportion to their numbers," whether in politics or in culture or, not least, in the military.[75]

The biggest challenge to the kibbutzim, however, derives from the ongoing transformation of the overall Israeli economy from predominantly socialist to predominantly capitalist and the inevitable reduction, even in the once avowedly socialist kibbutzim, of the belief in and the practice of shared property and wealth. The very success of small kibbutzim industries, both high-tech and more traditional, has in many cases led to a competitive free-market capitalist spirit that would surely have delighted Henry Ford. Moreover, two Kibbutzim founded after World War II and long involved more in manufacturing than in farming, have more recently achieved stability and success in turning out soy meals and soy pellets. Interestingly, a typical dilemma is whether to allow for the purchase of cars by individual members at times of their own choosing, since in the past all cars were communally owned and were bought only with communal approval. Some defenders of these changes contend that "many high-tech industries thrive on teamwork" and that competition can enhance rather than undermine cooperation even in the capitalist workplace, be it high tech or more traditional.[76] Citing the example of the village industries, Ford might well have agreed. Nevertheless, the overall future of Israel's kibbutzim is quite uncertain.

By contrast, within the United States there have repeated been calls for the construction, or reconstruction, of small dams to replace millions of barrels of precious oil and tons of coal by water power and so to provide clean and efficient alternative energy sources. Writing in 1977, David Lilienthal, for example, former chairman of both the Tennessee Valley Authority and the Atomic Energy Commission—and a lifelong advocate of large-scale power systems—lamented that "lost megawatts flow over [the] nation's myriad spillways." Although "I do not embrace the notion that what is small is necessarily beautiful . . . I am nevertheless skeptical of the equally extreme doctrine that bigger is better, and that biggest is best," he conceded. Instead, "I suggest that 'bigness' and 'smallness' are not exclusives but rather complementary, as they have been in the Tennessee Valley Authority."[77] Surely, Ford would have approved this argument.[78]

Ford would likely have been still more delighted at the actual ongoing revival of the small-scale hydroelectric industry following the 1978 National Energy Act. That legislation mandated that regional power companies purchase electricity from anyone who produced it, no matter how small an amount, as a means of saving precious and ever more expensive oil. The act set prices greatly exceeding existing prices in order to spur investment but allowed for regional variations. Those involved in such efforts are not innocent romantics wishing to escape modern technology but rather practical-minded, technically skilled entrepreneurs who see "minihydros" as potentially lucrative enterprises. Yet all share a considerable idealism not merely for reviving small-scale hydroelectric power but also for integrating older and newer technologies. The parallels to the village industries are obvious.

There are others as well. Much like Henry Ford, but perhaps more systematically and certainly more efficiently, these persons investigate all possible streams, roads, and towns in a given region before proceeding further. What they seek are not virgin springs but precisely sites where "the power of falling water" had already been utilized, whether by utility companies, other businesses, or private individuals.[79] More specifically, they seek abandoned or at least available-for-purchase dams, mills, turbines, generators, governors, and the like. Left to rot in many cases by those for whom, by the mid-twentieth century, hydroelectric power was no longer profitable to produce, these sites can finally turn a profit again, thanks to the 1978 act.

In the process, much as in the intended impact of the Ford auto plants on the nineteen chosen communities, "more than power will be restored" in the affected towns. Although few of these contemporary locales "would be pictured on a wall calendar" and many are "fetid little cities half consumed by acid rains," in John McPhee's words, all are as appreciative of the opportunity for economic and social rebirth as were the original inhabitants of the village industries.[80] Moreover, the machinery in each power plant will be as up-to-date as was that in Ford's nineteen facilities. And a number of the plants will operate semiautomatically, with a limited workforce and with ample free time for other activities—including gardening, if not necessarily farming—for their employees. If then, relatively few local residents will work in the plants, those who do may nonetheless be fulfilling Ford's dreams of dual employment.

Such modern plants need not, however, be restricted to either rural areas or to areas with substantial water power. Ford's refusal to consider more populated sites and other power sources undermined both the practicality and the appeal of his scheme. The decentralization of electricity production, with many of the social and economic benefits that Ford envisioned for minihydros in the village industries, can now be accomplished in a variety of other ways, as through cogeneration (the sequential production of electricity and steam for heat or industrial processes), photovoltaics (solar cells), and wind, ocean thermal, solar thermal, and solid waste energy conversions. These can often be situated in heavily populated areas, and with greater efficiency and lower costs than conventional large-scale, centralized utility systems. As Richard Hirsh has shown, the "small scale and cost-effectiveness" of such new technologies has proved critical to their success. Thus "the compact size of quickly manufactured gas turbines, for example, meant that independent power companies could locate prepackaged generation units near load centers soon after the need for power became apparent." Customers could thereby avoid waiting for "regulated utilities to complete construction of large, centralized plants—plants that often came on line later than expected and at high cost."[81]

Like minihydros, moreover, these alternative energy technologies can be ecologically beneficial insofar as they utilize renewable natural resources that are indigenous, in one form or another, to all parts of the world. And like minihydros they do not preclude continued partial reliance on traditional large-scale, centralized power facilities—just as Ford expanded his Highland Park and especially Rouge plants as he simultaneously developed the village industries. The extent to which the American electric power industry has moved in these new directions has been on the basis of simultaneously retaining its traditional reliance on large-scale, centralized power facilities; whatever innovations it has allowed have come slowly and reluctantly, and usually because of overwhelming economic and technological problems. At the same time, however, these new electrical systems hark back to the origins of electrical power production in the United States (and elsewhere), which was initially dispersed among decentralized grids.[82]

Despite this growth in recent decades of minihydros and related developments, however, there may soon be a trend in the opposite direction: removing small dams whose modest contributions to hydroelectric power in their respective locales is outweighed by ecological considerations, such as improving or restoring fish populations and recreational activities. According to John McPhee, "Since 1960, over a hundred small-river dams have been removed in the United States," which leaves "sixty-six thousand river dams in the United States five or more feet high." The first such removal under federal order was that of the Edwards Dam on the Kennebec River in Augusta, Maine, in 1999. Built in 1837, the dam had had "an immediate impact on the fish populations," yet by the time of its removal it was generating merely one-tenth of 1 percent of the state's electrical power. It nevertheless took twelve years from the denial in 1987 of a relicensing request by the Federal Energy Regulatory Commission to the dam's actual removal. Still, this case may be trend-setting.[83]

Significantly, though, efforts are now under way to restore several of the barely used village industry sites, to register as many as possible with the state of Michigan for historical preservation status (for protection and fund-raising purposes), and to develop the Ford Heritage Trail for self-guided tours of the original village industries, among other historic locales associated with Ford and Ford Motor Company in southeastern Michigan. The trail consists of three routes, all beginning at Greenfield Village. Each of twenty stops will feature interpretive signs, and an overall brochure, book, and travel poster will be available. Nankin Mills, the first site to be so registered (in 1977; Newburg, Phoenix, and Plymouth were registered in 1989), has become the center of these activities by virtue of its current status as headquarters of the Wayne County Division of Parks (Wayne County includes but is not limited to the city of Detroit). In the words of the division's brochure:

> This leadership was historically spurred by the foresight of Henry Ford. His concept of Village Industries led to the conversion of millraces and the damming of the Rouge River for hydroelectric power. These early mills, impounded lakes, and other flood management aspects of Henry Ford's Village Industry projects are preserved and utilized in the design of the Wayne County Park System. Some of Ford's oldest facilities now house park offices, maintenance facilities, or provide the natural backdrop for our better inland boating and fishing. County residents are indeed fortunate that these flood plain lands have been preserved for recreation purposes since the 1920s. Population shifts and commercial development now limit park expansion and land acquisition.[84]

The hope of the organizers is that the tourism spurred by the Ford Heritage Trail will be "beneficial to the economies of the small towns through which it passes and will be an incentive for further historic preservation and adaptive reuse of historical buildings on the Trail." Tourism, then, more than new industry, has become the hope for saving village industry sites, although the trail's promotional material refers to them as a "living laboratory in one of the most visionary experiments of the twentieth century."[85]

In 2001 the Wayne County Division of Parks opened the Nankin Mills Interpretive Center. The exhibit focuses on the Rouge River's history from the glaciers to the present (including the current cleanup effort) and has four sections: Native American Era, European Settlement Era, Henry Ford Era, and Wayne County Era. Along with the Division of Parks headquarters, the Interpretive Center is housed in the actual former gristmill that was purchased by Ford in 1918 and rebuilt for his initial village industry. Ford's widow Clara donated the plant to Wayne County in 1948. The center operates tours of its exhibits, educational programs, and summer nature camps. The Henry Ford Era section includes a life-sized mannequin of the industrialist and an interactive display that allows visitors to hear Ford speak about his vision of the future.[86]

Equally important, in 1989 the Plymouth Historical Museum opened a permanent exhibit on the village industries, including photographs, artifacts, and a videotape of, among other things, interviews with several former workers. Funded in part through a Ford Motor Company grant—but the work of unpaid Plymouth Historical Society members—the exhibit is housed in a structure whose exterior is designed to resemble the original Nankin Mills building. The exhibit covers the opening of Northville in 1920 to the closing of most of the sites in the 1950s.[87]

In addition, efforts are under way to establish a Women's Museum at the Phoenix Mill—currently a Wayne Country maintenance yard—because of its predominantly female workforce. The proposed museum would illuminate the achievements of not just the Phoenix workers but also other American women workers. It would also have a coffee shop, for the county contends that Phoenix established the practice of the coffee break.[88]

No less important, in 1998 the Congress and President Bill Clinton designated the entire region of southeastern and central Michigan the MotorCities National Heritage Area, one of twenty-four National Heritage Areas. (All of them are affiliated with the National Park Service, which provides modest technical assistance, but the burden of funding is placed on local communities, governments, businesses, and other institutions.) This designation recognized the region as having the world's largest concentration of automobile-related enterprises, sites, and events. The hope is to use this concentration—and the rich history accompanying it—to spur further economic and cultural growth in southeastern Michigan as well as to educate citizens about that remarkable past. The MotorCities National Heritage Area has been divided into "Six Corridors of Automotive History," one of which is the Rouge River Corridor. The village industries in general and the Ford Heritage Trail, the Nankin Mills Interpretive Center, and the Plymouth Historical Museum in particular are in turn part of the Rouge River Corridor, as are other aspects of Henry Ford's life and of Ford Motor Company history. One of the MotorCities' goals is to restore and reuse historic structures such as Nankin Mills for education, business, and tourism.[89]

With this designation and these two exhibits, the village industries have finally begun to secure a place at least in the Michigan historical consciousness.

Conclusion

Henry Ford Evolves from Mechanical to Social Engineer

GIVEN THE VARIOUS DECENTRALIZATION EFFORTS CITED in chapter 11, one might quote approvingly the last line of the Ford Motor Company's 1948 press release: "It all adds up to a realization that the seeds of the project planted . . . years ago by Henry Ford are bearing fruit" at long last, if not necessarily "for both the workers and the company."[1] Were the village industries more widely known today, Ford might be a folk hero to a new generation of Americans, few of them raised on farms or in small towns. In his unsystematic, unorthodox way, Ford understood a good deal more about the direction of modern technology and society than did most of his seemingly more sophisticated contemporaries. In the village industries he sought a limitation on the ever greater size, scale, and impersonality of technological development and a concern for other aspects of the "good life," although the limits he would impose were hardly as severe as those of, say, Helen and Scott Nearing. Ford, then, accepted modern technology as a fact of life and offered means of accommodating it to the cultural values that he thought should prevail. His preferred values were clearly not shared by everyone, but the accommodation of technology to existing cultural values has been characteristic of Americans' responses to new technologies since colonial times.[2]

Ford should not, however, be put back on his pedestal solely because of those nineteen experiments. He almost certainly established and maintained them for a variety of reasons—for profits, for public relations, for union busting, for social control of the workforce, and for love of small towns and of water power—but it is impossible to be precise. Even his publicist W. J. Cameron conceded that "the motives were mixed."[3] What John Kasson observed about the Boston merchants who established Lowell in the early nineteenth century surely applies to Ford a century later: "A . . . satisfactory explanation of the founding of Lowell would recognize *both* commercial and social and ideological motives. For the Boston associates . . . were in fact both capitalists and concerned citizens, hard-dealing merchants and public-spirited philanthropists, entrepreneurs and ideologues."[4]

Simultaneously, as Donald Davis has argued in another context, an understanding of Ford and his enterprises must be extricated "from the premise of exceptionalism that has heretofore governed the literature on the early automotive industry. Too much emphasis on Ford's idiosyncrasies—or madness, as some would have it—has obscured the extent to which the individual and the company did fit the industry-wide pattern."[5] If both Ford and the Ford Motor Company clearly practiced decentralization to a far greater degree than did the rest of the industry, they just as clearly were not alone in their assessment of its practicality and potential.

By the same token, the village industries do constitute partial exceptions to the production system that was eventually termed Fordism. However much the nineteen plants resembled their larger counterparts, their ethos was certainly one of greater flexibility of operations and more diversified tasks for most workers than were found in the conventional plants. The contemporary debates about the continuation of Fordism in the automobile and other industries and about post-Fordism as a new stage invariably—with one notable exception[6]—overlook the village industries as themselves having been pioneering partial alternatives to Fordism.[7] Yet the "obvious nostalgia" on the part of some contemporary historians for what one reviewer terms "a golden age of small, independent, imaginative, and intelligently responsive producers of yesteryear" has important parallels with Ford's own feelings about the village industries as being such partial alternatives.[8] If Marx once claimed not to be a Marxist, so Ford might, to this extent, have claimed not to have been a Fordist. Just as it is tempting to reduce Ford's motives behind the village industries to one or two, likewise is it tempting to impose a rigid Fordist model upon the company he led, but both of those temptations must be firmly resisted.

The village industries must be seen as not simply amusing hobbies or historic relics, not merely the exotic products of an eccentric, eventually senile, mind and personality or the manifestations of a supremely self-centered man with the financial and administrative means to make the outside world conform to his values and prejudices. Nor were they merely futile efforts to "freeze" history, flights from reality having no relevance to Ford's time—or to ours.[9] On the contrary, these nineteen experiments ought properly to be appreciated as twentieth-century versions of the "machine in the garden," seeking new but still necessary balances between the all too common antitechnological and protechnological extremes. Certainly Ford's repeated emphasis on uniting agriculture and industry through this and related schemes suggests the need of that same search for a balance in modern America. Yet the extremes continue to shape much of the rhetoric—and the reality—of technology in American society and culture. Ford tried to overcome those extremes, and to this extent at least his efforts must be deemed progressive.[10]

Aldous Huxley, I believe, had such a vision in mind when he wrote his foreword to the 1946 reprint of Brave New World—a book that, as already noted, ironically uses Ford and Ford's large-scale, heavily centralized assembly lines as the focal point for its brilliant satire of future technological utopia or, more precisely, dystopia. As Huxley conceded in 1946 about his 1932 work:

> It seems worth while at least to mention the most serious defect in the story, which is this. The Savage is offered only two alternatives, an insane life in Utopia, or the life of a primitive in an Indian village, a life more human in some respects, but in others hardly less queer and abnormal. At the time the book was written this idea, that human beings are given free will in order to choose between insanity on one hand and lunacy on the other, was one that I found amusing and regarded as quite possibly true. . . . If I were now to rewrite the book, I would offer the Savage a third alternative. Between the utopian and the primitive horns of his dilemma would lie the possibility of sanity—a possibility already actualized, to some extent, in a community of exiles and refugees from the Brave New World, living within the borders of the Reservation. In this community economics would be decentralist and Henry Georgian, politics Kropotkinesque cooperative. Science and technology would be used as though, like the Sabbath, they had been made for man, not (as at present and still more so in the Brave New World) as though man were to be adapted and enslaved to them.[11]

Huxley, then, might have approved of the village industries—about which he probably knew little or nothing—despite condemning the rest of the Ford ethos and empire. One wonders if Huxley's contemporary Charlie Chaplin would have offered a similar kind of middle ground if he had ever rethought the ending of *Modern Times* (1936), a film in which the Little Tramp and his girlfriend leave the horrors of industrial life for a rural retreat down the road.

Similarly, the romanticized vision of small-town America that Walt Disney created in Disneyland and later theme parks—as reflected above all in his Main Street—leaves little room for modernity beyond its antique automobiles. Growing up in a rootless childhood and repeatedly moving about with his family left Disney nostalgic for a past that in large measure never existed. There are few if any connections between his idyllic small-town America and the rest of his theme parks, with their focus on high-tech exhibits and entertainment. By contrast, Ford was clearly rooted in rural agricultural Michigan but was able to embrace and help to shape evolving industrial America.[12]

Moreover, along with other projects of Ford's later life—from his educational programs and agricultural experiments to his industrial and world's fair exhibits to his Dearborn collections and institutions—the village industries provided a vision of a new social order in America. Far from just looking backward, as is usually assumed, Ford was also looking ahead—and with less guilt over what the automobile and mass production had done to agrarian values and ways of life than is usually assumed. For better or for worse, these activities served to "decentralize" Ford's time and interest away from his fundamental business concerns.[13]

"Who is the typical American of today," asked the famous journalist Ida Tarbell in 1927, "as Washington, Jefferson and Lincoln were in their times?" Ford, she replied, whose integration of these various projects she went on to describe as looking both behind and ahead in a most positive manner.[14] Having been given by Ford himself, twelve years earlier, her "first convincing glimpse of a possible future return to the [alleged] industrial practice of early America"—when farm and factory were supposedly combined—Tarbell now confirmed the initial success of this enterprise, as in the initial village industries.

Even H. G. Wells, the eminent British writer, historian, and visionary, was impressed by Ford's many connections between the past and the future and specifically endorsed "the several factories" in the United States that allowed "a man to work on the land in summer and come into the shelter and light of the factory in winter time." (Interestingly, Wells also praised Ford's alleged plan to take "factories to the mouth of his mines" in Kentucky and Virginia "so that the miners may be able to spend only half their working hours below ground and for the rest of their time earn their living as machinists.") Far from resenting Ford's fortune, Wells declared in 1936 that Ford "can be trusted with money. Let him make as much as he can—it will be used for important purposes and in a stimulating and individual way. The essential point is that he does not want money for its own sake, and money has never been his main incentive."[15]

Still, writing about the colonial revival movement in twentieth-century America, Kenneth Ames raises the "fundamental question" as to "whether deep immersion into the past can be read as a positive, affirmative action or whether it might be seen more accurately as an act of cultural desperation."[16] Although Ames sees the colonial revival as primarily the latter, the village industries, I contend, do not fall so readily into that category, for the reasons I have detailed. As Ford often remarked, the farther people could look back, the farther they could then look ahead.[17] Technology had admittedly created problems, but it had also solved many problems and, he believed, would continue to do so. And as Ford and Crowther had put it in *Today and Tomorrow*, "We have both lost and gained in the movement of modern industry. Our gains are many times greater than our losses; we can keep all of the gains and repair some of the losses."[18]

In this context, Ford's otherwise cranky and callous comments in the midst of the Great Depression, about the future being so bright and about technological unemployment being a false fear, take on a more complex meaning. As he had put it in 1933, "The machine age is barely started now. In the real machine age which is to come the dirt and ugliness and confusion and noise and disregard of human rights [as in the Ford Motor Company!] which are all about us today will be done away with." Moreover, the "real" machine age "will mean that the badly equipped factories which are in the great majority today"—presumably none within the Ford empire—"will have to give way to well equipped, scientifically run plants." Meanwhile, the automobiles of the coming machine age will be "really comfortable and fast and easy to handle. There will be no mechanical troubles and little or no service costs. And these cars will cost less because they will be perfectly made" in the scientifically run factories.[19]

The issue, however, was not simply greater efficiency, greater automation, or greater physical and administrative decentralization but, no less, a new sense of historical continuity and discontinuity. The critique of Technocracy that Ford had offered in 1933 reflected his deepened sense of the past, present, and future being at once parts of a vast continuum yet distinct entities in themselves. Just as the Technocrats had, according to Ford, for all their technical expertise, wrongly assumed that "present conditions are permanent," so he recognized that "life has a funny way of pushing out where we least expect it. It breaks up all our diagrams."[20] The Depression had indeed shaken Americans' historic assumptions that, thanks in no small measure to technology, the future would inevitably be better than—and march smoothly on from—the past and the present.

Ford did not, of course, share this anxiety about the future even as he embraced the past, as in his museums and related historical enterprises. The Depression did not shatter his version of the American Dream, as it did for so many ordinary citizens. But his attempted recasting of the Machine Age, as epitomized in the village industries, reflected a struggle to balance the often competing demands of the past and the future, a struggle paralleling that between industrial and managerial centralization and decentralization. By turns prophet and skeptic, Ford managed to carve out a middle ground that sometimes held together but sometimes broke apart.

Fittingly, perhaps, in 1995 the Ford Motor Company made its own peace of sorts with Henry Ford and history by using him and his words in national television advertisements for the first time in decades. Black-and-white images of the company's founder were incorporated with color shots of its newest vehicles. Ford was quoted as saying, "I want to build a motor car for the great multitude. . . . Any person making a good salary will be able to own one and enjoy with his family the blessing of hours of pleasure in God's great open spaces." The longtime fear of antagonizing potential buyers who associated Henry Ford with antiunionism, anti-Semitism, and other unappealing traits had finally diminished sufficiently to allow a celebration of his achievements once again. And these initial commercials were received so well—or at least generated so few complaints—that beginning the next year the company ran ads that starred elderly retirees who had been at Ford early enough to have "worked alongside Henry Ford" in theory if not in fact. These retirees endorsed the company's latest products and repeated its assertion that "Quality is Job 1."[21] In addition, the company's Web site detailed Ford's life and contributions to the enterprise without a trace of defensiveness. (By contrast, new exhibits at The Henry Ford, founded by Ford himself in 1929, included materials showing his darker side, such as his anti-Semitism, and placing his positive achievements, such as the 1908 Model T, in the context of others' contributions to the production of a vehicle for ordinary citizens.)[22]

Building on the celebration of Henry Ford's achievements, company print advertisements in 1999 praised the founder as a "passionate environmentalist." In the words of his great-grandson and the then newly appointed chairman of the board, William Clay Ford, Jr., "He developed ways to recycle lumber, use alcohol as fuel, slash manufacturing waste and conserve scarce resources with revolutionary research. He even used soybean-plastic parts in every car built in 1935." The famous photo of Henry Ford taking an ax to the trunk lid of a Ford in 1940 accompanies the advertisement, which has as its backdrop the cover of a container of soybeans, "Two Pounds of Soybeans in Every Car: Henry Ford, 1935." The great-grandson concludes, "He didn't just want Ford Motor Company to make cars. He wanted to make a difference."[23] Given William Clay Ford, Jr.'s self-image as a "passionate environmentalist"—as epitomized by his ongoing efforts to transform much of the Rouge complex into an environmentally progressive site[24]—these historical connections seemed legitimate. If, as the great-grandson put it, his great-grandfather was famous for having allegedly declared that "customers could have whatever color they wanted as long as it was black," he himself was now declaring that "customers can have any vehicle they want, as long as it is green."[25] Presumably, the elder Ford would have agreed.

Once the younger Ford also became chief executive officer of Ford Motor Company in 2001, it remained to be seen whether he could carry out his ambitious plans.[26] Interestingly, company print advertisements that appeared after this new appointment continued to invoke the elder Ford, followed by his great-grandson's concurrence. For example:

> Henry Ford, Founder—"I do not consider the machines which bear my name simply as machines. If that were all there were to it I would do something else. Power and machinery are useful only as they set us free to live. They are but means to an end."

> Bill Ford, Chairman and CEO—"If all we are as a company is a producer of cars and trucks, then to me that's not enough. If our cars and trucks make people's lives better, help them do their work better, give them the freedom to go wherever they want to go, then we've done our job."[27]

And again:

> Henry Ford, Founder—"The pioneer spirit is what America has over and above any other country. If ever we lose that spirit, if ever we get to the point where the people are afraid to do things because no one before them has done them or because they are hard to do, then we shall stop going forward."

> Bill Ford, Chairman and CEO—"Not every idea pans out, and that's fine. You open yourself up to criticism and you open yourself up to failure, but if you don't try and you don't push the envelope and you don't have a 'no

boundaries' mentality, you're never going to achieve greatness. That's what we aspire to."[28]

A similar statement appeared in a popular magazine: "We're a family company. We're not another faceless corporation. We want to use innovative technologies to build a stronger business and a better world. In the 20th century, we made automobiles economically affordable. Now, we want to make them affordable in every sense—economically, environmentally, and socially. That's a great way to honor our past and secure our future."[29] And related television advertisements that began running in 2002 and in 2003 carried similar messages.[30] Meanwhile, the company's 2001 annual report pictured Bill Ford in front of a photo of his great-grandfather.

These explicit connections drawn between the founder and his great-grandson illuminate a fundamental point about Henry Ford's life as reflected in the village industries: in the years after 1920, his orientation gradually shifted from that of a mechanical engineer to that of a social engineer. His concern was no longer just the automobile or even mass production but the whole of American society—and its future as much as its past.[31] Ford might insist, as he did in *Today and Tomorrow*, that "no man can say anything of the future. We need not bother about it. The future has always cared for itself in spite of our well-meant efforts to hamper it."[32] But his activities, like his book's very title, spoke otherwise. Just as the Michigan village industries were intended as experimental models for the rest of the country, if not the entire industrialized world, so Ford's museums and related historical projects were intended to provide as prototypes of a new American sense of historical evolution and progress. Ford's vision of America's future, of the new Machine Age, like so much else of his thought, was never clearly spelled out, and one need not endorse all of what can be uncovered. Yet in regard to decentralized technology, as he conceived and implemented it in his village industries, it is surely tempting to conclude that Henry Ford indeed had a better idea.

APPENDIX: BASIC FACTS ABOUT AND PRESENT STATUS OF THE NINETEEN VILLAGE INDUSTRIES

In these listings the name of each plant, river on which it operated, and its distance from Dearborn/Ford headquarters are followed by

(1) Dates when operations began and ended
(2) Type(s) of building(s)
(3) Principal part(s) made
(4) Peak size of workforce (in peacetime, *not* in wartime—except for Clarkston and Cherry Hill, which opened during World War II—as wartime numbers varied too much over four years to be useful here)
(5) Present status, ownership, condition

NORTHVILLE
(Rouge River; 23 miles from Dearborn)

(1) Opened in 1920; closed in 1981 but reopened in 1982; closed for good in 1989
(2) Old (1825) sawmill and renovated (1896) woodworking shop; replaced by new building in 1936 (designed by Albert Kahn)
(3) Valves; after 1982 reopening, fuel tanks and shipping racks
(4) 400 (in 1937)
(5) Since 1994, a multiuse, privately owned office building that includes a health club, offices, and light manufacturing; land around the mill now a Northville town park

NANKIN MILLS
(Rouge River; 12 miles from Dearborn; closest of the village industries)

(1) Opened in 1921; closed in 1948
(2) Old (1832) gristmill; replaced by new building in 1937

(3) From 1928 until its closing, nearly all the engravings—stencils, script dies, identification badges—for Ford vehicles

(4) 70 (in 1941)

(5) Since 1985, headquarters of Wayne County Department of Public Services, Division of Parks; as of 2001 also the site of the popular Nankin Mills Interpretive Center and the gateway for the MotorCities National Heritage Area (both described in chapter 11)

PHOENIX
(Rouge River; 16 miles from Dearborn)

(1) Opened in 1922; closed in 1948

(2) New building (designed by Albert Kahn) on site of old gristmill

(3) Gauges and taps, generator cutouts, voltage regulators, stoplight switches; from 1936 on, 50 percent of all Ford vehicle cutouts and regulators (remaining 50 percent purchased from non-Ford manufacturers)

(4) 184 (in 1946)

(5) Long a Wayne County Division of Parks garage and maintenance yard; also the site of a proposed Women's Museum (see chapter 11)

FLAT ROCK
(Huron River; 17 miles from Dearborn)

(1) Opened in 1923; closed in 1950

(2) New building (designed by Albert Kahn) on site of razed sawmill

(3) For many years, all of Ford vehicle lamps (front, tail, and interior)

(4) 1,200 (in 1929)

(5) Since 1950, occupied by privately owned manufacturing companies; land around the mill now part of a park being renovated, including bike trails, to bring visitors along the MotorCities National Heritage Trail System

PLYMOUTH
(Rouge River; 17 miles from Dearborn)

(1) Opened in 1923; closed in 1948

(2) New building (designed by Albert Kahn) on site of old gristmill

(3) For most of its years made 95 percent of the taps for threads for Ford vehicles; also tools and drills

(4) 35 (in 1936)

(5) Since 1949, a Wayne County Division of Parks garage, but is being leased out to a metal sculptor, who will renovate and repair it

WATERFORD
(Rouge River; 22 miles from Dearborn)

(1) Opened in 1925; closed in 1954
(2) New building (on site of old gristmill)
(3) For many years, all of Ford's inspection precision gauges and taps
(4) 210 (in 1952)
(5) Since the early 1980s, a privately owned window manufacturing company

YPSILANTI
(Huron River; 28 miles from Dearborn)

(1) Opened in 1932; merged with larger Ford complex in 1947
(2) New building (designed by Albert Kahn)
(3) For several years, all the starters and generators for Ford vehicles
(4) 1,500 (in 1948), largest workforce of all the village industries
(5) Since 1947, absorbed by large conventional Ford Motor Company factory making electrical components; its Rawsonville hydroplant, dam, and adjoining land donated in 1969 to the city of Ypsilanti and Ypsilanti Township for power production and parks

NEWBURGH
(Rouge River; 15 miles from Dearborn)

(1) Opened in 1935; closed in 1948
(2) New building on site of old cider mill
(3) For most of its years, 95 percent of the twist drills for larger Ford plants
(4) 32 (in 1946)
(5) Long used by Wayne County Division of Parks for maintenance operations and later also for law enforcement, including a horse barn; recently renovated in expectation of public use

TECUMSEH/HAYDEN MILLS
(Raisin River; 47 miles from Dearborn)

(1) Opened in 1935; closed in 1948
(2) Restored old (1898) flour mill
(3) Soybean cleaning, sacking, and storage
(4) 25 (in 1946)
(5) For years, a community center for teens, senior citizens, and others, plus a private gun club; powerhouse recently renovated to serve meals to senior citizens

Dundee
(Raisin River; 50 miles from Dearborn)

(1) Opened in 1936; closed in 1954
(2) Old (1832) gristmill and new building
(3) Copper welding tips
(4) 125 (in 1941)
(5) Between 1954 and 1970, owned and operated by Wolverine Fabricating and Manufacturing, which donated it to the village; since 1970, village offices, a community center, and a museum; recently renovated by the town as a banquet facility and part of revitalized town center

Milan
(Saline River; 41 miles from Dearborn)

(1) Opened in 1938; closed in 1947
(2) Old gristmill and new building
(3) Ignition coils; ammeters; soybean extraction, cleaning, and storage
(4) 186 (in 1946)
(5) Since 1947, various municipal units (city hall, public library, police); recently renovated for additional use in recreation programs

Milford
(Huron River; 38 miles from Dearborn)

(1) Opened in 1938; closed in 1948
(2) New building on site of old (autodash) factory
(3) For years, all the carburetors for Ford vehicles (save for screws, lock washers, and gaskets)
(4) 438 (in 1939)
(5) Since early 1980s, owned and operated by Kelsey-Hayes (valves)

Saline
(Saline River; 31 miles from Dearborn)

(1) Opened in 1938; closed in 1947
(2) Old (1845) gristmill
(3) Soybean processing (into oil for plastic auto parts, including steering wheels), soybean water paint
(4) 19 (in 1939)
(5) Once owned and operated by a small soybean processing company and a resident stock company; since 1962, houses both an antique shop/

general store and a reception hall for private parties; has more recently also become a café

Brooklyn
(Raisin River; 60 miles from Dearborn; most distant of the village industries)

(1) Opened in 1939; closed in 1967
(2) New building on site of old gristmill
(3) From 1945 to 1954, 50 percent of all Ford vehicle horn buttons and starter switches; from 1954 to 1967, plastic lamp lenses and armrests
(4) 130 (in 1952)
(5) Once owned and operated by Industrial Automotive Products, a subsidiary of Jackson Gear; since 1989, houses a collector's Model T's and antique engines that are being restored

Sharon Mills
(Raisin River; 57 miles from Dearborn)

(1) Opened in 1939; closed in 1947
(2) Old (1835) gristmill
(3) Cigar and cigarette lighters; electrical switches; generator ammeters
(4) 19 (in 1940)
(5) Longtime occupants operated an antique and wine shop; in 1999, purchased and restored by Washtenaw County Park Division for a museum and small conference center (with historic markers, picnic areas, canoe launches, river-viewing decks, terraces, and a pavilion); now called Sharon Mills Park, is a popular site for weddings and receptions

Manchester
(Raisin River; 55 miles from Dearborn)

(1) Opened in 1941; closed in 1957
(2) New building on site of old (1892) gristmill
(3) Ammeter, oil, fuel, temperature gauges; (for several years) made all the ammeters for instrument clusters and half the remaining instruments: gas, oil, water temperature
(4) 279 (1946)
(5) Owned and operated by several companies making or marketing various products (including compressors for paper balers and wax applicators); in part sold and in part donated to Manchester by last owner; since 2001, houses village offices and area's public library

WILLOW RUN
(Huron River; 17 miles from Dearborn)

(1) Opened in 1941; closed in 1944
(2) New building
(3) Ignition locks, door locks, keys
(4) 35 (in 1941)
(5) Long abandoned and partly dismantled

CLARKSTON
(Clinton River; 40 miles from Dearborn)

(1) Opened in 1942; closed in 1947
(2) Old gristmill
(3) Drill bushings, straps, seat covers (operated only in wartime)
(4) 40 (in 1942)
(5) Once Hawke Tool Company; since the 1980s, a small shopping mall

CHERRY HILL
(Rouge River; 25 miles from Dearborn)

(1) Opened in 1944; closed in 1945
(2) Converted milk depot building
(3) Ignition locks, door locks, keys, machined brass radiator petcocks
(4) 30 (in both years)
(5) Houses privately owned manufacturing companies; in addition, Canton
    Township building a Traditional Town Center around the mill, the first
    such development in southeastern Michigan

NOTES

INTRODUCTION

1. This was the subtitle of an article by Matthew L. Wald, "Back Offices Disperse from Downtowns," *Sunday New York Times*, May 13, 1984, Commercial Real Estate Report, 12-1.
2. See, for example, John F. Kasson, *Civilizing the Machine: Technology and Republican Values in America, 1776–1900* (New York: Grossman/Viking, 1976), chap. 1, esp. 25.
3. See, for example, Alfred D. Chandler, Jr., *Strategy and Structure: Chapters in the History of the American Industrial Enterprise* (Cambridge, Mass.: MIT Press, 1969); Chandler, *The Visible Hand: The Managerial Revolution in American Business* (Cambridge, Mass.: Harvard University Press, 1977); and Chandler, *Scale and Scope: The Dynamics of Industrial Capitalism* (Cambridge, Mass.: Harvard University Press, 1990). See also David A. Hounshell, *From the American System to Mass Production, 1800–1932* (Baltimore, Md.: Johns Hopkins University Press, 1984), chaps. 6, 7; Arthur J. Kuhn, *GM Passes Ford, 1918–1938: Designing the General Motors Performance-Control System* (University Park: Pennsylvania State University Press, 1986); and James J. Flink, *The Automobile Age* (Cambridge, Mass.: MIT Press, 1988), 240–42.
4. But see the implicit critique (summarized in chapter 11) of Chandler's "visible hand" thesis, as ignoring very different specialty production companies, in Philip Scranton, *Endless Novelty: Specialty Production and American Industrialization, 1865–1925* (Princeton, N.J.: Princeton University Press, 1997). See also John N. Ingham, "Business History: Theory-Driven and Theory-Starved," *Canadian Review of American Studies* 22 (Summer 1991): 101–9; and Richard R. John, "Elaborations, Revisions, Dissents: Alfred D. Chandler's *The Visible Hand* after Twenty Years," *Business History Review* 71 (Summer 1997): 151–200.
5. But see Chandler, *Scale and Scope*, 38, 208, regarding the more limited concern with vertical integration on the part of both General Motors and Chrysler and the wisdom of their strategies when, because of declining demand for automobiles, unit costs greatly increased for all three companies, but especially Ford.
6. See, for example, Allan Nevins and Frank E. Hill, *Ford: Expansion and Challenge, 1915–1933* (New York: Scribner, 1957), 295–99; Nevins and Hill, *Ford: Decline and Rebirth, 1933–1962* (New York: Scribner, 1963), 8; David L. Lewis, *The Public Image of Henry Ford: An American Folk Hero and His Company* (Detroit: Wayne State University Press, 1976), 160–62, 483; and Stephen Meyer III, *The Five*

Dollar Day: Labor Management and Social Control in the Ford Motor Company, 1908–1921 (Albany: State University of New York Press, 1981), introduction.

7. John H. Van Deventer, "Ford Principles and Practice at River Rouge, II: Links in a Complete Industrial Chain," *Industrial Management* 64 (September 1922): 131–32.

8. See "America's Ruggedest Individual Takes a $35,000 Crack at Depression," *Life* 4 (May 30,1938): 12.

9. Lewis, *Public Image*, 12. In confirmation of Ford's enigmatic personality see, for example, Stanley Ruddiman, *The Reminiscences of Mr. Stanley Ruddiman*, October 1951, 5; and Mrs. Stanley Ruddiman, *The Reminiscences of Mrs. Stanley Ruddiman*, March 1952, 84, both in Ford Motor Company Archives, Oral History Section, Benson Ford Research Center, The Henry Ford, Dearborn, Michigan. The Ruddimans were close friends of Ford. See Ford R. Bryan, *Henry's Lieutenants* (Detroit: Wayne State University Press, 1993), 298, 315. See also such illuminating semischolarly studies as Gamaliel Bradford, "The Great American Enigma: An Exploration of Henry Ford," *Harper's Magazine* 161 (October 1930): 513–24; Dixon Wecter, *The Hero in America: A Chronicle of Hero-Worship* (1941; rept., Ann Arbor: University of Michigan Press, 1963), 419–22; and Sigmund Diamond, *The Reputation of the American Businessman* (1955; rept., New York: Harper Colophon Books, 1966), chap. 6.

10. Ford confessed, "I was born and raised on a farm and have followed the plow for many a weary mile" (introduction to *Fordson: The Universal Tractor* [Detroit: Ford Motor Company, n.d.], 3). Despite the absence of a publication date, *Fordson* was almost certainly published between 1917, when the Ford Motor Company began making Fordsons, and 1928, when it stopped making them, at least in North America. See Robert C. Williams, *Fordson, Farmall, and Poppin' Johnny: A History of the Farm Tractor and Its Impact on America* (Urbana: University of Illinois Press, 1987), chap. 3.

11. Quoted in Drew Pearson, "Ford Predicts the Passing of Big Cities and Decentralizing of Industry," *Motor World* 80 (August 28, 1924): 9. The same interview appeared simultaneously, and virtually unchanged, in *Automotive Industries* and *Motor Age* and was later summarized in *Literary Digest*. On Ford's overall antiurbanism, see Morton and Lucia White, *The Intellectual versus the City: From Thomas Jefferson to Frank Lloyd Wright* (New York: New American Library, 1964), 201–2, and John R. Mullin, "Henry Ford and Field and Factory: An Analysis of the Ford Sponsored Village Industries Experiment in Michigan, 1918–1941," *Journal of the American Planning Association* 48 (Autumn 1982): 426–27.

12. On these retreats, see Lewis, *Public Image*, 223, 258; Dorothy Boyle Huyck, "Over Hill and Dale with Henry Ford and Famous Friends," *Smithsonian* 9 (June 1978): 88–95; and David Lewis, "Ford Country" (column), *Cars and Parts* 38 (October 1995): 64. On the controversy over the safety of Firestone tires on Ford sport utility vehicles, which ended those corporations' nearly century-long relationship, see Keith Bradsher, "Firestone to Stop Sales to Ford, Saying It Was Used as Scapegoat," *New York Times*, May 22, 2001, A1, C4.

13. As Joseph Interrante observes, "Farmers bought Tin Lizzies sooner and in greater numbers than urban residents during the prewar period. In 1910, 0.17 percent of farm families owned 0.50 percent of the 450,000 registered motor vehicles in the

United States; by 1930, 53.1 percent of the rural population owned 50.3 percent of the nation's 23 million cars" ("The Road to Autopia: The Automobile and the Spatial Transformation of American Culture," *Michigan Quarterly Review* 19–20 [Fall 1980 and Winter 1981, combined special issue]: 508). See also Reynold M. Wik, "The Early Automobile and the American Farmer," in *The Automobile and American Culture*, ed. Lewis and Laurence Goldstein (Ann Arbor: University of Michigan Press, 1983), 37–47. (This book grew out of the *Review*'s special issue, cited above, which included the Interrante but not the Wik article.)

14. On these revivals, see Lewis, *Public Image*, 223–24, 226–28, 259, 311; and Ford R. Bryan, *The Fords of Dearborn*, rev. ed. (Detroit: Harlo, 1989), chap. 16.

15. I do not intend either to overlook or to slight the earlier studies of the village industries by such scholars as Nevins and Hill, Lewis, and Mullin (cited above and throughout this book); or the master's thesis by John Tobin, Jr. (cited in chapter 2, n. 1); or Rusty Davis's two-part article "Ford Motor Company Village Industries," *V-8 Times* 20 (July/August 1983):24–29 and (September/October 1983): 28–34. I am greatly indebted to these prior studies, but all of them are briefer, less comprehensive, and less contextual than mine; otherwise, I would have had no reason to pursue this project. It was after writing earlier drafts of this book that I came upon the ongoing research of Bruce Pietrykowski, whose illuminating articles on the village industries are cited in chapters 4, 6, 7, 10, and 11 (I am grateful to him for providing me with copies). As I was completing this book I was interviewed for a brief article on it by Michelle Krebs, "Farm to Factory: Village Industries Brought 20th Century Industry to Rural Towns," *Crain's Detroit Business: The Ford Legacy*, Summer 2003, 14.

16. A complementary critique of technological determinism in American automotive history is Clay McShane, *Down the Asphalt Path: The Automobile and the American City* (New York: Columbia University Press, 1994). McShane's focus, however, is the gradual acceptance by most Americans of the need for cars as integral rather than as alien components of cities, and the changing social and cultural values that largely account for that change. Henry Ford, of course, held an antithetical position on cities. Another complementary critique of technological determinism—as it applies to the decline of post-World War II Detroit from America's "arsenal of democracy" to its most impoverished and most physically decayed large city—is Thomas J. Sugrue, *The Origins of the Urban Crisis: Race and Inequality in Postwar Detroit* (Princeton, N.J.: Princeton University Press, 1996), as outlined in his introduction.

17. Charles A. Beard, epilogue to *Whither Mankind? A Panorama of Modern Civilization*, ed. Beard (New York: Longmans, Green, 1928), 403–4. Lewis Mumford, himself a contributor to that volume—which included the work of philosophers, economists, and other humanists and social scientists—reviewed rather negatively the companion *Toward Civilization*, which included work by engineers and scientists. See Mumford, "Toward Civilization?" *New Republic* 63 (May 28, 1930): 49–50.

18. See, for example, Silas Bent, *Machine Made Man* (New York: Farrar & Rinehart, 1930), a book that, like Beard's two works, was intended for a general, educated readership. See also the wide-ranging and illuminating *The Machine Age in America, 1918–1941*, ed. Richard Guy Wilson, Dianne H. Pilgrim, and Dickran Tashjian

(New York: Brooklyn Museum/Harry N. Abrams, 1986). The 1986–87 Brooklyn Museum exhibit that this book accompanied is detailed in Phil Patton, "How Art Geared Up to Face Industry in Modern America," *Smithsonian* 17 (November 1986): 156–67.

19. Lee Iacocca, "Henry Ford," *Time* 152 (December 7, 1998): 79 (special issue: *100 Builders and Titans of the Twentieth Century*). See also the complementary article on Ford and others by Alex Taylor III, "Giants of the 20th Century: Kings of the Road," *Fortune* 139 (June 7, 1999): 150–51, 154. See also the *Fortune* advertisement for a later issue designating Ford as "Businessman of the Century," cited in *New York Times*, November 9, 1999, C15; and David Lewis, "Henry Ford and the 20th Century," *Automotive History Review* 32 (Spring 1998): 4–6.

CHAPTER 1

1. Arthur Van Vlissingen, "The BIG Idea behind Those SMALL Plants of Ford's," *Factory Management and Maintenance* 96 (April 1938): 46.
2. See "Ford's Little Plants in the Country," *Reader's Digest* 32 (July 1938): 62–64.
3. See Leo Marx, *The Machine in the Garden: Technology and the Pastoral Ideal in America* (New York: Oxford University Press, 1964); and Howard P. Segal, "The 'Middle Landscape': A Critique, a Revision, and an Appreciation," in Segal, *Future Imperfect: The Mixed Blessings of Technology in America* (Amherst: University of Massachusetts Press, 1994), 13–26.
4. On those colonial settlements, see Alan I Marcus and Howard P. Segal, *Technology in America: A Brief History*, 2d ed. (Fort Worth, Tex.: Harcourt Brace, 1999), 3–4, 8–10, 15–16, 23–24; and, on Lowell, etc., 57–61.
5. William A. Simonds, "Rural Factories along Little Streams," *Stone and Webster Journal* 41 (November 1927): 653. On Simonds, see Bryan, *Henry's Lieutenants* 242–49.
6. W. J. Cameron, "The Spread of Industry," *Ford Sunday Evening Talk*, Detroit, May 5, 1935 (reprint, n.p.), Ford Motor Company Archives. On Cameron, see Bryan, *Henry's Lieutenants*, 52–57. On the overall content of Cameron's radio broadcasts, see Harvey Pinney, "The Radio Pastor of Dearborn," *Nation* 145 (October 9, 1937): 374–76. Pinney's analysis of nine months' worth of these weekly six-minute talks reveals not simply inordinate, if understandable, praise for both Ford and the Ford Motor Company but also gross ignorance and distortion of history, economics, and politics akin to his employer's own controversial views over the years.
7. Letter to me from Donn P. Werling, director, Fair Lane, September 25, 1989. Once totally self-sufficient by its harnessing of the Rouge River, the estate fell into disrepair after Henry Ford's death but has since been restored and is now the principal site of the University of Michigan's branch campus at Dearborn. See the update by Doug Moffat, "The Histories of the Henry Ford Estate: A National Treasure on the U-M Dearborn Campus," *Michigan Today* 30 (Fall 1998): 21–23. On Fair Lane and its power system, see Bryan, *The Fords of Dearborn*, chaps. 10, 11; and David L. Lewis, "Ford Country" (column), *Cars and Parts* 39 (June 1996): 54–55.
8. Van Vlissingen, "BIG Idea," 46.

9. See James Rubenstein, *The Changing US Auto Industry: A Geographical Analysis* (London: Routledge, 1992), chap. 3; on the more recent trend within the industry toward spatial centralization, see chap. 1. See also Rubenstein, "Changing Distribution of the American Automobile Industry," *Geographical Review* 76 (July 1986): 288–89.

10. Back in 1904, well before any of he village industries were established, one journalist fantasized about workers in, presumably, still urban factories driving home to more pleasant surroundings: "Imagine a healthier race of workingmen, toiling in cheerful and sanitary factories, with mechanical skill and tradecraft developed to the highest, as the machinery grows more delicate and perfect, who, in late afternoon, glide away in their own comfortable vehicles to their little farms or houses in the country or by the sea twenty or thirty miles distant! They will be healthier, happier, more intelligent and self-respecting citizens because of the chance to live among the meadows and flowers of the country instead of in crowded city streets." William E. Dix, "The Automobile as a Vacation Agent," *Independent* 56 (June 2, 1904): 1259–60, quoted in Rudi Volti, *Society and Technological Change*, 2d ed. (New York: St. Martin's, 1992), 25.

11. Quoted in Paul V. Kellogg, "The Play of a Big Man with a Little River, Part I," *Survey Graphic* 52 (March 1, 1924): 641. On Kellogg, see Clarke A. Chambers, *Paul U. Kellogg and the Survey: Voices for Social Welfare and Social Justice* (Minneapolis: University of Minnesota Press, 1971). The book does not, however, even mention Ford.

12. On these public relations efforts, see Lewis, *Public Image*, 233–34, 281; and Mullin, "Henry Ford and Field and Factory," 431 n. 45. Ford Motor Company's films on the village industries at the National Archives, which I watched in 1991, were made primarily in the 1930s and early 1940s and were of varying length and quality. There was usually no narration but only brief views of construction, renovation, operations, and transportation. Mayfield Bray's *Guide to the Ford Film Collection in the National Archives* (Washington, D.C.: National Archives, 1970) was a useful introduction but too general to be of extensive help. In addition, sympathetic, sometimes worshipful contemporary biographers of Ford mentioned the village industries but rarely devoted much space to them. An exception is Allan L. Benson, *The New Henry Ford* (New York: Funk & Wagnalls, 1923), chaps. 18, 19.

13. See, for example, the numerous articles on these separate developments clipped from the Detroit newspapers in the Joe Brown Collection, Archives of Labor History and Urban Affairs, Reuther Library, Wayne State University, boxes 9, 10, and 12. Some Detroit newspapers, following Ford's lead, happily linked the two, as, for example, "Fifteen Little Industries United to 30,000 Ford Acres," *Detroit Saturday Night*, June 15, 1935, 23–25, 28; and "Ford's Village Industries," *Detroit Sunday Times*, January 15, 1939, sec. 5, 2.

14. *The Ford Industries: Facts about the Ford Motor Company and Its Subsidiaries* (Detroit: Ford Motor Company, 1924), foreword, n.p. The typical headline is from an article in *Ford News* 5 (May 15, 1925): 3–5,8. On Ford's own ambivalence toward the Rouge plant, see Nevins and Hill, *Ford: Decline and Rebirth*, 71–72; Lewis, *Public Image*, 237; and "Mr. Ford Doesn't Care," *Fortune* 8 (December 1933): 65, 122. As David A. Hounshell notes in *From the American System to Mass Production, 1800–1932* (Baltimore, Md.: Johns Hopkins University Press, 1984),

260–61, Ford was happy to provide technical information for contemporaries and potential rivals—as well as more popular materials for more general audiences—once the company's supremacy was secure.

15. With characteristic wit and wisdom, John Kenneth Galbraith debunked Ford's "genius" as mechanic, inventor, manager, or corporate executive in a superb essay, "Was Ford a Fraud?" in Galbraith, *The Liberal Hour* (Boston: Houghton Mifflin, 1960), 141–65. Galbraith noted Ford's willingness to be portrayed as a genius, not least by his own public relations staff. See also the complementary but more restrained comments by Flink, *Automobile Age*, 50–51.

16. See, for example, Louis C. Hunter, "The Heroic Theory of Invention," in *Technology and Social Change in America*, ed. Edwin T. Layton, Jr. (New York: Harper & Row, 1973), 25–46; and James J. Flink, "Henry Ford and the Triumph of the Automobile," in *Technology in America: A History of Individuals and Ideas*, ed. Carroll W. Pursell, Jr. (Cambridge, Mass.: MIT Press, 1981), 163–75.

17. W. J. Cameron, "Decentralization of Industry," *Mechanical Engineering* 59 (July 1937): 485.

18. See Ernest G. Liebold, *The Reminiscences of Mr. E. G. Liebold*, Ford Motor Company Archives, Oral History Section, January 1953, 528–33. On Liebold, see Bryan, *Henry's Lieutenants*, 168–74, 310. See also Roscoe M. Smith, *The Reminiscences of Mr. Roscoe M. Smith*, Ford Motor Company Archives, Oral History Section, April 1954, 48–49; and Charles Voorhess, "Information regarding Village Industries," July 12, 1944 (one-page memorandum), Ford Motor Company Archives.

19. On Edgar Chambless's scheme, see Howard P. Segal, *Technological Utopianism in American Culture* (Chicago: University of Chicago Press, 1985), 49 and illus. 1. The most recent example of undocumented speculation, this one suggesting Edison as the source, is Peter Collier and David Horowitz, *The Fords: An American Epic* (New York: Summit Books, 1987), 107, which describes the village industries as an "archipelago."

20. "It is interesting that . . . Mr. Ford . . . perhaps has never heard of Kropotkin and other apostles of industrial decentralization" ("Milk and Motor Cars," *Survey* 45 [February 26, 1921]: 750). But see Peter Kropotkin, *Fields, Factories, and Workshops Tomorrow*, ed. Colin Ward (New York: Harper & Row, 1975), for a comparison with Ford's scheme. Mullin, "Henry Ford and Field and Factory," 428–29, also compares them.

21. Some relatively recent writings on the transition from the "cottage industries" in England and the Continent to the English Industrial Revolution have argued for a more complex evolution. See, for example, Franklin F. Mendels, "Proto-industrialization: The First Phase of the Industrialization Process," *Journal of Economic History* 32 (March 1972): 241–61; Peter Kriedte, Hans Medick, and Jurgen Schlumbohm, *Industrialization before Industrialization* (New York: Cambridge University Press, 1981); and Robert S. DuPlessis and Martha C. Howell, "Reconsidering the Early Modern Urban Economy: The Cases of Leiden and Lille," *Past and Present* 94 (1982): 49–84. But see the critiques of "proto-industrialization" in Lawrence Stone, "The New Eighteenth Century," *New York Review of Books* 31 (March 29, 1984): 42–48, and in David Herlihy, review of *Peasants, Landlords, and Merchant Capitalists: Europe and the World Economy, 1500–1800* by Peter Kriedte, *Business History Review* 59 (Autumn 1985): 530–31.

22. Without for a moment defending Ford's lack of systematic thinking about the village industries, it is interesting that as late as 1980 two eminent social scientists, Manfred Kochen and Karl W. Deutsch, published a book titled *Decentralization: Sketches Toward a Rational Theory* (Cambridge, Mass.: Oelgeschlager, Gunn, and Hain, 1980). Their avowed focus, moreover, is not on manufacturing and production but on administration and management. "Above all," they state, "we are concerned with developing a consistent theory that can help elucidate value positions for decentralization" (xviii). On the need for greater precision about decentralization in the context of technology, society, politics, and culture, see Langdon Winner, "Decentralization Clarified," in Winner, *The Whale and the Reactor: A Search for Limits in an Age of High Technology* (Chicago: University of Chicago Press, 1986), 85–97.

23. Charles Voorhess, *The Reminiscences of Mr. Charles Voorhess*, Ford Motor Company Archives, Oral History Section, November 1952, 96. (On Voorhess, see Bryan, *Henry's Lieutenants*, 318–19). As Voorhess recalled, "As far as I know, this idea of the village industries was Mr. Ford's alone. I don't have any information that anyone brought it to his mind" (94). Kenneth Edwards, chief clerk of all the village industries from 1943 to 1946 and before that a worker and then clerk at the Milan plant, confirmed this lack of an overall plan in my June 13, 1988, interview with him. Arthur J. Kuhn details Ford's hostility toward planning in virtually all aspects of corporate management and administration, whereas Sloan of General Motors, as he makes abundantly clear, pioneered corporate planning; see Kuhn, *GM Passes Ford*.

24. Rubenstein, *Changing US Auto Industry*, 48, 68.

25. Liebold, *Reminiscences*, 540–41.

26. As Ford told Drew Pearson in a 1924 interview, "Go out and see for yourself. Go into the country and visit some of our village factories where we are manufacturing small parts. We have been doing some experimenting" (Pearson, "Ford Predicts the Passing of Big Cities," 9).

27. "America's Ruggedest Individual," 13. Roger Burlingame, *Henry Ford* (New York: Knopf, 1954), 96, suggests (though he offers no evidence) that Ford's principal motivation for establishing the village industries "may have sprung from his observation that the Rouge was too big."

28. Kellogg, "Play of a Big Man with a Little River, Part I," 639–40.

29. See Davis Lowe et al., *Ten Minutes ahead of the Rest of the World: A History of Milford* (Milford, Mich.: Milford Historical Society, 1982), 288–89; a June 18, 1988, letter to me from Rodes Walters, who worked at the Milford plant from its opening until its merger with the Rawsonville plant in 1958, confirms the statement. Not surprisingly, Kenneth Edwards, the chief clerk of all the village industries from 1943 to 1946, whom I interviewed in 1988, could not recall any serious criticism of the village industries from their respective local communities.

30. "Dundee Ford Employees Join in Drive to Assure Operation of Plant There," *Monroe Evening News*, March 5, 1936, 1, 19.

31. "Business Men Ask Co-Operation," *Dundee Reporter*, March 5, 1936, 1; the article lists no author.

32. Cameron, "Spread of Industry," n.p.

33. See, for example, Harold N. Denny, "Times Good, Not Bad, Ford Says: Sees the Dawn of a Bright Future," *New York Times*, February 1, 1933, 3.

34. The extremely negative portrayal of Ford in "A Job at Ford's," one of the seven segments of the 1993 PBS series *The Great Depression*, exemplifies this aspect of Ford's legacy. The program condemns virtually everything Ford did, from dehumanizing the workplace and destroying countless workers' lives to opposing by every means possible the formation of a union at the Ford Motor Company. As a result, in my view, the program is insufficiently balanced.

35. See Flink, *Automobile Age*, 125, 220–22.

36. On the *Peace Ship*, see Douglas Brinkley, *Wheels for the World: Henry Ford, His Company and a Century of Progress* (New York: Viking, 2003), 195–98. On the broader context of Ford's anti-Semitism, see Leo P. Ribuffo, "Henry Ford and *The International Jew*," *American Jewish History* 69 (June 1980): 437–77, revised and reprinted in Ribuffo, *Right Center Left: Essays in American History* (New Brunswick, N.J.: Rutgers University Press, 1992), 70–105; and Neil Baldwin, *Henry Ford and the Jews: The Mass Production of Hate* (New York: Public Affairs, 2001). Ribuffo and Baldwin alike cite both Cameron and Liebold as readily embracing as well as promoting Ford's anti-Semitism.

37. On the actual decline of wages for most Ford Motor Company employees a few years after Ford's much-heralded $5.00 per day minimum wage went into effect in 1914, see Flink, *Automobile Age*, 123–24, 220–21. On this larger context of American capitalism in crisis and of attacks on its leading figures, see Diamond, *Reputation of the American Businessman*, conclusion.

38. On this larger context of American capitalism in crisis and of attacks on its leading figures, see Diamond, *Reputation of the American Businessman*, conclusion.

39. See John Dos Passos, "Tin Lizzie," in his trilogy *U.S.A.: III. The Big Money* (New York: Modern Library/Random House, 1937), 47–57; Upton Sinclair, *The Flivver King: A Story of Ford-America* (1937; rept., Chicago: Charles H. Kerr, 1984), 110; and Aldous Huxley, *Brave New World* (1932; rept., New York: Harper Perennial Books, 1969), 29. Interestingly, Dos Passos writes that "in 1922 there started the Ford boom for President (high wages, waterpower, industry scattered to the small towns)" (54–55). On earlier critiques of the man and his methods which may have influenced Huxley, see Peter Edgerly Firchow, *The End of Utopia: A Study of Aldous Huxley's Brave New World* (Lewisburg, Pa.: Bucknell University Press, 1984), 103–4.

40. On *Modern Times* and technology, see the useful overview by George Basalla, "Keaton and Chaplin: The Silent Film's Response to Technology," in Pursell, *Technology in America*, 192–201. On Chaplin's 1923 visit to Detroit and meeting with Henry (and Edsel) Ford, see Hounshell, *From the American System to Mass Production*, 319–20; and Brinkley, *Wheels for the World*, 363–64.

41. John Bird, "One Foot on the Land," *Saturday Evening Post* 216 (March 18, 1944): 12.

CHAPTER 2

1. See John Tobin, Jr., "Henry Ford and His Village Industries in Southeastern Michigan" (M.A. thesis, Eastern Michigan University, 1985), 45.

2. "Valves by Northville," (Ford) *Rouge News*, August 2, 1947, 3. The article was the

second in a series of seven on different village industries described in this post–World War II Ford Motor Company publication circulated among southeastern Michigan employees. The series, which ran for just a year, was akin to that noted earlier in the 1920s and 1930s *Ford News*.

3. Smith, *Reminiscences*, 49. The term "electronic tornado" is used in Burnham Finney, "Ford Makes Starters and Generators in Model Small Plant," *Iron Age* 132 (November 9, 1933): 11; this detailed outsider's analysis of the Ypsilanti plant is as laudatory as Smith's insider one. On Smith, see Bryan, *Henry's Lieutenants*, 258–64, 316–17.

4. Finney, "Ford Champions the Small Plant," *Iron Age* 131 (May 4, 1933): 697. Liebold, *Reminiscences*, 543, recalled the use of radios for communicating quickly between Dearborn headquarters and the initial village industry in Northville. On the actual tools and machines within several of the plants, see the detailed descriptions in Finney, "Ford Makes Starters and Generators," 10–14, 60; Frank J. Oliver, "Ford Modernizes Northville Valve Plant," *Iron Age* 140 (August 12, 1937): 34–38; and J. B. Nealey, "Drill Making at Ford's Village Unit," *Iron Age* 140 (November 4, 1937): 46–48. As Finney (10) concluded about the Ypsilanti plant, "Above all, the fact has been fully recognized that efficient, low-cost production is dependent upon machine tools of latest design. . . . [T]he plant might well be studied as a model for small manufacturers."

5. Voorhess, "Information Regarding Village Industries," also quoting Ford. In our June 13, 1988, interview, Kenneth Edwards confirmed all these points but noted that the size of the machinery in a particular village industry plant "would depend a great deal on the product." Some items required smaller machinery than in conventional plants in order to fit inside the smaller building. See also J. B. Nealey, "Drill Making at Ford's Village Industry," *Iron Age* 140 (November 4, 1937): 46–48, regarding the use of new machines to make twist drills.

6. See E. F. Schumacher, *Small Is Beautiful: Economics as If People Mattered* (New York: Harper & Row, 1973), the key work of this orientation.

7. Voorhess, *Reminiscences*, 100–101.

8. Smith, *Reminiscences*, 51, 43. On Ford's system and its historical context, see Thomas P. Hughes, *American Genesis: A Century of Invention and Technological Enthusiasm, 1870–1970* (New York: Viking, 1989), 8–9, 184–87, 203–20, chap. 6. Confirmation of the village industries as constituting a system in terms of management as well as production comes from my June 13, 1988, interview with Edwards, who recalled visiting the plants regularly to make sure that their clerical practices, like their production practices, conformed to company standards. He also characterized Smith as "a person that liked jobs well done. He was a difficult taskmaster if a person didn't do his job"—a description reinforced in a letter to me of May 27, 1989, from former Milford worker Rodes Walters, who recounted Smith's demanding inspections of that plant. In addition, the publisher of the *Saline Reporter*, Paul Tull, recounted in a letter to me of March 14, 1987, the duties of his father, an assistant paymaster at the Highland Park plant, in the 1920s and 1930s.

9. See Tobin, "Henry Ford and His Village Industries," 61 and, on the transfer of operations from the Highland Park and Rouge facilities to the village industries, 16. On earlier names for the Rouge complex, see Lewis, "Ford Country" (column), *Cars and Parts* 41 (March 1998): 52.

10. Lindy Biggs, *The Rational Factory: Architecture, Technology, and Work in America's Age of Mass Production* (Baltimore, Md.: Johns Hopkins University Press, 1996), 140, 104, 140. It is not clear if "new industrial village" is Mayo's or Biggs's term. Biggs's book never mentions the village industries.

11. See ibid., 152–55. See also Robert B. Gordon and Patrick M. Malone, *The Texture of Industry: An Archaeological View of the Industrialization of North America* (New York: Oxford University Press, 1994), 332–39.

12. As Donald F. Davis demonstrates, Detroit in the 1910s and 1920s was unique among major American cities in its domination by and dependency upon a single industry. See Davis, "The City Remodelled: The Limits of Automotive Industry Leadership in Detroit, 1910–1929," *Histoire sociale/Social History* 13 (November 1980), 451–86. On the reasons for the concentration of automobile manufacturers and related businesses in the Detroit area, see John B. Rae, "Why Michigan?" in *Michigan Quarterly Review* 19–20 (Fall 1980 and Winter 1981 combined special issue): 436–44; and Rubenstein, *Changing US Auto Industry*, chap. 2. On Ford Motor Company's power over Dearborn, see Carl Raushenbush, *Fordism: Ford and the Workers; Ford and the Community* (New York: League for Industrial Democracy, 1937), 39–60.

13. Thomas J. Ticknor, "Motor City: The Impact of the Automobile Industry upon Detroit, 1900–1975" (Ph.D. thesis, University of Michigan, 1978), 180; the Detroit and Los Angeles figures are from 135–36.

14. Davis, "City Remodelled," 473.

15. Ibid., 482.

16. Ibid., 486.

17. "Ford Will Build Small Factory," *Detroit News*, April 22, 1938, n.p., in the Joe Brown Collection, Archives of Labor History and Urban Affairs, Reuther Library, Wayne State University, box 12. On the Wayside Inn, see Lewis, *Public Image*, 225–26, 487.

18. Quoted in Denny, "Times Good, Not Bad, Ford Says," 3.

19. "Henry Ford Wants Cowless Milk and Crowdless Cities," *Literary Digest* 68 (February 26, 1921): 42; Wilbur Forrest, "The Secret of an Interview with Henry Ford; Lucky Reporter Had Appearance of a Mechanic," *New York Herald Tribune*, February 20, 1921, sec. 7, 1.

20. Burnham Finney, "Ford Decentralizes," *American Machinist* 81 (April 21, 1937): 320.

21. See Tobin, "Henry Ford and His Village Industries," 20–21, 143–46. Macon is on Macon Creek, whereas the nineteen sites are on rivers.

22. Quoted in *The Ford Industries*, 101.

23. See Nevins and Hill, *Ford: Decline and Rebirth*, 73.

24. Quoted in Hauck, "Over Hill and Dale," 91.

25. "Fords and Staff Visit Milford Tuesday," *Milford Times*, April 10, 1936, n.p. The article does mention the then ongoing series of *Ford News* articles on the other sites. Not surprisingly, subsequent *Milford Times* articles updated readers on the village industry's progress through final site selection, factory construction, factory opening, and other developments.

26. "Dundee Speculates on the Ownership of Old Grist Mill," *Monroe Evening News*, November 20, 1931, 1. Like the *Milford Times*, the *Monroe Evening News* updated

readers on the village industry's progress from final site selection through its opening.

27. Editorial quoted in Lewis, *Public Image*, 163. Nevertheless, Ford was quoted that same year as boasting that "our plan is not to be confined to one portion of the United States, but will extend throughout the country. We will probably not limit it to the United States. England offers many opportunities of this kind" (*Literary Digest* 68 [February 26, 1921]: 42). However, as Liebold recalled, "We wouldn't extend this decentralization system to Canada because the Ford Motor Company of Canada had an exclusive contract with the [American] Ford Motor Company which gave them the rights to manufacture and distribute Ford cars in Canada and all British possessions other than the British Isles. . . . I don't see how this would fit in with anything we were trying to do" (*Reminiscences*, 559).

28. This is not, however, to deny the local interest aroused by the prospect of a conventional branch plant, even if most of those were located in cities not as dependent upon one possible new plant as were the village industry towns. See Rubenstein, *Changing US Auto Industry*, 55.

29. "Invites Ford to Walkill; Walden Woman Suggests That He View Water Power Chances," *New York Times*, February 12, 1922, 21. Other representative inquiries and responses can be found in Ford Motor Company Archives, Ford Museum, accession 23, box 5 ("Mill Sites, 1929"), and accession 288, boxes 1–13 ("Water Power, 1918–1945: General-Water Power in Michigan").

30. See the Ford Motor Company Archives, accessions 23 and 288.

31. See Reynold M. Wik, *Henry Ford and Grass-roots America* (Ann Arbor: University of Michigan Press, 1972), 193–94. Ford's "Industrialized American Barn" (discussed in chapter 3) *was* intended to unite farm and factory.

32. "Ford Plans a $100,000 Power Project to Give Farmers Winter Work at City Wages," *New York Times*, April 27, 1923, 1. The project referred to was the developing village industry at Ypsilanti. See also "Lets Ford Get Power Sites," *New York Times*, May 5, 1923, 21.

33. On these facilities, see *The Ford Industries*, 81, 85–89, 103–5; Nevins and Hill, *Ford: Expansion and Challenge*, 228, 298; Nevins and Hill, *Ford: Decline and Rebirth*, 9; Mullin, "Henry Ford and Field and Factory," 419; Liebold, *Reminiscences*, 559, 572–73; and Henry Ford and Samuel Crowther, *Today and Tomorrow* (Garden City, N.Y.: Doubleday, Page, 1926), 125–27, 146. On various administrative problems at the Upper Peninsula sites, see Smith, *Reminiscences*, 49–50.

34. Voorhess, *Reminiscences*, 124–25. This is confirmed by W. J. Cameron, *The Decentralization of Industry* (Washington, D.C.: Seventh International Management Congress, 1938), 37. The publication is similar to but, despite the same title, not identical to his 1937 article in *Mechanical Engineering* cited in chapter 9, n. 32.

35. See also David Lewis, "The Rise and Fall of Old Henry's Northern Empire," Part I, *Cars and Parts* 17 (December 1973): 90–97, and Part II, 18 (January–February 1974): 100–105; and Ford R. Bryan, *Beyond the Model T: The Other Ventures of Henry Ford*, rev. ed. (Detroit: Wayne State University Press, 1997), 53–56, 107.

36. See Robert L. Dorman, *Revolt of the Provinces: The Regionalist Movement in America, 1920–1945* (Chapel Hill: University of North Carolina Press, 1993), the most comprehensive of many works on this topic. Not surprisingly, though, it does not mention Ford.

37. On Ford and the Muscle Shoals incident, see Ford and Crowther, *Today and Tomorrow*, 169–70; Nevins and Hill, *Ford: Expansion and Challenge*, 305–11; Preston J. Hubbard, *Origins of the TVA: The Muscle Shoals Controversy, 1920–1932* (Nashville, Tenn.: Vanderbilt University Press, 1961), chaps. 1–5; Wik, *Henry Ford and Grass-roots America*, 106–25; and "To Ford, Hydro Was a Top Job," *Hydro Review* 12 (August 1993): 86.

38. *New York Times*, January 12, 1922. A fairly detailed description of the "city" is in *Literary Digest* 73 (April 8, 1922): 72, 74.

39. Quoted in Nevins and Hill, *Ford: Expansion and Challenge*, 310.

40. On Norris's suspicions, see "To Ford, Hydro Was a Top Job," 86. See also Anthony Menke, "The Conflict for Muscle Shoals: How a $100,000,000 Industrial Project Became a Political Issue and Divided a Nation's Opinion," *Michigan Manufacturer and Financial Record*, February 17, 1923, 1; and "Muscle Shoals Development: Henry Ford Still Desirous of Acquiring the Property," *Pipp's Weekly* (Detroit), September 26, 1925, 15.

41. See Lewis, "Ford Country" (column), *Cars and Parts* 37 (March 1994): 46.

42. See Dorman, preface and introduction to *Revolt of the Provinces*. On the resurgence of interest in and scholarship about regionalism, see "A Sense of Place: Regionalism," a special issue of *Humanities: The Magazine of the National Endowment for the Humanities* 20 (July/August 1999).

43. Kellogg, "The Play of a Big Man with a Little River, Part I," 637.

44. Liebold, *Reminiscences*, 596, also 580–97.

CHAPTER 3

1. Quoted in Bruce Barton, "'It would be Fun to Start Over Again,'" *American Magazine* 91 (April 1921): 122.

2. On those fears of local businessmen, see Liebold, *Reminiscences*, 541–42.

3. On Ford's Thrift Gardens, see "Garden-Minded Employees," *Ford News* 15 (October 1935): 187, 196–97; and "Ford Workers Produce Much Food," *Hydro Plants News* 1 (September 1, 1946): 4. This was another post–World War II company publication akin to the *Rouge News* in its focus on southeastern Michigan employees, but here those specifically in the village industries.

4. Van Vlissingen, "BIG Idea," 50. See also John Bird, "One Foot on the Land," *Saturday Evening Post* 216 (March 18, 1944): 48.

5. See Paul K. Conkin, *Tomorrow a New World: The New Deal Community Program* (Ithaca, N.Y.: Cornell University Press, 1959), 29.

6. Quoted in Pearson, "Ford Predicts," 9. For a similar summary of Ford's views see, among other interviews, one conducted by the famous journalist Ida Tarbell, "Every Man a Trade and a Farm," *McCall's* 54 (July 1927), 5, 79–80.

7. Henry Ford and Samuel Crowther, *My Life and Work* (Garden City, N.Y.: Doubleday, Page, 1922), 189; see also 188–90, 192. On Crowther, see David E. Nye, *Henry Ford: "Ignorant Idealist"* (Port Washington, N.Y.: Kennikat Press, 1979), 139; and Bryan, *Henry's Lieutenants*, 295. Crowther was not a Ford Motor Company employee but rather an employee of Doubleday, Page, not coincidentally the publisher of several of Ford's—and Crowther's—books. Like so much else allegedly written by Ford, these could hardly have been written by Ford alone or even

primarily, given his limited formal education and his sheer lack of time. As John Kenneth Galbraith observed, "A few samples of Ford's real writing have survived in the form of letters. His syntax and spelling have many of the rough-and-ready qualities of the planetary transmission" ("Was Ford a Fraud?" 144). Yet in regard to the village industries and related developments, *My Life and Work* and *Today and Tomorrow* (1926) do accurately represent Ford's ideas as embodied in actual projects. More generally, on the need to take Ford's ideas seriously, and as something more than rationalizations for his business practices, see Flink, *Automobile Age*, 114–17; Martha Banta, *Taylored Lives: Narrative Productions in the Age of Taylor, Veblen, and Ford* (Chicago: University of Chicago Press, 1993); and Gib Prettyman, "Criticism, Business, and the Problem of Complicity: The Case of Henry Ford," *Interdisciplinary Literary Studies: A Journal of Criticism and Theory* 2 (Fall 2000): 49–66.

8. Quoted in *Ford News* 17 (April 1937): 62. The quotation appeared originally in a series of three "messages" from Ford—"Unemployment," "Self-Help," and "Farm and Factory"—that were published in major American newspapers during the week of May 30, 1932. As Francis Michaels, a long-time Milford employee, wrote to me in August 1989, this idea proved practical when, as often occurred prior to World War II, the village industries "plants would only operate 6 to 9 months out of the year." There being no unemployment insurance, one "would have to look elsewhere for work"—including one's own farm or garden plot. Michaels had been employed at the Rouge plant earlier and had planted a garden then as well for the identical reason.

9. See Ford R. Bryan, *Henry's Attic: Some Fascinating Gifts to Henry Ford and His Museum*, ed. Sarah Evans (Dearborn, Mich.: Ford Books, 1995), 10.

10. The estimate appears in, among other places, Ford and Crowther, *My Life and Work*, 204.

11. Ford quoted in Paul V. Kellogg, "The Play of a Big Man with a Little River, Part II," *Survey Graphic* 52 (April 1, 1924): 14. On Ford's agricultural policies, see Henry Ford and Samuel Crowther, *Today and Tomorrow* (Garden City, NY: Doubleday, Page, 1926), 210–13, 218–19, and my discussion below of his efforts to promote the industrial use of soybeans and other farm crops.

12. Flink, *Automobile Age*, 114.

13. Ford and Crowther, *My Life and Work*, 204, 15.

14. Williams, *Fordson, Farmall, and Poppin' Johnny*, 157.

15. Ford, introduction to *Fordson*, 4–5.

16. On Ford's overall conception of "the New Industrial Proletariat," see Flink, *Automobile Age*, 117–20.

17. Quoted in Baldwin, *Henry Ford and the Jews*, 207 (regarding Ford's aversion to alleged Jewish control over American farmers, see 204–10).

18. A. Hurford Crosman et al., "One Foot in Industry and One Foot in the Soil," typescript, n.d., 8. This illuminating report was "based on a five-day visit in July 1945 to the Ford Motor Co., Dearborn, Michigan, with Mr. [Maurice] Gerry, in charge of Rural Reconstruction in the French Ministry of Agriculture, and A. Hurford Crosman of the American Friends Services Committee (AFSC). Interviewed about 35 persons, 15 of whom were executives, and 20 regular factory workers, foremen, and other top non-executives" (1). To be sure, as Crosman

reported in a one-page memorandum to Clarence Pickett, the AFSC executive secretary, on September 10, 1945, "In Detroit, the Ford Motor Company treated us royally, placing at our disposal a car and driver, and for five days the heads of various phases of the Ford setup personally saw to it that we learned all about each particular phase." Such fine treatment no doubt influenced their findings, which were generally favorable. So, too, did the modest number of ordinary workers whom they interviewed. Like the report, the memorandum was found in a 1945 folder on General Administration, Social-Industrial Section, American Friends Service Committee Archives, Philadelphia. That same folder has four other reports by Crosman, all written in 1944, on his visits to Penn-Craft, a private cooperative community in southwestern Pennsylvania which was founded and supported by the AFSC; those reports provide useful autobiographical information as well about Crosman and his prior experiences in small business. On Penn-Craft, see Joseph D. Conwill, "Back to the Land: Pennsylvania's New Deal Era Communities," *Pennsylvania Heritage* 10 (summer 1984): 13–17. Significantly, as Crosman also reported in his September 10, 1945, memorandum: "I was much impressed with Mr. Gerry, and he feels that Ford's experiments in decentralization are extremely applicable to France. He will carry back the story, particularly to Citroen, the 'Ford of France.'"

19. See Press Release, Ford News Bureau, Dearborn, August 16, 1948, 3. Ruddiman, *Reminiscences*, 5–6, confirms these unexpected developments.

20. Douglas Reynolds, "Engines of Struggle: Technology, Skill, and Unionization at General Motors, 1930–1940," *Michigan Historical Review* 15 (Spring 1989): 70–76; the quotations are from 71–72.

21. W. J. Rorabaugh, *The Craft Apprentice: From Franklin to the Machine Age in America* (New York: Oxford University Press, 1986), 66.

22. See James Sweinhart, *The Industrialized American Barn* (n.p., 1934).

23. See also Nevins and Hill, *Ford: Expansion and Challenge*, 490–91; Nevins and Hill, *Ford: Decline and Rebirth*, 71–72; Lewis, *Public Image*, 282–87; and Reynold M. Wik, "Henry Ford's Science and Technology for Rural America," *Technology and Culture* 3 (Summer 1962): 247–58.

24. Quoted in Arthur Van Vlissingen, "Henry Ford Discusses the Farm Surplus Problem: An Authorized Interview," *American Legion Monthly* 21 (September 1936): 8. Bryan, *Henry's Attic*, 52, suggests that Ford envisioned soybeans as the potential "salvation of his village industries, which were foundering because of the expense of shipping raw materials out to the country and shipping the finished products back." Bryan provides no sources, much less any figures, to support this claim and concedes, "Although the soybean was a raw material that could be grown on site, Henry's hope did not materialize" (52). See also Lewis, "Ford Country" (column), *Cars and Parts* 45 (February 2002): 52–53.

25. Quoted in Van Vlissingen, "Henry Ford Discusses the Farm Surplus Problem," 9. On Ford's plastic car, see David Lewis, "Henry Ford's Plastic Car," *Michigan History* 56 (Winter 1972): 319–30. See also John Holusha, "Detroit Experimenting with the Plastic Look," *New York Times*, November 29, 1985, D1, D3; Reuters, "GM Cancels Project on Plastic-body Car," *Boston Globe*, October 20, 1986, 15; and Tim Moran, "A Look Ahead: Nylon in the Engine, Plastic for the Body," *New York Times*, October 21, 1998, in *Cars: A Special Section*, 21.

26. Smith, *Reminiscences*, 55, however, describes the "soybean operation at Saline" as "another job that we couldn't make pay due to the size of the operation. If we had a mill that handled 100 ton a day we would have been all right, but we had this little bit of a place there. He wanted to keep it small. Saline was no town for a large operation."

27. See "messages" cited in n. 8 above.

28. On Ford and the chemurgy movement, see Lewis, *Public Image*, 282–87; Lewis, "Henry Ford's Plastic Car"; Christy Borth, *Pioneers of Plenty: The Story of Chemurgy*, rev. ed. (Indianapolis: Bobbs-Merrill, 1942); and Carroll W. Pursell, Jr., "The Farm Chemurgic Council and the United States Department of Agriculture, 1935–1939," *Isis* 60 (Fall 1969): 307–17.

29. See Sweinhart, *Industrialized American Barn*; and Lewis, *Public Image*, 186–88, chap. 18.

30. Quoted in Merrill Gregory, "One Foot on the Land: Henry Ford's Dream of Combining Farm and Factory Becomes a Reality," *Prairie Farmer*, 109 (June 19, 1937): 26. A variation of this scheme was noted in a letter to me from James Lincoln, editor of the *Tecumseh Herald*, September 15, 1986.

31. "The Song of the Water Wheel," typed paper, n.p., 1945; no author given, but other portions appeared as Ford's interview in Van Vlissingen, "Henry Ford Discusses the Farm Surplus Problem," so the paper's author may have been Ford himself. See also R. H. McCarroll, "Increasing the Use of Agricultural Products in Industry," *Ford News* 16 (April 1936): 65–66, 75.

32. James Sweinhart, "Ford and the Coming Agrindustrial Age," reprint from *Dallas Dispatch and Dallas Times-Herald*, June 7, 1936, 1. See also Voorhess, *Reminiscences*, 94. As Benson had proclaimed in a glowing biography of Ford thirteen years earlier, "Future generations may never know that Ford ever built automobiles or was a billionaire. A thousand years hence Ford may be known only as the Father of Modern Agriculture" (*New Henry Ford*, 252).

33. See the similarities between Ford's notion of the "agro-industrialist" and Sweinhart's of "The Agrindustrial Age" and those later ideas of E. F. Schumacher regarding India and other "developing countries," as detailed in Jordan B. Kleiman, "The Appropriate Technology Movement in American Political Culture" (Ph.D. diss., University of Rochester, 2000), 86–88. Schumacher even used the term "agro-industrial culture." On the greater success by the 1980s of China versus Tanzania in becoming industrialized while remaining overwhelmingly agricultural, see Gavin Kitching, *Development and Underdevelopment in Historical Perspective: Populism, Nationalism, and Industrialization*, 2d. ed. (London: Routledge, 1989), chap. 5. As Kitching correctly notes, "If the comparison of China and Tanzania reveals anything, it is the familiar truth that social, cultural, and historical factors may be as important in development as any economic variable" (139).

34. William J. Hale, *The Farm Chemurgic* (Boston: Stratford, 1934), ii.

Chapter 4

1. See Voorhess, *Reminiscences*, 100, 101, 104, 113.

2. Tobin, "Henry Ford and His Village Industries," 31.

3. See Mullin, "Henry Ford and Field and Factory," 425; David L. Lewis, "Ford and

Kahn," *Michigan History* 64 (September/October 1980): 17–28; and Bryan, *Henry's Lieutenants*, 138–45. See also W. Hawkins Ferry, *The Legacy of Albert Kahn* (Detroit: Wayne State University Press, 1987). By contrast, Ford paid comparatively little attention to the actual design of his cars, unlike Alfred Sloan and General Motors. See C. Edson Armi, *The Art of American Car Design: The Profession and Personalities* (University Park: Pennsylvania State University Press, 1988).

4. On the (re)construction of various village industries, see Liebold, *Reminiscences*, 541–42, 543–49; F. W. Loskowske, *The Reminiscences of Mr. F. W. Loskowske*, Ford Motor Company Archives, Oral History Section, November 1951, 81–83; Smith, *Reminiscences*, 36–37, 49; and Voorhess, *Reminiscences*, 101–2, 110. The contemporary newspaper accounts of Dundee and Milford, among others (quoted in chapter 1) reflect an excitement largely missing from the oral histories.

5. Biggs, *The Rational Factory*, 6.

6. Ibid. Biggs characterizes her illuminating book as "the story of the recasting of the workplace in the image of the machine that could manufacture goods without regard to recalcitrant workers" (7). As I repeatedly make clear, the village industries do not fit this mold.

7. Smith, *Reminiscences*, 52.

8. According to Finney, "Part of the power for the Northville plant, as for every one of Ford's village industries, is supplied by water. The River Rouge has been dammed to form an artificial lake, the water operating an overshot wheel" ("Ford Decentralizes," 322).

9. Biggs, *The Rational Factory*, 104.

10. Quoted in Kellogg, "The Play of a Big Man with a Little River," Part I, 641. See also Fay Leone Faurote, "The Ford Hydro-Electric Developments," *Industrial Management* 74 (December 1927): 322–29.

11. Hughes, *American Genesis*, 307.

12. See Louis C. Hunter, *A History of Industrial Power in the United States, 1780–1930*, vol. 1, *Waterpower in the Century of the Steam Engine* (Charlottesville: University Press of Virginia and Eleutherian Mills-Hagley Foundation, 1979), and vol. 2, *Steam Power* (Charlottesville: University Press of Virginia and Hagley Museum and Library, 1985). Significantly, as Edwin T. Layton, Jr., observed in his review of *Steam Power*, "Hunter rejects simplistic theories of economic or technological determinism. Instead, he emphasizes the role of culture, as in the preference for large-scale factories, the desire to mechanize urban industry, and the freedom that steam gave for both the size and the location of factories" (*Journal of American History* 73 [September 1986]: 463). My interpretation of the village industries likewise stresses the nontechnological reasons behind their establishment.

13. Rubenstein, *Changing US Auto Industry*, 69; the selection of these second-generation branch assembly plants reflected Ford's "increasingly irrational behavior" (68).

14. Liebold, *Reminiscences*, 542–43. Crosman et al., "One Foot in Industry and One Foot in the Soil," 8–9, says the same about Ford's priorities. And Edward J. Cutler recalled that "the only time he [Ford] tried to estimate the number of people that would work in these mills by the available man power in the surrounding area, so they wouldn't have to bring in people from the outside area to work, was when we

were working on Dundee, to the best of my knowledge" (*The Reminiscences of Mr. Edward J. Cutler*, Ford Motor Company Archives, Oral History Section, March 1952, 149–50). On Cutler, see Bryan, *Henry's Lieutenants*, 80–87, 304.

15. See Tobin, "Henry Ford and His Village Industries," 86. Tobin (103), does note that other, more practical, considerations determined the size of at least the Dundee and Ypsilanti workforces.

16. Ibid., 48.

17. Louis C. Hunter and Lynwood Bryant, *A History of Industrial Power in the United States, 1780–1930*, vol. 3, *The Transmission of Power* (Cambridge, Mass.: MIT Press, 1991), 133, 134, 135; see also the entire section "A Trend toward Decentralization of Power Supply," 133–39.

18. Ford and Crowther, *My Life and Work*, 193.

19. Ford quoted by Nevins and Hill in *Ford: Expansion and Challenge*, 228. They list Waterford as the village industry in question, but both Liebold (*Reminiscences*, 537), and Tobin, "Henry Ford and His Village Industries," 30) list Phoenix and are more reliable sources in this regard. Voorhess (*Reminiscences*, 125–26) claims that Nankin Mills was the site but also uses a different Ford quotation, though with the same meaning. On the (allegedly) limited use of generators with Ford's approval, see Voorhess, *Reminiscences*, 93, and Smith, *Reminiscences*, 36–37, 42, 52. On Clarence Avery, see Bryan, *Henry's Lieutenants*, 14–19.

20. Transcript of Kenneth Truesdell interview, 1989, Plymouth Historical Society Village Industries Exhibit, Plymouth, Michigan. I am indebted to Bruce Richard, then director of the society, for transcripts of this and other interviews cited below.

21. Biggs, *The Rational Factory*, 75. As she notes, "In Ford's first two factories, workers and managers had enjoyed close working arrangements that reinforced the lack of rigid hierarchy"; beginning with Highland Park, however, "the highest level of management was housed in a fancy, segregated building, a fact that reflected a new relationship between management and worker" (103).

22. Charles La Croix, *Village Industries: Record of War Effort*, 2 vols. (Dearborn, Mich.: Ford Motor Company, 1942), 2: 4. Despite its subtitle, the work also details prewar operations at each of the village industries then in existence. See also Oliver, "Ford Modernizes Northville Valve Plant," 34–38, and "Valves by Northville," 3.

23. La Croix, *Village Industries*, 2:4 (each section of each volume is numbered separately).

24. See ibid., 1:1, 4.

25. Ibid., 2: 5, 6, and 1–2; and Finney, "Ford Makes Starters and Generators," 10–14, 60.

26. See chapter 6 on my interview with Bruce Richard, who worked at the Ypsilanti plant for thirty years.

27. For example, "Ypsilanti, Largest Hydro Plant, Supplies Ford's Electrical Parts," *Rouge News*, July 5, 1947, 4 (initial article about the post-World War II village industries): "The story of the Ford team at Ypsilanti is one of both men and women. Of the 1152 employees, 215 are women and 937 men. . . . Ypsilanti's women workers are scattered throughout the plant. They are very efficient on some light assembly operations, such as hand assembly of commutators, taping of coils and insertion of small parts."

28. On Phoenix, see, for example, *Ford Industries*, 103; and "Village Industries by Little Rivers," *Ford News* 16 (April 1936): 63–64, 71.

29. See Sam Hudson, "Ford 'Village Industry' was in Plymouth," *Observer and Eccentric*, October 17, 1974, 7A.

30. For elaboration, see Bruce Pietrykowski, "Fordism at Ford: Spatial Decentralization and Labor Segmentation at the Ford Motor Company, 1920–1950," *Economic Geography* 71 (October 1995): 392; and Pietrykowski, "Gendered Employment in the U.S. Auto Industry: A Case Study of the Ford Motor Co. Phoenix Plant, 1922–1940," *Review of Radical Political Economics* 27 (September 1995): 40–41.

31. "Women Outnumber Men," *Rouge News*, November 22, 1947, 6. On these employees' previous work experience, see Pietrykowski, "Fordism at Ford," 392–93, and Pietrykowski, "Gendered Employment," 40–41.

32. Pietrykowski, "Fordism at Ford," 392.

33. "Women Outnumber Men," 6. On comparisons between the Phoenix women and other (male) automobile industry workers, see Pietrykowski, "Fordism at Ford," 393–94; and Pietrykowski, "Gendered Employment," 41–45.

34. Edwards interview, June 13, 1988; he added that the two got married after the plant closed.

35. Pietrykowski, "Fordism at Ford," 393, makes this explicit comparison.

36. Pietrykowski, "Gendered Employment," 44–46 (quotation on 44).

37. "Another Ford Ideal to Help Mankind Crumbles to Earth with Closing of the Phoenix Plant," *Plymouth Mail*, April 2, 1948, 1. The article names Ivor Evans as having come from the Highland Park plant to become Phoenix's manager. Sullivan also came from Highland Park.

38. Marian Zayti, "Zaytis' Rare Personal Glimpse of Henry Ford and His Plant," *Mill Race Quarterly* 17 (Summer 1989): 4. An editor's note states that "this is an excerpt from an oral history dictated by Marian and Benny Zayti" and conducted by the Northville Historical Society, which publishes the *Quarterly*. Benny Zayti worked at the Northville plant and, like his wife, was grateful to Ford for many things. A similar expression of gratitude to Ford for the Home Arts Program is a letter to the superintendent of the Plymouth schools by a 1938 Plymouth High School graduate, written in 1988 on the fiftieth anniversary of her graduation. She herself "went on to work at Children's Hospital in Farmington, Michigan, in the physiotherapy department and loved every minute of it" (letter of Helen E. [Norgrove] Shepard, Plymouth Historical Society, Ford Village Industries Exhibit Display Notebook, vol. 2).

39. Steve Babson, *Building the Union: Skilled Workers and Anglo-Gaelic Immigrants in the Rise of the UAW* (New Brunswick, N.J.: Rutgers University Press, 1991), 53.

40. For example, *Craftsman* 4 (October 7, 1938): 1, 4 (an issue sent to me by Fred Winstanley of Milford), mentioned an alumnus as going to work in the then new Milford plant. The Henry Ford Trade School remained in operation until 1952, when, along with some of the village industries and other allegedly peripheral company enterprises, it was closed. On its many grateful alumni, see Lewis, "Ford Country" (column), *Cars and Parts* 39 (February 1996): 64, and 40 (January 1977): 30; and on the opening in 1997 of a kindred enterprise, the Henry Ford Academy of Manufacturing Arts and Sciences, 40 (August 1997): 48.

41. On these formal and informal educational programs, see Tobin, "Henry Ford and His Village Industries," 44–45, 83–84, 91.
42. See Babson, *Building the Union*, 53–54.
43. See, for example, "Training Offered All Hydro Plant Workers," *Hydro Plants News* 1 (September 1, 1946): 2.
44. See "Apprenticeship Training Offered in Skilled Trades," *Hydro Plants News* 2 (September 1, 1947): 1.
45. Quoted in Van Vlissingen, "BIG Idea," 48.
46. See Tobin, "Henry Ford and His Village Industries," 38 n. 34, and La Croix, *Village Industries*, 2: 1–4.
47. Van Vlissingen, "BIG Idea," 50.
48. Letters to me from John Peters, May 1989; Fred Winstanley, July 25, 1988; and Rodes Walters, September 3, 1988. On dwarfs at Willow Run, see Lewis, "Ford Country" (column), *Cars and Parts* 37 (August 1994): 66.
49. See, for example, J. E. Mead, "Rehabilitating Cripples at Ford Plant," *Iron Age* 102 (September 26, 1918): 739–42; Mead, "Rehabilitation: Training and Employment of Disabled Workmen in the Ford Plant," *Monthly Labor Review* 17 (November 1923): 1163–64; "Henry Ford's Viewpoint on the Elderly Worker," *Monthly Labor Review* 29 (August 1929): 337–38; Edsel Ford, "Why We Employ Aged and Handicapped Workers," *Saturday Evening Post* 215 (February 6, 1943): 16–17; and Charles B. Coates, "Rehabilitation of Veterans Must Begin Now," *Factory Management and Maintenance* 102 (February 1944): 82–92. On Cherry Hill, see Tobin, "Ford's Factory at Cherry Hill," *Michigan History* 71 (September/October 1987): 36–41; and Lewis, "Ford Country" (column), *Cars and Parts* 38 (April 1995): 62. As Tobin notes, Cherry Hill was also unique among the village industries in not having an agricultural component, given the limitations of its workforce. On various deviations from and inconsistencies within this positive record, see Raushenbush, *Fordism*, 55–56: "There is no evidence that the handicapped workers are men who were injured in Ford's employ. Most of them seem to be hard-luck cases that have attracted Ford's attention; he responds to these appeals on the one hand while on the other hand he evades his obligations . . . to men injured in his service."
50. See Lloyd H. Bailer, "Negro Labor in the Automobile Industry" (Ph.D. diss., University of Michigan, 1943), 43, 64. There are, however, occasional photographs of the Ypsilanti plant showing an African American working with whites in nonjanitorial positions; see, for example, *Rouge News*, July 5, 1947, 4—but this is, of course, after unionization and World War II had changed employment practices.
51. Bailer, "Negro Labor," 43.
52. Charlie Oestrike, quoted in letter to me from his friend Winifred Hamilton, February 10, 1987.
53. The figure is from John Barnard, *Walter Reuther and the Rise of the Auto Workers* (Boston: Little, Brown, 1983), 21. See also Heather Ann Thompson, *Whose Detroit? Politics, Labor, and Race in a Modern American City* (Ithaca, N.Y.: Cornell University Press, 2001), 12–13. On the situation in Pittsburgh in the same period, see Michelle Isham, "A Long Way from Home: Blacks in Pittsburgh during the Great Migration" (graduate seminar paper, University of Maine, 1996).

54. These figures come from Joyce Shaw Peterson, "Black Automobile Workers in Detroit, 1910–1930," *Journal of Negro History* 64 (Summer 1979): 177, 187.
55. These figures come from Zaragosa Vargas, *Proletarians of the North: A History of Mexican Industrial Workers in Detroit and the Midwest, 1917–1933* (Berkeley: University of California Press, 1993), 1, 51, 6. Vargas's pioneering study is the principal source of my comments on Mexican workers here and below.
56. But see the qualifications of this situation provided in Peterson, "Black Automobile Workers," 180–81.
57. On African American workers at the Ford Motor Company overall, see the convenient summary in Lewis, "Ford Country" (column), *Cars and Parts* 31 (June 1988): 178. The most detailed account is August Meier and Elliot Rudwick, *Black Detroit and the Rise of the UAW* (New York: Oxford University Press, 1979). The figures for 1926 are from Barnard, *Walter Reuther*, 21; for 1937, from Bailer, "Negro Labor," 66 (table 10). See also the brief mention of the company's recordkeeping of employees' racial (and religious and national) characteristics in Lewis, "Ford Country" (column), *Cars and Parts* 47 (January 2004): 54–55.
58. Bailer, "The Negro Automobile Worker," *Journal of Political Economy* 51 (October 1943): 416. As Sugrue (*Origins of the Urban Crisis*, 25, 95) notes, "Before World War II, only a handful of Detroit's major manufacturers had employed African Americans," and, among the city's other automakers, only Briggs and Dodge employed any significant numbers, though nothing as compared with Ford. Interestingly, when World War II began, "blacks made up only 4 per cent of auto work force; by 1945, they comprised 15 per cent; by 1960, they made up about 16 per cent." Thompson points out, however (in *Whose Detroit?* 58), that after World War II "it was Chrysler that took the lead in black hiring" in Detroit.
59. Vargas, *Proletarians of the North*, 52; the figures come from 51.
60. Ibid., 105–9; Bailer, "The Negro Automobile Worker," 417–18; and Bailer, "Negro Labor," 66–68.
61. Letter to me from Peters, March 16, 1989.
62. See Lewis, "Working Side by Side," *Michigan History* 77 (January 1993): 26–27: "Despite his poor health and advancing age, as well as the company mass layoffs during the 1920s and 1930s, Perry remained on the Ford payroll until his death at the age of eighty-seven years on 9 October 1940. He remains the oldest employee to have graced the company's active-service payroll."
63. On Ford's relationship with George Washington Carver, see Bryan, *Fords of Dearborn*, chap. 19; and Lewis, "Ford Country" (column), *Cars and Parts* 29 (April 1986): 48, 36 (May 1993): 64, and 37 (September 1994): 62. Interestingly, a Ford Motor Company special advertising section, "Conserving, Cataloging, and Complementing Nature," in *Newsweek* 131 (May 18, 1998), included a page headed "Carver: Missouri's Man for All Seasons" (16), as presented in the George Washington Carver National Monument.
64. Meier and Rudwick, *Black Detroit*, 9–11. See also Sugrue, *Origins of the Urban Crisis*, 25–26; and for a much more positive assessment, Lewis, "Working Side by Side," 28–29.
65. See Babson, *Building the Union*, 55–56; and Peterson, "Black Automobile Workers," 180.
66. Peterson, "Black Automobile Workers," 187 and, for details, 182–87.

67. Lewis, "Ford Country" (column), *Cars and Parts* 34 (December 1991): 157.
68. Sugrue, *Origins of the Urban Crisis*, 96; see also 95–105.
69. Vargas, *Proletarians of the North*, 77.
70. See ibid., 106–9, 122–23.
71. See ibid., 197–98, 207–8. The 1,000 figure comes from p. 197, but on p. 208 Vargas writes, in seeming contradiction, that "by the late 1930s several thousand of the original Mexican settlers remained in Detroit." And on p. 189, in another seeming contradiction, he writes, "By the middle of December 1932, only 3,000 Mexicans remained in Detroit. By 1936 the population dwindled to 1,200, a nearly 90 percent reduction of the population residing in the city in 1928." Whichever figures are accurate, new waves of Mexicans—but now largely Mexican Americans, if still also from Texas—came to Detroit in the late 1930s as the auto industry revived (208).
72. See ibid., 50.
73. See Peterson, "Black Automobile Workers," 181; Flink, *Automobile Age*, 226–28; and Lewis, "Working Side by Side," 30. Lewis contends that most African American employees willingly sided with Ford and his efforts to block unionization.
74. Bailer, "Negro Labor," 180.
75. See Nelson Lichtenstein, *The Most Dangerous Man in Detroit: Walter Reuther and the Fate of American Labor* (New York: Basic Books, 1995), 179, 207–9, and (for later years until Reuther's death in 1970) 372–75.

CHAPTER 5

1. Van Vlissingen, "BIG Idea," 47.
2. Hartley W. Barclay, *Ford Production Methods* (New York: Harper, 1936), 28. The book's contents had earlier appeared in the form of articles in *Mill and Factory*.
3. For example, materials in the Ford Motor Company Archives titled "Auditing Records," accession 33, box 100 (including "Village Industries, 1931–36"), and "Office of Henry Ford," accession 288, boxes 1–13 ("Water Power in Michigan, 1918–1945," including fifteen village industries), are too diffuse to be at all useful here. And no other records I have found come close to these in terms of seemingly appropriate figures.
4. Drew Pearson, "Henry Ford Says Farmer-Workmen Will Build Automobile of the Future," *Automotive Industries*, August 28, 1924, 389.
5. Kellogg, "The Play of a Big Man with a Little River, Part II," 16.
6. Voorhess, *Reminiscences*, 121.
7. Edwards interview, June 13, 1988.
8. Liebold, *Reminiscences*, 577.
9. Nevins and Hill, *Ford: Decline and Rebirth*, 73.
10. Ford and Crowther, *Today and Tomorrow*, 145.
11. Voorhess, *Reminiscences*, 121.
12. Illuminating examples are provided in Karel Williams, Colin Haslam, and John Williams, "Ford versus 'Fordism': The Beginning of Mass Production?" *Work, Employment and Society* 6 (December 1992): 541–44.
13. "The Rebirth of Ford," *Fortune* 35 (May 1947): 84. On Ford's overall aversion to formal management throughout the company, see Collier and Horowitz, *The*

Fords, 149–50. On Ford's aversion to paperwork, office space, office staff, business equipment, and organizational structure, see Bryan, *Henry's Attic*, 371–72.

14. Flink, *Automobile Age*, 246.

15. Thomas J. Peters and Robert H. Waterman Jr., *In Search of Excellence: Lessons from America's Best-Run Companies* (New York: Harper & Row, 1982), 15, 113; see also 16, 31–32, 65, 112, 321.

16. Smith, *Reminiscences*, 47–48, 43, 48.

17. Ibid., 46.

18. The percentages are from Tobin, "Henry Ford and His Village Industries," 87, 89, 96. In the name of efficiency, Ford insisted that one village industry use the scrap of another. Thus the copper used at Dundee to make welding tips was trucked twenty miles from Ypsilanti, where it had fallen in the manufacture of commutators for generators.

19. "You Play Vital Part in Ford Truck Job: All Assembly Plants Use Hydro Parts, Accessories," *Hydro Plants News* 3 (February 1, 1948):1.

20. See "Supplies Rushed By Air: Plane Freight Helps Lick Parts Shortage at Hydro Plants," *Hydro Plants News* 2 (June 1, 1947):1.

21. Press Release, Ford News Bureau, August 16, 1948, 2.

22. Kellogg, "The Play of a Big Man with a Little River, Part I," 639–40, 641.

23. Voorhess, *Reminiscences*, 122. On the particulars about Highland Park's losses to the village industries, see Pietrykowski, "Fordism at Ford," 389–90.

24. This possibility is suggested in Tobin, "Henry Ford and His Village Industries," 63.

25. See Biggs, *The Rational Factory*, 152; see also 158–59. Biggs notes that "despite the amount of activity at the Rouge, for several years it was considered as a feeder plant to Highland Park. A 1924 Company publication described the Rouge as the plant that 'deals primarily in raw materials.'" On the contemporary ruins of Highland Park, see Brinkley, *Wheels for the World*, 761.

26. Smith, *Reminiscences*, 45. Smith nevertheless recalled his own frequent travels to each of the village industries "to see that they were operating efficiently. . . . I was continually on the road" (51). And Voorhess recalled that the "Rouge executives went to the various plants, perhaps not on a regular schedule, but they did visit the plants" (*Reminiscences*, 125).

27. On Ford's employee garden program, see Tobin, "Henry Ford and His Village Industries," 81–82; "Ford Promotes His Hobby to Unite Farm and Factory," *Business Week* 104 (September 2, 1931): 23; and "Stirred Up by Henry Ford's 'Shotgun Gardens,'" *Literary Digest* 110 (September 12, 1931): 10. The last two articles are brief discussions of Ford's threat to fire any workers at his Iron Mountain, Michigan, woodworking plant who did not maintain gardens. In addition, former Flat Rock and Rouge employee John Peters recalled that in "the old days they would give out cards to have a Ford garden. And you had to give a reason if you didn't want it" (letter to me from Peters, May 1989). Former Milford plant employee Raymond Pflug also remembered "the pressure on employees to garden—I heard of men being fired because they did not comply" (letter to me from Pflug, August 17, 1989).

28. Quoted in Pearson, "Ford Predicts," 11.

29. Voorhess recalled that Ford "never took any *active* political interest in the way

these towns were run. . . . When he first went into a town, and it didn't seem reasonably good politically, he'd talk about it so the people would find out about it. If they didn't clean up, he didn't go in there" (*Reminiscences*, 113).

30. See "America's Ruggedest Individual," 12.

31. On these contributions to various communities, see Liebold, *Reminiscences*, 98; and Voorhess, *Reminiscences*, 542.

32. Robert Strother, "Village Makes Good: The Success Story of Dundee, the Town that Came Back," Press Release, Ford News Bureau, May 18, 1938, 1–6. This article became the basis for several local newspaper stories in later years. As with the other village industries, so with Dundee, the press release was not a wholesale distortion of the truth even though, to be sure, it exaggerated the facts in Ford Motor Company's characteristically uncritical fashion. Letters to me from the former village industry employees (cited above and below) unanimously agree on the company's overall positive presence in their respective communities, differ though they do on the work environments in the plants themselves.

33. "Efforts to Be Made to Clean River Bank," *Dundee Reporter*, April 25, 1935, 1.

34. On Ford's educational efforts and the philosophy behind them, see Ford and Crowther, *Today and Tomorrow*, chap. 15; *The Ford Industries*, 29–30; Voorhess, *Reminiscences*, 114–16; Wik, *Henry Ford and Grass-roots America*, 196–206; and Lewis, *Public Image*, 281–82. That Ford's educational orientation has not lost its appeal is reflected in a full-page Amway advertisement in a 1988 issue of *Newsweek* praising one Claude Harvard, a black graduate of Detroit's Ford Trade School who became a successful engineer and, now retired, helps teach poor Detroit youths, black and white alike. Not only did Harvard, while working for Ford Motor Company in 1934, invent "an automated machine for inspecting piston pins that replaced a time-consuming manual task"; he also, in that same year, introduced Henry Ford to George Washington Carver, whom Ford admired and supported. Like Ford and Carver, Harvard is praised as a hard-working "self-made man" (just like those whom Amway employs). Interestingly, the then *New York Times* education editor Edward B. Fiske, in his February 8, 1989, column "Lessons," B10, cites the contemporary Ford Motor Company's varied and flexible employee-management relations programs as a possible model for ailing American public schools wedded to excessive rigidity and hierarchy.

Chapter 6

1. Letters to me from Francis Michaels, August 1 and August 9, 1988.

2. This and the following three paragraphs quote a letter to me from Fred Winstanley, July 25, 1988.

3. Rodes Walters's recollections are quoted from his letters to me of March 24, April 8, June 18, and September 3, 1988.

4. Transcript of Tom Levandowski interview, Plymouth Historical Society Village Industries Exhibit, 1989. His exact number of years at Plymouth is not provided. This permanent exhibit, probably the first one ever on the village industries, opened on April 23, 1989.

5. Transcript of Louis Norman interview, Plymouth Historical Society Village Industries Exhibit, 1989; Julie Brown, "Plant Staffers Took Pride in Job Well Done,"

Observer and Eccentric, April 27, 1989, 1, an article about the Plymouth Historical Society exhibit. James Gallimore was superintendent of both the Newburgh and Plymouth plants, according to a short biography of him that accompanied the dedication program of the James S. Gallimore Elementary School in Plymouth on March 10, 1957 (the program is at the Plymouth Historical Society). The influence of village industry plant managers on the hiring of employees is also noted in an oral history by Benny Zayti, who worked at the Northville plant for an unspecified length of time beginning in 1935, the year before the original facility was replaced by a new one. See Zayti, "Zaytis' Rare Personal Glimpse," 4.

6. Transcript of Kenneth Gates interview, Plymouth Historical Society Village Industries Exhibit, 1989. His exact number of years at Nankin Mills is not provided.

7. Quoted in Ken Abramczyk, "Village Industry Vets Return to Nankin Mills," *Observer and Eccentric*, October 3, 1999, A5. His exact number of years at Nankin Mills is not provided.

8. Ibid. His exact number of years at Nankin Mills and the Rouge is not provided.

9. Gates interview.

10. Quoted in Abramczyk, "Village Industry Vets," A5, A7.

11. My interview with Bruce Richard of the Plymouth Historical Society, October 9, 1999 (Richard helped to found the society).

12. Irene Shaw's quotations are from the transcript of her interview, Plymouth Historical Society Village Industries Exhibit, 1989.

13. Richard, "Henry Ford's Village Industries," *Plymouth Historical Society Newsletter*, October 11, 1984, 6. Ironically, an article by Sandra Steele in the *Crier*, May 10, 1989, n.p., titled "Ford Welcomed Women Workers," is subtitled "Village Industries Gave Equal Opportunity."

14. Edwards's comments are quoted from my interview with him, June 13, 1988.

15. Letter to me from Dale Noble, April 2, 1987.

16. John Peters, quoted from letters to me of March 16 and April 1989.

17. Ralph Cameron, quoted in letter to me from his friend Winifred Hamilton, February 10, 1987. The letter does not specify how many years he worked at Flat Rock.

18. Bill Carter, quoted in ibid.

19. Charlie Oestrike, quoted in ibid.

20. See Sugrue, *Origins of the Urban Crisis*, 95–105.

21. Letters to me from Raymond Pflug, January 5 and October 8, 1988.

22. With the short biography of Gallimore cited in n. 5 above there is a typed paragraph stating that Gallimore "was the only superintendent of the six plants who made his home locally." Which other five plants are referred to is not clear— though Newburgh is presumably among them—nor is the situation with the other village industries indicated. Still, it is a revealing comment.

23. Letter to me from Peters, March 16, 1989.

24. On Ford Motor Company's wage policy until 1937, when his pamphlet appeared, see Raushenbush, *Fordism*, 6–13. See also Samuel M. Levin, *Essays on American Industrialism: Selected Papers of Samuel M. Levin* (Detroit: Wayne State University College of Liberal Arts, 1973), chaps. 3, 4, 6; Daniel Martin Gorodetsky Raff, "Wage Determination and the Five-Dollar Day at Ford: A Detailed Examination" (Ph.D. diss., Massachusetts Institute of Technology, 1987); and Raff, "Looking

Back at the Five-Dollar Day," *Harvard Business Review* 67 (January–February 1989): 180–82.

25. Examples of these various recreational and social activities can be found in, among other places, all the issues of the *Hydro Plants News*, the post–World War II (begun in 1946) company publication intended for village industries employees and, Bruce Pietrykowski notes, "the only nonrecreational institutional link among workers in the village plants" ("Fordism at Ford," 396).

26. Wayne A. Lewchuk, "Men and Monotony: Fraternalism as a Managerial Strategy at the Ford Motor Company," *Journal of Economic History* 53 (December 1993): 825.

27. Van Vlissingen, "BIG Idea," 47–48; Bird, "One Foot on the Land." See also, for example, Ralph W. Cessna, "Down by the New Mill Stream," *Christian Science Monitor Weekly Magazine* 32 (December 30, 1939): 8–9.

28. Quoted in Kellogg, "The Play of a Big Man with a Little River," Part II, 18. Ford unintentionally confirmed these sentiments in Ford and Crowther, *Today and Tomorrow*, 211, 213: farming "is a part-time job in a world that asks for a living on the basis of a full-time job," and farming "never has given such a living. Few have ever made any money out of farming." Voorhess, *Reminiscences*, confirms this dilemma.

29. Tobin, "Henry Ford and His Village Industries," 182.

30. Voorhess, *Reminiscences*, 121–22.

31. Kellogg, "The Play of a Big Man with a Little River," Part II, 19. As Ford himself conceded about the nature of work in Phoenix and, presumably, other village industries, "In this factory there is not a task which cannot be learned by any one of ordinary intelligence within a week" (*Today and Tomorrow*, 143).

32. Letters to me from Michaels, August 9, 1988, and Peters, April 1989.

33. Ford and Crowther, *Today and Tomorrow*, 160. David Gartman, *Auto Slavery: The Labor Process in the American Automobile Industry, 1897–1950* (New Brunswick, N.J.: Rutgers University Press, 1986), 128–29, 138–41, 148–49, 163–64, provides a good summary of critiques of Ford's position here. See also Stephen Meyer III, "The Persistence of Fordism: Workers and Technology in the American Automobile Industry, 1900–1960," in *On the Line: Essays in the History of Auto Work*, ed. Nelson Lichtenstein and Stephen Meyer (Urbana: University of Illinois Press, 1989), 73–99.

34. Kellogg, "The Play of a Big Man with a Little River," Part II, 52; Ford and Crowther, *Today and Tomorrow*, 12.

35. Letters to me from Michaels, August 9, 1988; from Winstanley, July 25, 1988; and from Walters, June 18, 1988; and Edwards interview, June 13, 1988.

CHAPTER 7

1. See, for example, Thomas H. Wright, "Why Ford's Men Strike," *Christian Century* 50 (November 29, 1933): 1501–4; Victor Weybright, "Henry Ford at the Wheel," *Survey Graphic* 26 (December 1937): 686–88, 717–21, 723; and Weybright, "Ford Puts on the Union Label," *Survey Graphic* 30 (November 1941): 554–59, 651–53. On the early history of Detroit's union movement, which did not succeed for several decades, see the summary in Wayne Lewchuk, "Fordism and the Moving

Assembly Line: The British and American Experience, 1895–1930," in Lichtenstein and Meyer, *On the Line*, 19–24; and the more detailed account in Thomas Klug, "Employers' Strategies in the Detroit Labor Market, 1900–1929," also in *On the Line*, 42–72.

2. See, for example, Meier and Rudwick, *Black Detroit*; Meyer, *The Five Dollar Day*; Barnard, *Walter Reuther*, esp. 51–53, 66–69; and Brock Yates, *The Decline and Fall of the American Automobile Industry* (New York: Random House, 1983), chap. 8. Diamond, *Reputation of the American Businessman*, chap. 6, notes that a majority of union leaders, including UAW President Walter Reuther if not necessarily a majority of rank-and-file members, nevertheless praised Ford upon his death despite all of this opposition a few years earlier.

3. Raushenbush, *Fordism*, 3.

4. Quoted in Collier and Horowitz, *The Fords*, 165.

5. For details of Ford antiunion policies and practices, see Raushenbush, *Fordism*, 8–38.

6. Gartman, *Auto Slavery*, 195.

7. "G.M. and Ford Are Moving Out," *Business Week* 396 (April 3, 1937), 16.

8. Ibid. See also "Auto Industry Decentralizing," *Business Week* 345 (April 11, 1936); and Sidney Fine, *Sit-Down: The General Motors Strike of 1936–1937* (Ann Arbor: University of Michigan Press, 1969), 48–50.

9. Sugrue, *Origins of the Urban Crisis*, 128.

10. See Pietrykowski, "Fordism at Ford," 395. Pietrykowski (384–87) does see Ford's antiunionism behind the establishment of the village industries but also sees other motives.

11. The cartoon is from a UAW local publication of August 23, 1939, n.p., found in the Joe Brown Collection, box 12, but was undoubtedly first published elsewhere.

12. See Gartman, *Auto Slavery*, 166–69, 262.

13. Article is from an unspecified UAW publication, May 13, 1939, n.p., found in the Joe Brown Collection, box 12.

14. Unnamed delegate quoted in Pietrykowski, "Fordism at Ford," 395.

15. On Detroit's weak union movement before the 1930s, see Ticknor, "Motor City," 209–11.

16. Raushenbush, *Fordism*, 31.

17. This argument was made most forcefully in the letter to me of April 21, 1987, from Dale Noble, who also saw antiunionism in the village industries enterprise. As he put it in a follow-up letter of May 17, 1987, "You seem surprised that I worked only one summer [in the early 1930s] for Ford. I don't believe anyone with any self-respect would have stayed longer in that setting unless economics dictated otherwise." Raushenbush (*Fordism*, 47–51) details Ford Motor Company's massive layoffs during the 1927 conversion from the Model T to the Model A and Henry Ford's—and so the company's—aversion to charity.

18. Cf. letters to me from Noble, April 21, 1987, and from Francis Michaels, August 1989 (discussed in chapter 3, n. 8). Michaels is less cynical than Noble about Henry Ford's motives. John Peters's letter to me of April 1989 discusses this slack period without criticism of Henry Ford and with implicit praise of farms as supplemental income. Edwards, however, in his June 13, 1988, interview, mentioned village industry employees' inability to plan farm work because of the changing demands

for car parts and the consequent changing employment schedules over those slack periods.

19. "Decentralization," editorial in unspecified Dodge UAW Local #3 publication, August 9, 1939, n.p., in the Joe Brown Collection, box 12.

20. Editorial, unspecified UAW publication, October 30, 1937, n.p., in the Joe Brown Collection, box 12.

21. "GM Builds Plant To Thwart Labor Organizations," unspecified Briggs' UAW Local #212 publication, December 10, 1938, n.p., in the Joe Brown Collection, box 12. That such fears were justified in the case of General Motors is confirmed by Kuhn, *GM Passes Ford*, 147–48.

22. On "technological unemployment" in American history, see Amy Sue Bix, *Inventing Ourselves Out of Jobs? America's Debate over Technological Unemployment, 1929–1981* (Baltimore, Md.: Johns Hopkins University Press, 2000).

23. Interview with John Eldon, October 28, 1938, 1 (mimeograph), in the Joe Brown Collection, box 9.

24. Emil Mazey, "Are They Better Off? Mazey Answers *Free Press*," editorial reply in unspecified Briggs' UAW Local #212 publication, August 30, 1939, n.p., in the Joe Brown Collection, box 9. The same point is made in, among other places, an editorial in the *West Side Officer*, November 7, 1938, 1, a mimeographed publication from West Side Detroit UAW Local #174; the editorial is at the end of an article titled "Present Employment in West Side Plants." (Detroit's West Side contained many auto parts and assembly plants; just outside its boundaries was the Rouge complex.) According to a Reuther biographer, "Reuther never opposed new technology. . . . If handled correctly, new technology would raise the standard of living for all" (Barnard, *Walter Reuther*, 154). See also Kevin Boyle, *The UAW and the Heyday of American Liberalism, 1945–1968* (Ithaca, N.Y.: Cornell University Press, 1995), 93–97.

25. The resolution, titled "Technological Unemployment" and proposed by Chrysler UAW Local #7 on May 20, 1939, was found in the Joe Brown Collection, box 9, accompanied by a seven-page mimeographed elaboration, prepared by the same local, titled "Help Solve Mankind's Greatest Problem: Technological Unemployment."

26. Unidentified worker quoted in Reynolds, "Engines of Struggle," 86–87; see also 86–90.

27. Quoted in Denny, "Times Good, Not Bad, Ford Says," 3. A similar argument was made by the then president of the Studebaker Corporation, Paul G. Hoffman, as reported in a *Detroit Free Press* article, April 16, 1934, n.p., "Machines Help Employment, Automobile Leader Asserts," in the Joe Brown Collection, box 9.

28. Stuart Chase, "Labor-Saving Devices Have Stolen the Show," *Detroit News*, August 12, 1934, n.p., in the Joe Brown Collection, box 9.

29. Rowland Smith, "River Rouge: Industrial Marvel of the Age Most Callous and Inhuman in Treatment of Its Workers," *United Automobile Worker*, September 10, 1938, 10, in the Joe Brown Collection, box 10.

30. On ongoing efforts to improve both the site of the 1937 attack and the nearby Miller Road, see Lewis, "Ford Country" (column), *Cars and Parts* 45 (January 2003): 63.

31. Pietrykowski, "Fordism at Ford," 395.

32. Crosman et al., "One Foot in Industry and One Foot in the Soil." Ironically, this team may have been persuaded by their "royal" treatment (see chapter 3) that labor relations in the village industries were almost idyllic, when clearly, according to former employees, they were not.

33. See Boyle, *The UAW*, 76–77.

34. The figures are from Tobin, "Henry Ford and His Village Industries," 154. Barnard gives these same figures for just the Rouge but says the "results at other Ford plants were equally decisive" (*Walter Reuther*, 68). This is not to suggest that some local AFL unions in other industries and in other contexts were any less militant than their CIO counterparts; see, for example, Staughton Lynd, ed., *"We Are All Leaders": The Alternative Unionism of the Early 1930s* (Urbana: University of Illinois Press, 1996).

35. Letters to me from Michaels, August 1, 1988; from Winstanley, July 25, 1988; from Walters, June 18, 1988; and from Peters, April 1989.

36. Edwards interview, June 13, 1988.

37. Letters to me from Pflug, January 5, August 17, and October 8, 1988.

38. Letter to me from Winstanley, July 25, 1988.

39. For some reason there were two locals at Plymouth, and one of them may have included these other six sites; Tobin ("Henry Ford and His Village Industries," 155) says Plymouth was joined with them originally.

40. Letter to me from Michaels, August 1989.

41. On these unionization developments and their impact on the village industries, see Tobin, "Henry Ford and His Village Industries," 154–56; and Pietryskowski, "Fordism at Ford," 397–98. One consequence of union recognition was dissolution of the Ford Service Department. Another was the centralization of power within the UAW—previously a comparatively decentralized and democratic organization—which is among the principal criticisms of Reuther made by Lichtenstein in *The Most Dangerous Man in Detroit*.

42. On these post–World War II developments, see Elizabeth A. Fones-Wolf, *Selling Free Enterprise: The Business Assault on Labor and Liberalism, 1945–60* (Urbana: University of Illinois Press, 1994), 68, 92, 94, 110–13, 124–27.

CHAPTER 8

1. Dorman, *Revolt of the Provinces*, xi. Interestingly, the introduction to the important study commissioned by President Herbert Hoover, *Recent Social Trends: Report of the President's Research Committee on Social Trends* (New York: McGraw-Hill, 1933), lxxv, saw conflict between "the new tools and the new technique"—that is, urban industrial life—and "the family, religion, the economic order, the political system," and, by implication, rural village life. Yet that same introduction acknowledged growing "centralization in social life, in domestic politics, and in international relations" (xxvi) and conceded that "regional isolation is being broken down all over the world" (xxvii). In his own way, Ford agreed with all these points.

2. See, for example, George C. S. Benson, *The New Centralization: A Study of Intergovernmental Relationships in the United States* (New York: Farrar & Rinehart, 1941), a small book by a prominent political scientist. Despite its title, his book advocates "A Program for American Decentralization" (168) regarding the admin-

istration of various federal, regional, state, and local programs. Although none of those programs related to industrialization and manufacturing, the larger point is the demonstration from this period of the popular use of "decentralization" itself. Nevertheless, in the next paragraph, as throughout this chapter and the entire book, I have specified what "decentralization" meant for Henry Ford and others concerned with industrialization and manufacturing, keeping in mind Benson's observation that it is "a somewhat protean word" (9). A complementary work is Thomas Hewes, *Decentralize For Liberty* (New York: Richard Smith, 1945). Published at the end of World War II, the book reflects concerns for postwar America in economics, politics, civil liberties, and other areas. Far from being a conservative Republican or an independent libertarian, however, Hewes was a Democrat who had served in the Treasury Department during the New Deal and held various state posts in his native Connecticut for many years.

3. On the broader historical context of these and other private and public efforts for electricity-based decentralization projects, see Thomas P. Hughes, "The Industrial Revolution That Never Came," *American Heritage of Invention and Technology* 3 (Winter 1988): 58–64. Hughes's analysis includes both Ford and Lewis Mumford (discussed below). For elaboration, see Hughes, *American Genesis.*

4. Carolyn Marvin, "Dazzling the Multitude: Imagining the Electric Light as a Communications Medium," in *Imagining Tomorrow: History, Technology, and the American Future*, ed. Joseph J. Corn (Cambridge, Mass.: MIT Press, 1986), 203.

5. See, for example, Jean Christie, "Morris L. Cooke and Energy for America," in Pursell, *Technology in America*, 202–12; and Ronald C. Tobey, *Technology as Freedom: The New Deal and the Electrical Modernization of the American Home* (Berkeley: University of California Press, 1996). See also Ralph L. Woods, *America Reborn: A Plan for Decentralization of Industry* (New York: Longmans, Green, 1939), chap. 12, "The New Deal and Decentralization." This is a good contemporary overview by someone in favor of decentralization in both the public and the private sectors.

6. See Carol Willis, "Skyscraper Utopias: Visionary Urbanism in the 1920s," in Corn, *Imagining Tomorrow*, 164–87; on 183–84 she treats regionalism as a critique of skyscraper utopias.

7. Harry Hopkins quoted in Lewis, *Public Image*, 163.

8. Rexford Guy Tugwell, "Henry Ford in This World," *Saturday Review of Literature* 3 (August 7, 1926): 19; the article reviews Ford and Crowther's *Today and Tomorrow* (1926). Although this praise predated the New Deal, there is no reason to believe that Tugwell's opinion changed substantially during the New Deal.

9. See Wik, *Henry Ford and Grass-roots America*, 193.

10. The definitive account remains Conkin, *Tomorrow a New World.*

11. *Ibid.*, 267.

12. Besides *ibid.*, chap. 11, see Ben Shahn, "In Homage," *New Yorker* 38 (September 29, 1962): 31–33; and Joseph Brandes, *Immigrants to Freedom: Jewish Communities in Rural New Jersey since 1882* (Philadelphia: Jewish Publication Society of America, 1971), 287, 316–18.

13. Crosman et al., "One Foot in Industry and One Foot in the Soil," 13. See also 13–14 for specific points, though the authors cite no particular government projects. Conkin, *Tomorrow a New World*, 23–24, 27, 29, mentions Ford's belief in the

decentralization of industry but never cites the village industries themselves. The same holds true for Conwill, "Back to the Land," 13–17, which compares Norvelt and Penn-Craft, Pennsylvania's only two "rural resettlement communities," the former "a government project," the latter "a private enterprise" (17).

14. Even such fundamentally positive assessments of modern technology (and science) as the two volumes edited by Charles A. Beard, *Whither Mankind: A Panorama of Modern Civilization* (1928) and *Toward Civilization* (1930), acknowledged contemporary criticism from various quarters about the course of "industrial civilization"—and of these works the former appeared just before the Great Depression struck and the latter before the worst of the Depression. See Beard's introduction to each volume. See also Daniel T. Rodgers, "Regionalism and the Burdens of Progress," in *Region, Race, and Reconstruction: Essays in Honor of C. Vann Woodward*, ed. J. Morgan Kousser and James M. McPherson (New York: Oxford University Press, 1982), 3–26, on the eventual disillusionment of Howard W. Odum, the foremost scholar and advocate of regionalism, with unadulterated technological "progress."

15. Warren Susman, "The Thirties," in *The Development of an American Culture*, ed. Stanley Coben and Lorman Ratner (Englewood Cliffs, N.J.: Prentice-Hall, 1970), 188.

16. See Bix, *Inventing Ourselves Out of Jobs?*

17. Ralph Borsodi, *This Ugly Civilization* (1929; rept., Philadelphia: Porcupine Press, 1975), 1, 3.

18. Scott Nearing, *The Making of a Radical: A Political Autobiography* (New York: Harper & Row, 1972), 211.

19. Arthur E. Morgan, *The Small Community: Foundation of Democratic Life* (1942; rept., Yellow Springs, Ohio: Community Service, 1984), 87.

20. See David E. Shi, *The Simple Life: Plain Living and High Thinking in American Culture* (New York: Oxford University Press, 1985).

21. See Kasson, *Civilizing the Machine*, which examines the years 1776–1900.

22. Mildred J. Loomis, *Alternative Americas* (New York: Universe Books, 1982), 58.

23. Borsodi, *This Ugly Civilization*, 7, 13–14. I therefore differ with Conkin, who characterizes Borsodi as wishing "to retreat from modernity and industrialization" (*Tomorrow a New World*, 99). As Conkin himself notes, Borsodi tried to establish "a Negro project near Dayton" (201) but was defeated by local whites hostile toward African Americans and fearful of depreciated property values. Surely such a person cannot be reduced to a political "reactionary" (327).

24. Borsodi, *This Ugly Civilization*, 115.

25. On Borsodi's life and achievements, see also William H. Issel, "Ralph Borsodi and the Agrarian Response to Modern America," *Agricultural History* 41 (April 1967): 155–66; Jacob H. Dorn, "Subsistence Homesteading in Dayton, Ohio, 1933–1935," *Ohio History* 78 (spring 1969), 75–93; William E. Leverette Jr., and David E. Shi, "Agrarianism for Commuters," *South Atlantic Quarterly* 79 (spring 1980): 204–18; and Richard D. Schubart, "Ralph Borsodi: The Political Biography of a Utopian Decentralist, 1886–1977" (Ph.D. diss., State University of New York at Binghamton, 1983). On Borsodi's views in the context of a related development, see Kleiman, "Appropriate Technology Movement," 336–37, 367–73.

26. Borsodi, *This Ugly Civilization*, 193.

27. Helen and Scott Nearing, *The Good Life: Helen and Scott Nearing's Sixty Years of Self-Sufficient Living* (New York: Schocken, 1989), 3. The book combines their *Living the Good Life* (1954) with their *Continuing the Good Life* (1979).

28. Helen and Scott Nearing, *The Maple Sugar Book* (1950; rept. New York: Schocken, 1970), 241, 243, 269.

29. *Ibid.*, 232–33, 223, 225.

30. See Stephen J. Whitfield, *Scott Nearing: Apostle of American Radicalism* (New York: Columbia University Press, 1974), 179–80, 220–21.

31. See Roy Talbert Jr., *FDR's Utopian: Arthur Morgan of the TVA* (Jackson: University Press of Mississippi, 1987), 116–22, 126. See also "New Town to Give 2,000 Better Living: Norris, Tennessee, Near Big Dam, Soon Ready for Permanent Housing," *Washington Star*, November 17, 1933, 4. Conkin (*Tomorrow a New World*, 113) notes that the New Deal agencies he discusses had no ties to TVA, though a loan to help build Norris had been contemplated.

32. Arthur E. Morgan, *A Business of My Own: Possibilities in Small Community Occupations and Industries* (Yellow Springs, Ohio: Community Service, 1945), 160. To be sure, Morgan was not referring to the TVA specifically here, but the same expectations held for the TVA, just as they did for other areas he wrote about before and after his TVA years.

33. *Ibid.*, 7, 9.

34. Morgan, *Small Community*, 86.

35. Arthur E. Morgan, *Industries for Small Communities* (Yellow Springs, Ohio: Community Service, 1953), 96, 104. For historical perspective on Morgan's endorsement of small industries, see Stuart W. Bruchey, ed., *Small Business in American Life*, (New York: Columbia University Press, 1980); the introduction and the essays that follow illuminate the persistence of small business in America despite the growth of large corporations and, no less important, the persistent identification of small business with core American values.

36. Morgan, *A Business of My Own*, 154.

37. Morgan, *Industries for Small Communities*, 4. In this context, it is interesting to quote Kleiman: "Central to the economic vision of the AT [appropriate technology] movement has been a call for the revitalization of the small business sector" ("Appropriate Technology Movement," 360).

38. See Edward S. Shapiro, "The Southern Agrarians and the Tennessee Valley Authority," *American Quarterly* 22 (Winter 1970): 791–806; and Shapiro, "Decentralist Intellectuals and the New Deal," *Journal of American History* 58 (March 1972): 938–57. I therefore differ with Conkin, who characterizes the southern Agrarians, along with Borsodi, as wishing "to retreat from modernity and industrialization" (*Tomorrow a New World*, 99).

39. On *Who Owns America?* see the retrospective essay by Edward S. Shapiro, "*Who Owns America?*: A Forgotten American Classic," *Intercollegiate Review* 35 (Fall 1999): 37–45. See also William E. Leverette, Jr., and David E. Shi, "Herbert Agar and *Free America*: A Jeffersonian Alternative to the New Deal," *American Studies* 16 (August 1982): 189–206; and George M. Lubick, "Restoring the American Dream: The Agrarian-Decentralist Movement, 1930–1946," *South Atlantic Quarterly* 84 (Winter 1985): 63–80.

40. David Cushman Coyle, "The Fallacy of Mass Production," in *Who Owns America?*

A New Declaration of Independence, ed. Herbert Agar and Allen Tate (Boston: Houghton Mifflin, 1936), 3, 7, 12, 13.

41. Ibid., 8.

42. The Agrarians might therefore not have appreciated a fairly recent TVA pamphlet that connected TVA with Henry Ford, albeit in comparing TVA's cheap electricity its earlier days to Ford's cheap automobiles. See *TVA and Regional Development* (Knoxville, Tenn.: TVA, n.d.), 3, 7. On Donald Davidson, the southern Agrarian most hostile to TVA, see Edward S. Shapiro, "Donald Davidson and the Tennessee Valley Authority: The Response of a Southern Conservative," *Tennessee Historical Quarterly* 33 (Winter 1974): 436–51. On Davidson's contempt for Ford, see his 1930 newspaper essay, "The World as Ford Factory," reprinted in *The Superfluous Men: Conservative Critics of American Culture*, ed. Robert M. Crunden (Austin: University of Texas Press, 1977), 81–84.

43. See John A. Piquet, "Bibliography: Decentralization of Industry," Agricultural Industries Division, Tennessee Valley Authority, Knoxville, 1935; and "Bibliography: Decentralization," Industry Unit Files, microfilm reel 75, Tennessee Valley Authority, Knoxville, 1935.

44. On the continuing popularity of the Nearings' Maine homestead, see Clarke Canfield, Associated Press, "Nearing Spirit Lives On," *Bangor Daily News*, September 22–23, 2001, G1, G2. On the continuing popularity of books on living the good life, see Julie Flaherty, "Living by the Books: Vermont Publisher Succeeds with Guides for a Simpler Life," *New York Times*, June 19, 1999, B1, B14; significantly, there is no mention here of the Nearings or, in contrast to the heavily commercial thrust of these contemporary writers and publishers, of their moral authority and conviction.

45. On such "back to the land" schemes, see the summary in Conkin, *Tomorrow a New World*, chap. 1. As with Borsodi and the Agrarians, so again here, Conkin does not distinguish between those persons and groups either hostile or indifferent toward modern technology and those favoring its employment in order to depopulate large cities and renew rural life. Consequently, his following statement, while certainly relevant to the village industries, is nevertheless inadequate: "One ever-present assumption of the back-to-the-land movement was that there were too many people in the cities for complete employment" (17).

46. Helen and Scott Nearing, *Maple Sugar Book*, 220. See, by contrast, the avowedly reactionary stance of Allan Carlson, *The New Agrarian Mind: The Movement toward Decentralist Thought in Twentieth-Century America* (New Brunswick, N.J.: Transaction, 2000). Carlson faults most twentieth-century decentralists for a misplaced faith in the alleged benefits of modern science and technology.

47. For elaboration on these aspects of Mumford's work, see Howard P. Segal, "Lewis Mumford's Alternatives to the Megamachine: Critical Utopianism, Regionalism, and Decentralization," in Segal, *Future Imperfect*, 147–59.

48. Lewis Mumford to George Weller, 1939 (no specific date), Mumford Correspondence, Lewis Mumford Papers, Special Collections, Van Pelt Library, University of Pennsylvania.

49. Lewis Mumford, *Technics and Civilization* (1934; rept., New York: Harcourt, Brace & World, 1963), 225.

50. Lewis Mumford, *The Culture of Cities* (1938; rept., New York: Harcourt Brace Jovanovich, 1970), 342, 400, 325.

51. Mumford, *Technics and Civilization*, 226.

52. See Mumford, *The Culture of Cities*, 303. Mumford nevertheless romanticized the organic qualities of those medieval communities no less than Ford and his associates and admirers romanticized those of the village industries.

53. For elaboration on this and the following paragraph, see Segal, introduction to Harold Loeb, *Life in a Technocracy: What It Might Be Like* (1933; rept., Syracuse: Syracuse University Press, 1996).

54. Denny, "Times Good, Not Bad, Ford Says," 1.

55. For elaboration, see Segal, introduction to Loeb, *Life in a Technocracy*, xxiii–xxiv, xxx–xxxi.

56. Alfred H. Jones, "The Search for a Usable American Past in the New Deal Era," *American Quarterly* 23 (December 1971): 710–24. On this search, see also Dorman, *Revolt of the Provinces*. Diamond, *Reputation of the American Businessman*, 168–69, 174–75, discusses the association of Henry Ford and his enterprises with American values beyond those of business alone.

57. Kenneth L. Ames, introduction to *The Colonial Revival in America*, ed. Alan Axelrod (New York: Winterthur Museum/Norton, 1985), 11.

58. See Dona Brown, *Inventing New England: Regional Tourism in the Nineteenth Century* (Washington, D.C.: Smithsonian Institution Press, 1995).

59. T. J. Jackson Lears, *No Place of Grace: Antimodernism and the Transformation of American Culture, 1880–1920* (New York: Pantheon, 1981), 89, 91.

60. Terry Smith, *Making the Modern: Industry, Art, and Design in America* (Chicago: University of Chicago Press, 1993), 138.

61. Dorman, *Revolt of the Provinces*, 262. Dorman discusses the failure of what he calls the regionalist movement in America to become politically active in order to achieve some material successes and the movement's consequent relegation to the margins of American society and culture.

62. See Jay Anderson, *Time Machines: The World of Living History* (Nashville, Tenn.: American Association for State and Local History, 1984). Anderson discusses both Dearborn museums and the Wayside Inn (28–29), but they are not simply escapist enterprises either.

63. Raymond B. Fosdick, *John D. Rockefeller, Jr.: A Portrait* (New York: Harper, 1956), 273, 274.

64. William Goodwin to Edsel Ford, June 13, 1924, in the Rockefeller Family Archives, Rockefeller Archive Center, North Tarrytown, N.Y., Record Group 2E, Cultural Interests Series, box 150, folder 1316. The other correspondence noted here is in the same folder.

65. For details, see Fosdick, *John D. Rockefeller, Jr.*, 278–96.

66. "Those Factories on the James," editorial, *Richmond Times-Dispatch*, July 23, 1956, 10, from Rockefeller Family Archives, Record Group 2E, box 143, folder 1254.

67. See also "Perfection at Williamsburg," an editorial in the *Norfolk Ledger-Dispatch*, October 27, 1958, which endorses the ongoing "perfection" of the community achieved by eliminating "automobile traffic and other 20th Century aspects" such

as paved roads and streets: Rockefeller Family Archives, Record Group 2E, box 150, folder 1318. By contrast, Maureen Milford, "Land-Rich Museums Find New Income Source," *New York Times*, April 2, 2003, C12, details the current expansion of Williamsburg's Merchant Square, a growing number of upscale, for-profit stores on the museum's grounds which generate revenue for the historical complex.

68. On these utopian communities, see Howard P. Segal, *Technological Utopianism in American Culture* (Chicago: University of Chicago Press, 1985), 97 and 216 n. 77.

69. See Segal, "The 'Middle Landscape,'" 13–26.

70. Peter F. Drucker, "Henry Ford: Success and Failure," *Harper's Magazine* 195 (July 1947): 6. Drucker refers to the huge sums Ford "poured into 'chemurgy' or into utopian village communities of self-sufficient, sturdy, yeoman farmers" who exemplified Ford's "belief in decentralization" and concludes that "it was Ford's personal tragedy to live long enough to see his Utopia crumble" (7). On Ford as a utopian industrialist, see also Banta, *Taylored Lives*; and Prettyman, "Criticism, Business, and the Problem of Complicity," 49–66. As noted above, Dorman characterizes the regionalist movement as having been "launched for the utopian reconstruction of modern civilization" (*Revolt of the Provinces*, xi).

71. Smith, *Making the Modern*, 139, 140.

72. See exhibition review by Craig R. Olson in *Journal of American History* 84 (June 1997): 181–87. Olson himself does not criticize the exhibition on this point but instead accepts the antithesis between farm and factory as conventional wisdom.

73. Michael Kammen, *Mystic Chords of Memory: The Transformation of Tradition in American Culture* (New York: Knopf, 1991), 300. On these tensions in the context of American "modernism" overall, see Daniel Joseph Singal, "Towards a Definition of American Modernism," in *Modernist Culture in America*, ed. Singal (Belmont, Calf.: Wadsworth, 1991), 1–27, esp. 10–11.

74. On a roughly comparable situation of the complex, often painful transition from predominantly agrarian to partially industrialized societies in many Third World countries in recent decades, see Kitching, *Development and Underdevelopment in Historical Perspective*.

CHAPTER 9

1. Sugrue, *Origins of the Urban Crisis*, 128.

2. Press Release, Automobile Manufacturers Association, March 26, 1936, 1, in the Joe Brown Collection, box 12. On the decentralization of automobile final assembly plants in much of the twentieth century, see Rubenstein, *Changing US Auto Industry*, chap. 1, and 102–4, for brief discussion of the village industries.

3. See "Auto Industry Decentralizing," 28–29; "G.M. and Ford Are Moving Out," 16–17; and Hounshell, *From the American System to Mass Production*, 264–66. As I noted in chapter 7, citing the second *Business Week* article here, some of GM's decentralization moves reflected corporate hostility toward sit-down strikes and other labor unrest in Detroit and Flint, but not all; there were other factors at work besides antiunionism.

4. R. D. Sangster, "Industry: Los Angeles County Automotive Center for Pacific Coast," *Los Angeles Times*, January 2, 1936, Part I-9, in the Joe Brown Collection, box 12. This was apparently a supplement to an insert in the paper, as Sangster was

identified as "Manager, Industrial Department, Los Angeles Chamber of Commerce." In this regard see also "149 Automobile Plants," unspecified UAW publication, October 30, 1937, n.p., in the Joe Brown Collection, box 12.

5. Joseph Geschelin, "Is Decentralization Industry's Next Step?" *Automotive Industries* 68 (May 13, 1933): 584.

6. See Irving Salomon, "Why We Moved to a Smaller Town," *Factory and Industrial Management* 76 (November 1928): 910–13; Paul S. Clapp, "Electric Power Transforms Main Street," *Magazine of Wall Street* 44 (June 29, 1929): 422, 424; A. W. Robertson, "Modern Transportation and Power Aid Decentralization," *Iron Age* 127 (January 15, 1931): 222–23; Martin J. Insull, "Engineering Progress: 1731–1831–1931," *Electrical Engineering* 50 (September 1931): 741; "Industry on the Move: 'Why and Where Plants and Industries are Migrating, What the Decentralization Trend Means, How New Competition Is Changing the Geography of Industry," special report in *Business Week* 391 (February 27, 1937): 43–52; John A. Piquet, "Is the Big City Doomed as an Industrial Center?" *Industrial Management* 68 (September 1924): 139–44; and Burnham Finney, "Has the Small Plant a Future?" *Iron Age* 127 (May 7, 1931): 1499–501, 1518.

7. See "Great Cities Are Declining in Population," *Current Opinion* 75 (August 1923): 207–8; Edward Mott Woolley, "Wanted—Ten Million People," *North American Review* 235 (March 1933): 207–15; Charles Merz, "Let's Go Back to the Small Town," *Collier's Weekly* 72 (July 28, 1923): 13; and Silas Bent, "Factories in the Country," *World's Work* 47 (March 1924): 529–33.

8. Carl J. Friedrich, introduction to *Alfred Weber's Theory of the Location of Industries*, ed. Friedrich (Chicago: University of Chicago Press, 1929), xiii. "English economic theory," he continued, "has neglected a strictly theoretical analysis of the problem," which was his principal concern. A less theoretical academic study is W. Gerald Holmes, *Plant Location* (New York: McGraw-Hill, 1930). Holmes is identified (only) as an "Industrial Engineer."

9. Philip Cabot, "The New Industrial Era," *Harvard Business Review* 12 (January 1934): 224, 227. But see the qualifications of the degree of actual industrial decentralization provided a year after Cabot's article by Daniel B. Creamer, *Is Industry Decentralizing? A Statistical Analysis of Locational Changes in Manufacturing Employment, 1899–1933* (Philadelphia: University of Pennsylvania Press, 1935).

10. Edward A. Filene, *The Way Out: A Forecast of Coming Changes in American Business and Industry* (Garden City, N.Y.: Doubleday, Page, 1924), 178, 179, 180, 233, 231.

11. Ibid., 231.

12. Ibid., 228–29.

13. Ibid., 230.

14. Martin J. Insull, address before the American Society of Civil Engineers, Dallas, April 24, 1929, reprinted in Insull, *America's New Frontier* (Chicago: Middle West Utilities, 1929), iii.

15. Ibid., 26, 37.

16. Joseph K. Hart, "Power and Culture," *Survey Graphic* 51 (March 1, 1924): 627.

17. *Ibid.*, 628. See the similar stance in Glenn Frank, "Power, the Background of Our Present-Day Civilization," *Mechanical Engineering* 50 (April 1928): 275–79. Frank was president of the University of Wisconsin.

18. Hart, *Power and Culture*, 628.
19. Many, though not all, of the books and articles cited above and below came to my attention through Helen Almyra Jansky, "Forces and Trends in the Decentralization of Industry: A Selected Bibliography," which was "submitted as one of the requirements for the Diploma of the Library School," University of Wisconsin, 1933; and through Piquet, "Bibliography: Decentralization of Industry." I found Jansky's Bibliography in the Chairman's Office Files, Tennessee Valley Authority, Knoxville.
20. Woods, *America Reborn*, 302; see also entire chap. 12, "The New Deal and Decentralization."
21. Insull, *America's New Frontier*, 38.
22. For a summary of these developments, see Marcus and Segal, *Technology in America*, 219–20, 237–38.
23. Cabot, "The New Industrial Era," 227.
24. Mark Foster, "The Automobile and the City," *Michigan Quarterly Review* 19–20 (fall 1980 and winter 1981, combined special issue): 465, 466.
25. See, for example, Ebenezer Howard et al., *Report of the International Town Planning Conference, New York, 1925*; Herbert Warren and W. R. Davidge, eds., *Decentralisation of Population and Industry, A New Principle in Town Planning*, (London: P. S. Smith, 1930); John M. Gries and James Ford, eds., *Slums, Large-Scale Housing, and Decentralization* (Washington, D.C.: President's Conference on Home Building and Home Ownership, 1932); and Edmund de S. Brunner and J. H. Kolb, *Rural Social Trends* (New York: McGraw-Hill, 1933).
26. Interrante, "The Road to Autopia," 508, 509, 510. As Interrante notes, "Studies of rural villages in 28 states in 1924–1930 found that the socioeconomic hinterland of two-thirds of them did not expand by as much as two square miles. And studies of car travel in five states between 1926 and 1928 found that one-third to one-half of all automobile trips measured under 20 miles. This was the approximate distance of a horse and a wagon, but cars took less time to traverse it. Automobile use encouraged not longer trips, but more frequent ones" (509–10).
27. Walter Cary, "Henry Ford—and the Decentralization of Industry," *Businessman-about-Town* 1 (June 1938): 16.
28. See Lewis, *Public Image*, 163. Regarding the Nazi plan, see also "Reich Would Cut City Populations," *Sunday New York Times*, January 7, 1934, 2E. On Ford's acclaim by the Nazis and the Russian Communists alike, see Flink, *Automobile Age*, 112–13. On recent revelations about the ties between Ford Motor Company and other major American corporations and the Nazis, see Michael Hirsh, "Dirty Business," *Newsweek* (International Edition) 132 (December 14, 1998): 24–28; and Ken Silverstein, "Ford and the Ruhrer," *Nation* 270 (January 24, 2000): 11–16. Significantly, the sole mention of Henry Ford in Edwin Black's controversial *IBM and the Holocaust: The Strategic Alliance between Nazi Germany and America's Most Powerful Corporation* (New York: Crown, 2001), is this: "Hitler's fascism resonated with certain men of great vision, such as Henry Ford. Another who found Hitlerism compelling was Thomas J. Watson, president of one of America's most prestigious companies: International Business Machines" (23). On the ideological connections between Ford and Hitler, see Kjetil Jakobsen, Ketil G. Andersen, Tor Halvorsen, and Sissel Myklebust, "Engineering Cultures: European Ap-

propriations of Americanism," in *The Intellectual Appropriation of Technology: Discourses on Modernity, 1900–1939,* ed. Mikael Hard and Andrew Jamison (Cambridge, Mass.: MIT Press, 1998), 117, 122–26.

29. See Charles S. Maier, "Between Taylorism and Technocracy: European Ideologies and the Vision of Industrial Productivity in the 1920s," *Journal of Contemporary History* 5 (1970): 27–61.

30. See Christopher Bailey, "Progress and Preservation: The Role of Rural Industries in the Making of the Modern Image of the Countryside," *Journal of Design History* 9 (1996): 35–53.

31. Charles Buxton Going, "Village Communities of the Factory, Machine Works, and Mine," *Engineering Magazine* 21 (April 1901): 59–74.

32. Cameron, "Decentralization of Industry," 483.

33. *Ibid.* 484. A similar argument by a sympathetic outsider is in Barclay, *Ford Production Methods,* 25.Yet Henry Ford, Charles Voorhess recalled, "felt he had overdeveloped the Rouge. It was too large a plant, and he felt it wasn't what he should have done. Development of the small, so-called village industries resulted from a lesson that he got in developing the Rouge" (*Reminiscences,* 92); see also 93. Ford's rethinking of the Rouge is also indicated in Harold N. Denny, "Small-Unit Plants Ford's Final Goal," *New York Times,* February 5, 1933, 1, 22. On the contradictions between Ford's theory of mass production and its implementation, see Cynthia Monaco, "Henry Ford's Ethos of Mass Production and the Assembly Line Worker" (undergraduate paper, Science, Technology, and Society Program, MIT, 1986).

34. Cameron, "Decentralization of Industry," 487. Ford and Crowther had also discussed conditions requiring centralization, but in far less detail, in *My Life and Work,* 191–92. See also Liebold, *Reminiscences,* 539, in confirmation of this point. Interestingly, even E. F. Schumacher, who became famous for his *Small Is Beautiful* (1973) and its advocacy of smaller-scale and decentralized technology, was, like Ford, open to both larger-scale and centralized technology, depending on the circumstances. See Kleiman, "Appropriate Technology Movement," 88–89.

35. See "Ford Aide Tells Rural Plant Gains: Cameron in Paper Written for Management Congress Urges Advantages to Employees," *Sunday New York Times,* August 21, 1938, sec. 3, 7. Cameron's paper was reprinted in *Proceedings, Seventh International Management Congress,* Production Section (Washington, D.C., 1938), 36–38.

36. Henry Ford, "If My Business Were Small," *System: The Magazine of Business* 43 (June 1923): 735. As Ford and Crowther argued three years later in *Today and Tomorrow,* "Size is only a stage; at one stage your finances will let you do only this. In the next stage you can do a little more. And so on" (242); "Size is purely an incident to a policy of manufacturing. It is nothing in itself" (243); and finally, "The way for the little man to use the best methods is to get big" (249).

37. Ford, "If My Business Were Small," 788. As Ford and Crowther also argued in *Today and Tomorrow,* "To effect the economies, to bring in the power, to cut out the waste, and thus fully to realize the wage motive, we must have big business— which does not, however, necessarily mean centralized business. We are decentralizing" (10; see also 136).

38. Ford and Crowther, *Today and Tomorrow,* 12. I used the same quotation near the end of chapter 6 regarding the degree to which Ford's village industries were (or

were not) akin to scientific experiments. On Ford's belief in the outright empirical nature of his evolving business practices, see Prettyman, "Criticism, Business, and the Problem of Complicity," 49–66.

39. Ford and Crowther, "Management and Size," *Saturday Evening Post* 203 (September 20, 1930): 153, 150; and "Ford Explains Policy of Letting Out Work," *New York Times*, March 24, 1930, 2. See also Liebold, *Reminiscences*, 538–39, in confirmation of Ford's intentions.

40. Quoted in Denny, "Small-Unit Plants," 22.

41. Ford and Crowther, "Management and Size," 153.

42. See Denny, "Small-Unit Plants," 1, 22.

43. Kuhn, *GM Passes Ford*, 8. See also Stuart W. Leslie, *Boss Kettering: Wizard of General Motors* (New York: Columbia University Press, 1983), 202.

44. Cameron, "Decentralization of Industry," 484. A collection of articles from the late 1960s and early 1970s reprinted from the influential *Harvard Business Review* suggests no consensus by even then about the value of centralization versus decentralization: see John Dearden, ed., *Centralization and Decentralization: Which, When, and How Much? Reprints from Harvard Business Review* (Cambridge, Mass.: Harvard Business Review, n.d.).

45. Editorial in *Commerce and Finance* 22 (February 8, 1933), 145.

46. Cameron "Decentralization of Industry," 487.

47. Cameron reported and quoted in "Ford's Plan Is Success: Decentralization Proves Advantage," *Detroit News*, August 21, 1938, n.p., in the Joe Brown Collection, box 12.

48. Quoted in Denny, "Banker Ford Aims to Aid Rural Shops," *New York Times*, February 28, 1933, n.p.

CHAPTER 10

1. La Croix, *Village Industries*; and "Village Industries," typed report, n. d. (though it is clearly from 1944 or 1945), Ford Motor Company Archives.

2. See "Willow Run: Another Village Industry," *Ford News* 21 (March 1941): 72, 80; E. L. Warner Jr., "Decentralization of Willow Run," *Automotive and Aviation Industries* 90 (April 15, 1944): 18–20, 85, 86, 88; Lowell J. Carr and James E. Stermer, *Willow Run: A Study of Industrialization and Cultural Inadequacy* (New York: Harper, 1952); Marion F. Wilson, *The Story of Willow Run* (Ann Arbor: University of Michigan Press 1956); and Cathy Stromme Horste and Diane Follmer Wilson, *Water under the Bridge: A History of Van Buren Township*, 2d ed. (Belleville, Mich.: Van Buren Township Bicentennial Commission, 1980), chap 6. Warner's article is useful regarding the decentralization of bomber production and assembly during World War II, including the use of the Rouge facilities as a branch plant. Willow Run Airport, now used primarily by corporate clients, is being renovated; the former bomber plant currently produces transmissions for General Motors vehicles. See Lewis, "Ford Country" (column), *Cars and Parts* 42 (August 1999): 23.

3. Letters to me from Michaels, August 1, 1988, and Walters, June 18, 1988.

4. Edwards interview, June 13, 1988.

5. See Tobin, "Henry Ford and His Village Industries," 161, 164.

6. Voorhess, *Reminiscences*, 124.

7. See Tobin, "Henry Ford and His Village Industries," 159–60; and "Ford to Drop Farming: Starts Program to Dispose of Its Sideline Activities," *New York Times*, March 28, 1946, 26.

8. See letter to me from Peters, March 16, 1989. Interestingly, the lengthy obituary of Ford that appeared in the *New York Times* on April 7, 1947 (reprinted in the *Times* online version in April 2002 under "On This Day"), mentioned neither the village industries nor decentralization. The reprint comes from the Associated Press and lists no author.

9. Lawrence J. White, *The Automobile Industry since 1945* (Cambridge, Mass.: Harvard University Press, 1971), 12.

10. Lewis, *Public Image*, 425–26. As Lewis notes, the contentions that the company was virtually bankrupt when Henry Ford II took over in 1945 were not made at the time but only later, and were not based on the actual financial and other conditions.

11. Press Release, Ford News Bureau, August 16, 1948, 2. Meanwhile the local *Plymouth Mail Weekly* had ominously reported, in a front-page story on June 21, 1946, regarding the end of a national coal strike and the reopening of Plymouth and other village industries, "It is generally understood that in the future these outlying plants must produce a normal day's production if they are to be continued in operation by the Ford Company."

12. Tobin, "Henry Ford and His Village Industries," 126. See also "Consolidation of Two Plants Effected; Four Others Will Be Merged," *Hydro Plants News* 1 (August 1, 1946): 2; and "Ford Reshapes His Empire," *Business Week* 1043 (August 27, 1949): 20–22.

13. See "Ford Motor Company Properties: Small Plants," Ford Motor Company Industrial Archives, Redford, Michigan, accession AR-65-101 (June 1946; the data sheets on each plant have varying June dates).

14. "Four Hydro Plants Become One," *Hydro Plants News* 2 (October 1, 1948): 1.

15. "Another Ford Ideal to Help Mankind Crumbles to Earth with Closing of the Phoenix Plant," *Plymouth Mail*, April 2, 1948, 1. True, the "Ford Ideal" mentioned here was the hiring of widowed and divorced women, whereas only married women could work at the other village industries—and only if their spouses were unemployed. But the overall lamentation is for the fate of all of the village industries.

16. See "New Division Headed by Roscoe M. Smith," *Hydro Plants News* 2 (May 1, 1947): 1.

17. Del S. Harder, address at Ypsilanti, October 1, 1948, in Press Release, Ford News Bureau, Dearborn, October 1, 1948, 1–2.

18. See "$70,000 'Ypsi' Remodeling Under Way," *Hydro Plants News* 1 (August 1, 1946): 2.

19. On Del Harder and automation at Ford Motor Company, see Flink, *Automobile Age*, 243.

20. According to Pietrykowski ("Fordism at Ford," 396) the real purpose of the *Hydro Plants News* "was an attempt to create a common identity among workers at village

plants at variance with the identity that workers were forming as union members."
This may be in part true, but my examples of more negative reports carried in that
same publication suggest more than one reason for its existence.

21. See Press Release, Ford News Department, Dearborn, March 20, 1970.

22. Quoted in Val Corbin, "Village Industries: Northville Closing Is Final Chapter in
    Their History," *Ford World* 18 (n.d.): n.p.

23. See Lewis, "Ford Country" (column), *Cars and Parts* 26 (August 1983): 158.

24. Kevin Wilson, "Ford Reopens Plant to Assemble Fuel Tanks," *Northville Record*,
    September 1, 1982, 1A. I am indebted to Tobin for this article.

25. Letter to me from Sally Henrikson, Office Manager, Northville Historical Society,
    September 15, 1986.

26. See the Northville Historical Society's *Welcome to the Mill Race Historical Village*
    brochure, kindly enclosed in ibid.

27. *Mill Race Quarterly* 17 (summer 1989): 1. See also Bob Needham, "Ford An-
    nounces June 9 Shutdown," *Northville Record*, March 23, 1989, 1, 10; "Pursue
    Ford Recognition," editorial, *Northville Record*, March 30, 1989, 5; Needham,
    "UAW Charges Violation of Ford Accord," *Northville Record*, April 20, 1989, 1,
    12; Needham, "Local Union President Thinks Ford Move Will Waste Money,"
    Northville Record, April 20, 1989, 1; Needham, "Company Resolves UAW Tiff:
    Ford Allows Northville Plant Workers to Transfer to Livonia," *Northville Record*,
    May 25, 1989, 1, 18; "Ford Manufacturing Set to End This Friday," *Northville
    Record*, June 8, 1989, 1, 6; and "Plant Study Done; City Waits on Ford," *Northville
    Record*, June 15, 1989, 1. Livonia was really Newburgh. See also Needham, "Love
    among the Ducks: Couple Find Romance at Ford Plant," *Northville Record*, June
    1, 1989, 5A, about a couple who met at the plant in 1987 and got married the next
    year, only to have their idyllic workplace close down a few months later.

28. On the profound administrative changes undertaken by Henry Ford II after he
    replaced his grandfather, see Kuhn, *GM Passes Ford*, chaps. 12, 13. As Kuhn puts
    it, "It is doubtful that FM [Ford Motor Company] under Henry Ford would qualify
    as a system" (271).

29. *The Decentralization Story* (Dearborn: Ford Motor Company, 1952), 1, 9. For an
    example of how this played out in administrative reorganization, see A. H. Allen,
    "Ford's Administrative Organization Gets Another Reshuffling, Latest Plan Being
    Another Step in Company's Decentralization Plan," *Steel* 124 (February 21, 1949):
    79. See also "Henry Ford II Speaks Out: A Conversation with Tom Lilley," *Atlantic
    Monthly* 180 (December 1947): 25–32.

30. Pietrykowski, "Fordism at Ford," 398. Pietrykowski contends (397–98) that the
    Ford Motor Company did not intend to dismantle all the village industries, or else
    it would not have established the new Parts and Equipment Manufacturing Divi-
    sion in 1947. Instead, he argues, persistent antiunionism on management's part
    (even after the acceptance of the United Auto Workers in 1941, there were many
    work stoppages and wildcat strikes at the Rouge and other larger plants during and
    after World War II, contrary to the UAW's "wartime no-strike pledge") saved sev-
    eral of the plants from being closed, since they could remain relatively free of work
    shutdowns and might absorb some of the troublesome workers elsewhere. But if
    that was the case, why shut down any of the nineteen village industries? The

creation of a new administrative structure was, in my view, primarily a reflection of management's uncertainty over the fate of the remaining sites.

31. Lilley, "Henry Ford II Speaks Out," 29.
32. "Ford Plans and Projects," *Hydro Plants News* 1 (May 1946): 3.
33. "Branch Buying Simplified," *Hydro Plants News*, 1 (August 1946): 1.
34. "*Fortune* Looks at the New Ford Team: How Auto Industry Battle Lines Are Drawn," *Hydro Plants News* 2 (June 1, 1947): 5.
35. See Sugrue, *Origins of the Urban Crisis*, 127–30, 140–41.
36. *Ibid.*, 129–30.

CHAPTER 11

1. David L. Lewis, "Old Henry Ford's Village Industries: A Tour of Practically Perfect Places to Work," *Detroit Magazine (Detroit Free Press)*, September 24, 1972, n.p.
2. See Roy E. Hamlin, "New Life for Old Dundee Mill," *Monroe Evening News*, November 1, 1982, n.p.; "Dundee Old Mill Open for Winter Hours," *Petersburg Sun*, December 4, 1986, n.p.; and "Dundee Gets $30,000 Grant for Old Mill Restoration," *Monroe Evening News*, January 6, 1988, n.p. See also Lewis, "Ford Country" (column), *Cars and Parts* 36 (June 1993): 65, for a further update.
3. These figures come from Diane E. Lewis, "Telecommuting," *Boston Sunday Globe*, March 28, 2004, G2; and Maggie Jackson, "Balancing Acts," *Boston Sunday Globe*, May 23, 2004, G1. See also such pioneering reports as Sarah Snyder, "Work Is Where the Computer Is," *Boston Globe*, July 26, 1988, 37, 43; Peter H. Lewis, "The Executive Computer: 'Electronic Cottages' Take Root," *Sunday New York Times*, October 16, 1988, Business Section, 10; John Schwartz and Dody Tsiantar, "Escape from the Office: High-tech Tools Spur a Work-at-Home Revolt," *Newsweek* 113 (April 24, 1989): 58–60; and Michael Alexander, "Home Tech: Telecommuting to the Office," *Boston Globe*, July 20, 1990, 46. See also, however, the less positive recent assessments by Matthew Brelis, "Work: Beyond Lonely: Life as a Telecommuter," *Boston Sunday Globe*, January 17, 1999, C1, C2; Michael Rosenwald, "Long-Distance Teamwork," *Boston Sunday Globe*, April 29, 2001, J1, J6; Jenn Director Knudsen, "All in a Day's Work . . . and Play: Working at Home Is on the Rise, Isolation and All," *Boston Globe*, May 10, 2001, H1, H5; Stephanie Armour, "Telecommuting Gets Stuck in the Slow Lane: Working from Home Loses Appeal for Harried Employees, Skeptical Bosses," *USA Today*, June 25, 2001, 1A, 2A; Martha E. Mangelsdorf, "When Home Starts Feeling a Lot like the Office," *Boston Sunday Globe*, February 24, 2002, D2; and Angela Lin, "View from the Cube: Couple Incorporate Living, Working in the Same Space," *Boston Sunday Globe*, Boston Works Section, May 19, 2002, G17.
4. On the envisioned "electronic cottage," see Eileen Boris, *Home to Work: Motherhood and the Politics of Industrial Homework in the United States* (New York: Cambridge University Press, 1994), 324–36.
5. A most ironic outcome of the growth of the home office has been the creation by an enterprising businesswoman of a tape recording of office sounds to be played by persons actually working at home to offset, during business-related telephone calls, the conventional sounds of home life: children, appliances, television, etc. So

popular did the tape become that its originator was forced to establish "a real office," one perhaps outside her home. See "How a Fake Office Created a Real Office," *New York Times*, October 12, 1988, D8.

6. See Henry J. Holcomb, "Young Companies Can Rent a Prime Address (and a Desk, too)," *Philadelphia Inquirer*, April 26, 1999, F1, F7; and Carol Kleiman, "Work Routines Become More Flexible," *Philadelphia Inquirer*, April 26, 1999, F14.

7. See Todd Lappin, "When the Cubicle Has a Crankshaft," *New York Times*, June 14, 2001, E1, E7.

8. D. C. Denison, "Business Intelligence: As Work Becomes Decentralized, Connection Is Crucial," *Boston Sunday Globe*, April 21, 2002, C2.

9. Ford and Crowther, *Today and Tomorrow*, 145.

10. "Ford Would Replace Plants with Small Contractor's Shops," June 28, 1933, n.p., Federated Press clipping in the Joe Brown Collection, box 12. On the general historical background to such concerns by organized labor, see David Montgomery, *Workers' Control in America: Studies in the History of Work, Technology, and Labor Struggles* (New York: Cambridge University Press, 1979).

11. See Kenneth B. Noble, "U.S. Will End Ban on Work in Home," *New York Times*, November 11, 1988, A1, A26; Alex Beam, "The Knitters Are Back," *Boston Globe*, April 5, 1989, 69; and Boris, *Home to Work*, chap. 11.

12. Maxine Berg, *The Age of Manufactures: Industry, Innovation, and Work in Britain, 1700–1820* (New York: Oxford University Press, 1986), 317.

13. See Wald, "Back Offices Disperse from Downtowns"; and Louis Uchitelle, "Outsider and an Insider: John Shepard Reed," *New York Times*, September 22, 2003, A12. As Uchitelle notes, the South Dakota legislature "had lifted the state usury laws, allowing the bank to charge higher interest rates."

14. Felicity Barringer, "Linton Journal: From Milking Cows to Manning Computers," *New York Times*, August 11, 1989, A10; Susan Carey, "Farmed Labor: A City-Slicker CEO Finds Fun and Profit at Home on the Range—Hal Rosenbluth Embraces Marvels of North Dakota and Spreads the Word—An Epiphany in Cow Dung," *Wall Street Journal*, April 10, 2000, A1; and Steve Cohn, "The Growth of the 'Global Office,'" *New York Times*, October 18, 1988, D1, D25. Now, ironically, it is Dublin, Ireland, that draws thousands of other Europeans to its high-tech call centers operated by more than sixty multinational corporations, many of them American. See William Underhill, "Ireland: Your Call is Important," *Newsweek* 135 (April 3, 2000): 67; and, for an update, Brian Lavery, "New Tech Surge in Ireland, and It Feels Like '99 Again," *New York Times*, June 17, 2004, W1, W7.

15. Ralph H. Kilmann, "Tomorrow's Company Won't Have Walls," *Sunday New York Times*, June 18, 1989, Business Section, 3. See also, as a case study of this kind of management thought and action, Sarah Bartlett, "John Reed Bumps Into Reality," *Sunday New York Times*, February 5, 1989, Business Section, 3, 12; significantly, the article's subtitle is "Fulfilling Citicorp's potential requires not more vision, but better nuts-and-bolts implementation."

16. See, for example, Zane L. Miller, *The Urbanization of Modern America* (New York: Harcourt Brace Jovanovich, 1973), 165–69, 207–10; Victor C. Ferkiss, "Bureaucracy," in *Technology and Change*, ed. John G. Burke and Marshall C. Eakin (San Francisco: Boyd & Fraser, 1979), 86–91; Joseph P. Charney, "In Mexico, an Urgent Need to Decentralize," Letter to the *New York Times*, October 11, 1985, A34; Al

Gore, "The Big Sweep," *Bangor Daily News*, September 14, 1993, 7 (regarding decentralization of the federal government through the use of "'massively parallel' computers"); David E. Sanger, "I.B.M. Forms Five Autonomous Units," *New York Times*, January 29, 1988, D1, D4; John Markoff, "I.B.M.'s Plan Can Work, Experts Say," *New York Times*, November 29, 1991, D1, D2; Neil A. Lewis, "New York's New Schools Chief Has a Super-Decentralization Plan," *Sunday New York Times*, September 24, 1989, Week in Review; Joseph Berger, "Board of Education: A Thing of the Past? Dismantling Decentralization—Again," *Sunday New York Times*, February 18, 1996, 39; Jayson Blair, "Harvey B. Scribner, New York Schools Chancellor in a Turbulent Era" (obituary), *New York Times*, December 24, 2002, C11; and Eric Bloom, "Teachers Find Scoring Tests a Treat," *Maine Sunday Telegram*, June 6, 1999, 1B, 8B (regarding "decentralized scoring" of statewide educational tests). Historian Walter LaFeber argues that contemporary technological advances have provided nonelites with unprecedented ability to spread information and culture around the world in ever more decentralized degrees; see LaFeber, *Michael Jordan and the New Global Capitalism* (New York: Norton, 1999).

17. Peter F. Drucker, "Information and the Future of the City," *Wall Street Journal*, April 4, 1989, A22.

18. See Gary Chapman, "Cities Starting to Get Smart about Technology," *Boston Sunday Globe*, August 2, 1998, E4; and Jonathan Alter, "Hope in Bloom," *Newsweek* 138 (November 19, 2001): 58. The latter observes the irony of efforts by New York City's then new mayor, Michael Bloomberg, to keep businesses from leaving town, thanks in part to the very decentralized real-time information systems that Bloomberg himself had earlier developed and marketed so effectively around the nation and the world. See also W. Warren Wagar, *The Next Three Futures: Paradigms of Things to Come* (Westport, Conn.: Praeger, 1991), 40–45, regarding projected decentralization in the writings of some, but hardly all, recent futurists.

19. On E. F. Schumacher's life, work, and legacy, see the detailed summary and analysis in Kleiman, "Appropriate Technology Movement," chap. 1. Kleiman (84–90) illuminates aspects of Schumacher's views of village industrial development in both the West and the Third World which have some similarities to—but, more often, differences from Ford's views of his village industries. See also Kitching, *Development and Underdevelopment*, 62–63, 84, 92–102, 176; and K. B. Suri, ed., *Small Scale Enterprises in Industrial Development: The Indian Experience* (New Delhi: Sage, 1988).

20. Kitching, *Development and Underdevelopment*, 100–01. Most of the book deals with the similarities and differences between preindustrial and industrial visions of Third World leaders, reformers, and theorists, or what Kitching calls "Populism" and "Neo-populism."

21. See Suri, introduction to *Small Scale Enterprises*.

22. Joseph Giovannini, "Carolina Industrialization: Factories amid Fields," *New York Times*, June 3, 1984, 36. On the persistence of these patterns, see introduction to Douglas M. Orr, Jr., and Alfred W. Stuart, eds., *The North Carolina Atlas: Portrait for a New Century* (Chapel Hill: University of North Carolina Press, 2000). On related developments in farming areas, see, for example, Steven Greenhouse, "New Farm Belt Crop: Industry," *New York Times*, June 26, 1986, D1, D7; and David Shribman, "A New Exodus: Populace Branches Out from Cities," *Boston*

Globe, April 1, 1994, 3. Additional useful facts and perspectives about North Carolina today came from the North Carolina Rural Economic Development Center in Raleigh.

23. "America's Ruggedest Individual," 12.

24. Steven E. Prokesch, "U.S. Companies Weed Out Many Operations," *New York Times*, September 30, 1985, A1, D5. See also James M. Rubenstein, *Making and Selling Cars: Innovation and Change in the U.S. Automotive Industry* (Baltimore: Johns Hopkins University Press, 2001), 57–58, 88–92; Saritha Rai, "Carmakers around World Are Turning to India for Parts," *New York Times*, June 20, 2003, W1, W7; and Brinkley, *Wheels for the World*, 763. Regarding Ford Motor Company's initial decision in 1928 to follow General Motors and Chrysler in obtaining ever more parts from outside suppliers, see Hounshell, *From the American System to Mass Production*, 300. See also Kim Moody, *Workers in a Lean World: Unions in the International Economy* (New York: Verso, 1997), 68–69. Martin Glaberman, in a 1997 review essay, says that thanks to outsourcing, at General Motors "in-house production is down from 70 percent [in the early 1980s] to 45 percent, Ford's is 39 percent, and Chrysler's [is] 36 percent" ("Labor in Crisis," *Contemporary Sociology* 26 [March 1997]: 167). See also Fred Andrews, "Dell, It Turns Out, Has a Better Idea than Ford," *New York Times*, January 26, 2000, C12. On General Motors continuing vertical integration longer than Ford, see Keith Bradsher, "G.M. Plans to Spin Off Parts Division," *New York Times*, August 4, 1998, D1, D9.

25. See Keith Bradsher, "Auto Negotiations Are Likely to Aim for a Longer Pact," *New York Times*, June 9, 1999, C2; Robyn Meredith, "Ford Planning to Spin Off Parts Division," *New York Times*, October 1, 1999, C1, C6; Meredith, "Ford's Deal with Auto Workers Had an Unusual Twist," *New York Times*, October 11, 1999, C2; Lewis, "Ford Country" (column), *Cars and Parts*, 45 (September 2002): 63; Rubenstein, *Making and Selling Cars*, 85–86; and Kenneth Gilpin, "Ford Will Take a Charge in Viste on Revamping Plan," *New York Times*, December 23, 2003, C2.

26. See John Holusha, "Helping the Big 3 Fill Their Niches," *New York Times*, September 6, 1988, D1, D9.

27. John Markoff, "A Web-Researched Ford in Microsoft's Future," *New York Times*, September 21, 1999, C2. See also Kathleen Kerwin, Marcia Stepanek, and David Welch, "At Ford, E-Commerce Is Job 1: No Other Manufacturer Is Pushing So Boldly onto the Web," *Business Week*, no. 3670 (February 28, 2000): 74–76, 78.

28. See Lewis, "Ford Country" (column), *Cars and Parts* 38 (June 1995): 62–63; 41 (July 1998): 51; and 42 (July 1999): 51.

29. See ibid., 26 (December 1983): 64, and 33 (April 1990): 62.

30. See ibid., 39 (February 1996): 64; 46 (May 2003): 49; and Mike Hudson, *Detroit News Autos Insider*, October 24, 2003, 1–3. On the origins of the Rouge complex's original steel mill, see Biggs, *The Rational Factory*, 150–51.

31. See Lewis, "Ford Country" (column), *Cars and Parts* 31 (May 1980): 170; 34 (April 1991): 187; 36 (August 1993): 44; 41 (July 1998): 50;42 (July 1999): 50; and 46 (March 2003): 52. A special tour of the Rouge plant on October 8, 1999, for interested members of the Society for the History of Technology, then holding its annual meeting in Detroit, made clear how different things had become from the early 1980s (and before that), beyond the reduction in workforce size: greater respect for workers' opinions and suggestions; greater cooperation between labor

and management; greater reliance on robots and on ergonomics for the most physically taxing jobs; greater concern for cleanliness (akin to that of the village industries); reduction but not elimination of belowground assembly pits in favor of those on the ground floor; and a much more diverse workforce. In addition, there was emphasis on Ford Motor Company's embrace of the "just-in-time" inventory system discussed below.

31. See Ford Motor Company's Web site: http:www.ford.com/en/company/rouge ReopensDoors.htm., and Dan McCosh, "History Bows at a Ford Plant," *New York Times*, April 16, 2004, D1, D9.

32. Charles Pappas, "Rebirth on the Rouge," *My Ford*, Special Centennial Edition, Summer 2003, 36–38; Ford Motor Company Web site; and Lewis, "Ford Country" (column), *Cars and Parts* 46 (June 2003): 48–49. See also Holusha, "Ford Thinks Green for River Rouge Plant," *Sunday New York Times*, November 26, 2000, 42; Martha Sherrill, "The Buddha of Detroit," *New York Times Magazine*, November 26, 2000, 112–16; Lewis, "Ford Country" (column), *Cars and Parts* 44 (December 2001): 64–65; and Rubenstein, *Making and Selling Cars*, 86–87.

33. Stephen Yokich quoted in Lewis, "Ford Country" (column), *Cars and Parts* 31 (May 1988): 170. Yokich later became the UAW's president, serving from 1995 to 2002. On Buick City, see Flink, *Automobile Age*, 400. Ironically, Buick City itself has by now been largely torn down or left vacant. See also Lewis, "Ford Country" (column), *Cars and Parts* 32 (December 1989): 160, regarding efforts by the UAW to erect a historical marker on the site of the 1937 Rouge "Battle of the Overpass" (see chapter 7).

34. Yokich quoted in Lewis, "Ford Country" (column), *Cars and Parts* 31 (May 1988): 170.

35. See Holusha, "Ford Leads in U.S. Car Profits," *New York Times*, February 18, 1987, D1, D5; and Lewis, "Ford Country" (column), *Cars and Parts* 31 (February 1988): 165. On the reasons for GM's declining profits, see Kuhn, *GM Passes Ford*, chap. 15, which attributes the company's problems to poor management, specifically to long-term deviations from Alfred Sloan's original policies, for which he blames Sloan himself as well as his successors. Like Ford's earlier, "Sloan's critical mistake occurred when he turned GM inward in the late 1930's" (348) and began to ignore changing external conditions—when, in effect, "centralization without the requisite corporate-level expertise" (8) took place.

36. See Steven Wilmsen, "GM Strike Cast as Final Battle for Power," *Boston Globe*, June 27, 1998, A1, A9; and Rubenstein, *Making and Selling Cars*, 176–79.

37. See Keith Bradsher, "Ford's 70-Year Itch Could Be Relieved: As GM Stumbles, Its Perch at the Top Is within Reach," *New York Times*, May 3, 2001, C1, C3; Danny Hakim, "The Big Three Fear that Toyota Is Becoming the Big One," *New York Times*, May 20, 2004, C8; and Todd Zaun, "Global Growth Gives Toyota 29% Rise in Profit," *New York Times*, August 4, 2004, W1, W7. But see also Andrea Gabor, "Management: Quality Revival, Part 2, Ford Embraces Six Sigma," *New York Times*, June 13, 2001, C5, regarding the company's abandonment in recent years of Total Quality Management in favor of the more cost-oriented Six Sigma management scheme. Ironically, Ford and Crowther's *My Life and Work* (1922) had for the prior fifteen or more years been praised as the Bible of "Total Quality Management," a management approach that, like the book itself, had earlier been

neglected for generations except in Japan. See Thomas R. Stuelpnagel, "Deja Vu: TQM Returns to Detroit and Elsewhere," *Quality Progress* 26 (September 1993): 91–95. As discussed below, Ford and Crowther's *Today and Tomorrow* (1926) has in the past fifteen or more years been deemed the principal—but also long neglected—source of a related management approach regarding inventory.

38. See, by contrast, Danny Hakim, "Big Loss at Nissan Seems to Undercut UAW Objectives," *New York Times*, October 5, 2001, C3, regarding the union's surprising failure to organize workers at Nissan's Smyrna, Tennessee, plant: "The union has never been able to organize a plant operated solely by a foreign automaker, though it has organized joint ventures" like that with Mazda/Ford. Regarding the UAW's ongoing efforts to unionize workers at Honda's four Ohio plants, see Hakim, "Auto Union and Honda Dispute Safety Record at Plants in Ohio," *New York Times*, June 26, 2002, C1, C2. See also Honda's full-page advertisement in *USA Today*, December 14, 2001, 9A, announcing the opening of its eighth plant in the United States in Lincoln, Alabama. On the overall unionization effort for Japanese carmakers in the United States by 2001, see Rubenstein, *Making and Selling Cars*, 170–75.

39. See Kenichi Yamamoto, President, Mazda Motor Corporation, "Remarks" at groundbreaking for Flat Rock plant, May 29, 1985, 6–7; Mazda Information Bureau Press Releases, May 29, 1985, and October 9, 1987; Susan Chira, "For Mazda, a U.S. Car Plant," *New York Times*, December 1, 1984, Business Section, 1, 33; Mazda Motor Corporation 1986, 1987, and 1988 Annual Reports; and Mazda's full-page *New York Times*, October 9, 1987, advertisement on opening day of the Flat Rock plant, which currently makes Ford Cougars for Europe, Mercury Cougars for the United States, and Mazda GT6's for both. When it opened, the plant built cars engineered by Mazda but styled by Ford to replace the then extremely popular Ford Mustang. Soon, however, the plant will begin making redesigned 2005 and subsequent Mustangs, following extensive expansion. See "Ford to Move Production of Mustangs," *New York Times*, February 11, 2003, C10.

40. See Joseph J. Fucini and Suzy Fucini, *Working for the Japanese: Inside Mazda's American Auto Plant* (New York: Free Press, 1990).

41. See James Sterngold, "Mazda Gives Ford Motor More Control," *New York Times*, December 28, 1993, D1, D2; Andrew Pollack, "Ford, in Mazda Investment, Is Revered as Well as Feared," *New York Times*, April 13, 1996, 35; and Stephanie Strom and Keith Bradsher, "Wedding or Wipe-Out? Lessons for Renault and Nissan in the Ford-Mazda Marriage," *Sunday New York Times*, May 23, 1999, Money and Business Section, 3, 13.

42. See Dennis Patrick Quinn Jr., *Restructuring the Automobile Industry: A Study of Firms and States in Modern Capitalism* (New York: Columbia University Press, 1988), 32–33, 120–21. See also John F. Krafcik, "A New Diet for U.S. Manufacturing," *Technology Review* 92 (January 1989): 28–34, 36, which treats the automobile industry; and, for an extended—if by now outdated—comparison of the Ford and Nissan Motor Companies' history and management, David Halberstam, *The Reckoning: The Challenge to America's Greatness* (New York: Morrow, 1986). On Halberstam, see Lewis, "Ford Country" (column) 44 (April 2001): 24. Ironically, in 1992, at least, JIT deliveries in Tokyo created serious traffic problems. See Michael Schrage, "Innovation," *Boston Sunday Globe* March 22, 1992, 76.

43. Norman Bodek, publisher's foreword to Ford and Cowther, *Today and Tomorrow*

(1926; rept., Portland, Ore.: Productivity Press, 1988), vii–viii. The press's seasonal catalogues continue to list and to praise the book. Bodek's position is forcefully supported by Williams, Haslam, and Williams, "Ford versus 'Fordism,'" 517–55. See also Lewis, "Ford Country" (column), *Cars and Parts* 40 (January 1997): 31; 40 (February 1997): 26; and 41 (March 1998), 52. On those pleas to emulate Toyota, see Lewis, "Ford Country" (column), *Cars and Parts* 36 (May 1993): 65. On the nature of Japanese automakers' centralized complexes in Japan, see Quinn, *Restructuring the Automobile Industry*, 32–33, 120–21. But see also the overseas decentralization of Toyota, Japan's largest automaker, from its base in Toyota City, in Ken Belson, "Rethinking the Town That Toyota Built," *New York Times*, October 21, 2003, C1, C4.

44. Quoted from *Assembly Engineering Magazine* in the summer catalogue of Productivity, Inc. (the company that owns Productivity Press), July 1999, 48. As Williams, Haslam, and Williams contend, "Ford's early twentieth century American achievement makes the late twentieth century Japanese look like sluggards" ("Ford versus 'Fordism,'" 522). On a later effort by Ford Motor Company to emulate allegedly original Japanese techniques, see Holusha, "Industry Is Learning to Love Agility," *New York Times*, May 25, 1994, D1, D5.

45. On "lean production" and its prospects, see the good summary in Ruth Milkman, *Farewell to the Factory: Auto Workers in the Late Twentieth Century* (Berkeley: University of California Press, 1997), 15, 141–46. On the allegedly wholly Japanese origins of "lean production," beginning with Toyota, see James P. Womack, Daniel T. Jones, and Daniel Roos, *The Machine That Changed the World* (New York: Rawson Associates/Macmillan, 1990). On their book's influence, see Rubenstein, *Making and Selling Cars*, 32–42. On the often negative effects of "lean production" on American (and Canadian) auto unions, see William C. Green and Ernest J. Yanarella, eds., *North American Auto Unions in Crisis: Lean Production as Contested Terrain* (Albany: State University of New York Press, 1996); and Rubenstein, *Making and Selling Cars*, 165–71. For additional historical context, see Meyer, "The Persistence of Fordism," 73–99. On the mixed blessings of "lean production" for a Massachusetts manufacturer of thermostats for automobiles, see Diane Lewis, "Lean and Mean," *Boston Globe*, November 11, 2003, C1, C4.

46. Biggs, *The Rational Factory*, 126. More detailed summaries of Fordism are in Flink, *Automobile Age*, chap. 4; and Milkman, *Farewell to the Factory*, 23–27. For historical—and international—context, see Hughes, *American Genesis*, 8–9, 184–87, 203–20, and chap. 6. But see Williams, Haslam, and Williams, "Ford versus 'Fordism,'" for a strong defense of the Highland Park complex as a precursor of Japanese continuous manufacturing improvement schemes—as an outright pioneer of "lean production"—more than of American rigid mass production ones (far better represented by the Rouge complex).

47. See Milkman., *Farewell to the Factory*, esp. chap. 5. See also Milkman's review both of Fucini and Fucini, and of Womack, Jones, and Roos, *Machine That Changed the World*, in *Tikkun* 6 (May/June 1991): 81–84; and Stephen Amberg, *The Union Inspiration in American Politics: The Autoworkers and the Making of a Liberal Industrial Order* (Philadelphia: Temple University Press, 1994), chap. 8.

48. Steve Babson, "UAW, Lean Production, and Labor-Management Relations at AutoAlliance," in Green and Yanarella, *North American Auto Unions in Crisis*, 82.

See also Fucini and Fucini, *Working for the Japanese*; and Keith Bradsher, "Nissan Workers at Tennessee Plant Want Union Vote," *New York Times*, August 15, 2001, C1, C2. On an earlier gap between rhetoric and reality in the attempted application of Fordism, see Stephen L. McIntrye, "The Failure of Fordism: Reform of the Automobile Repair Industry, 1913–1940," *Technology and Culture* 41 (April 2000): 269–99, which illuminates Ford's unsuccessful efforts in these years "to rationalize repair work using the company's successful factory methods as a model" (295).

49. Paul Boreham, "The Myth of Post-Fordist Management: Work Organization and Employee Discretion in Seven Countries," *Employee Relations* 14 (March 1992): 22–23.

50. Moody, *Workers in a Lean World*, 86. On the sometimes disappointing economic returns of "lean production," see Rubenstein, *Making and Selling Cars*, 42–55.

51. See Philip Scranton, *Endless Novelty: Specialty Production and American Industrialization, 1865–1925* (Princeton, N.J.: Princeton University Press, 1997).

52. See especially Michael Piore and Charles Sabel, *The Second Industrial Divide: Possibilities for Prosperity* (New York: Basic Books, 1984); Charles Sabel and Jonathan Zeitlin, "Historical Alternatives to Mass Production: Politics, Markets, and Technology in Nineteenth-Century Industrialization," *Past and Present* 108 (August 1985): 133–76; and Sabel and Zeitlin, eds.,*World of Possibilities: Flexibility and Mass Production in Western Industrialization* (New York: Cambridge University Press, 1997). The last work avowedly refines and qualifies the second, as the editors' introduction makes clear. But see Adam Tooze's illuminating review of these Sabel and Zeitlin works and of Scranton, *Endless Novelty*, as well in *Social History* 25 (May 2000): 247–50; see also the critical reviews of Sabel and Zeitlin, *World of Possibilities*, by Sidney Pollard in *English Historical Review* 113 (September 1998): 1025–26, and by William Lazonick in *Business History Review* 73 (summer 1999): 309–13. In addition, see the more general criticisms of the "flexible specialization" historical analysis as summarized in Ash Amin, "Post-Fordism: Models, Fantasies, and Phantoms of Transition," in *Post-Fordism: A Reader*, ed. Amin (Cambridge, Mass.: Blackwell, 1994), 13–16, 21–24; and by Bruce Pietrykowski, "Beyond the Fordist/Post-Fordist Dichotomy: Working Through [Piore and Sabel,] *The Second Industrial Divide*," *Review of Social Economy* 57 (June 1999): 177–98. Finally, see the several comparative analyses of the reception of Fordism in various European societies in Mikael Hard and Andrew Jamison, eds., *The Intellectual Appropriation of Technology: Discourses on Modernity, 1900–1939* (Cambridge, Mass.: MIT Press, 1998).

53. As noted in Pietrykowski, "Fordism at Ford," 398.

54. Ibid., 384, 398.

55. Pietrykowski, "Beyond the Fordist/Post-Fordist Dichotomy," 194. See also John Bellamy Foster, "The Fetish of Fordism," *Monthly Review* 39 (March 1988): 14–33.

56. Isabel Wilkerson, "Detroit's Symbol of Revival Now Epitomizes Its Problems," *New York Times*, September 1, 1986, 5.

57. See ibid.; Robyn Meredith, "G.M. Buys a Landmark of Detroit for Its Home," *New York Times*, May 17, 1996, A12; Keith Bradsher, "Ford Returning to Suburb, Souring Detroit Real Estate Shift," *New York Times*, December 11, 1996, B14; Paul Gargaro, "GM Begins a Game of Musical Chairs," *Sunday New York Times*,

July 20, 1997, Real Estate Section, 26; Lewis, "Ford Country" (column), *Cars and Parts* 40 (April 1997): 33, 40 (June 1997): 48, 41 (May 1998): 52, 43 (November 2000): 48, 44 (February 2001): 69; and Jim Utsler, *All Things Auto: The Visitor's Itinerary to Metro Detroit's Automotive Heritage* (Detroit: n.p., 2000), 32. The GM video is complemented by an undated brochure, *Progress Ahead: A Pocket Guide to Renaissance Center*. See also Keith Bradsher, "Ford Is Moving Lincoln-Mercury Headquarters to California," *New York Times*, January 23, 1998, C3.

58. Carolyn Kraus, "Patches of Eden amid Detroit's Ruins," *New York Times*, June 25, 1988, 27; Bill McGraw, "In Detroit, Urban Renewal Sprouts at the Top," undated *Detroit Free Press* article reprinted in *Boston Globe*, May 26, 2001, A2; and Kate Stohr, "In the Capital of the Car, Nature Stakes a Claim," *New York Times*, December 4, 2003, D10.

59. Ticknor, "Motor City," 298; see his chap. 5 for details.

60. See John Flesher, Associated Press, "Motor City Stuck in Reverse: Population Falls below One Million," *Boston Globe*, March 29, 2001, A10. But also see Jeffrey Ghannam, "Motor City Paves Road to a Renaissance," *Boston Sunday Globe*, December 7, 2003, A6.

61. Drucker, "Henry Ford: Success and Failure," 1. In his concluding paragraph Drucker noted that "there is today [in 1947] such a grim contrast between his [Ford's] social utopia and our social reality" (8).

62. See Robyn Meredith, "5 Days in 1967 Still Shake Detroit," *New York Times*, July 23, 1997, A10. But see also the more hopeful updates in Meredith, "Motown Enters the Zone: U.S. Program Helps Return Industry to an Inner City," *New York Times*, April 11, 1997, C1, C3; Robert Sharoff, "Testing Downtown Detroit for Housing," *Sunday New York Times*, May 17, 1998, Real Estate Page, A33; and Jim Suhr, "Motor City Has New Drive: Investors and Downtown Projects Help Momentum," *Boston Sunday Globe*, July 11, 1999, A8. For another, generally positive assessment of Detroit's history since the 1950s, see Thompson, *Whose Detroit?* Thompson's excellent work details many hopeful developments ignored or minimized by other historians and scholars.

63. See Lewis, "Ford Country" (column), *Cars and Parts* 32 (December 1989): 160, and 33 (July 1990): 65; also 29 (June 1986): 62, regarding the pollution of the Rouge River.

64. See ibid., 3 (April 1990): 64. Lewis himself informed me of the elimination of that soybean cultivation.

65. Ironically, though, tofu's principal non-Oriental producers in the United States are located, by choice, in high-tech Massachusetts. See Kristen o. Lundberg, "Move Over High Tech, Here Comes Tofu; or, Can Soybeans Fuel Massachusetts' Economy into the 21st Century?" *Boston Globe*, August 5, 1986, 25, 36. See also Associated Press, "Soy Protein Found to Benefit Cholesterol Levels in Humans," *Bangor Daily News*, August 3, 1995, A4; Philip Brasher, Associated Press, "Putting Tofu on the School Menu: U.S. Officials, Trying to Cut Fat, Want to Include Soy Products in Subsidized Lunches," *Boston Globe*, December 24, 1999, A3; and Marian Burros, "Eating Well: Doubts Cloud Rosy News on Soy," *New York Times*, January 26, 2000, D1, D9.

66. See Lewis, "Ford Country" (column), *Cars and Parts* 36 (June 1993): 18.

67. Letter to me from Paul Tull, publisher of the *Saline Reporter*, March 14, 1987.

68. See Guilford H. Rothfuss,'*Round the Square: A Story of the Brooklyn Area in Prose and Picture* (Brooklyn, Mich.: Exponent Press, 1981), 319.

69. Rubenstein, "Changing Distribution of the American Automobile Industry," 288; Rubenstein, "Further Changes in the American Automobile Industry," *Geographical Review* 77 (July 1987): 359–62; Rubenstein, *Changing US Auto Industry*, and Rubenstein, *Making and Selling Cars*, 94–96.

70. Rubenstein, *Changing US Auto Industry*, 1.

71. Mullin, "Henry Ford and Field and Factory," 429. Regarding this trend in a more rural state, see *The Flight of the Arrow of Change: Technology and Maine's Future, A Report to the Commission on Maine's Future* (Augusta, Maine, April 1989), 15–17. Berg, *The Age of Manufactures*, 19–20, notes similarities between small-scale English cottage industries at the early stages of the English Industrial Revolution and Third World manufacturing today.

72. See the Village Ventures Web site—http://www.villageventures.com—for elaboration on the company. It was cofounder Matt Harris who commented on the company's interest in Ford's village industries.

73. See Steven Levy, "The Hot New Tech Cities," *Newsweek* 132 (November 9, 1998): 44–48, 50–56. See also Charles Piller, "Innovation: Small ISPs Keep Big Boys at Bay: Firms Stress Human Touch in Bid to Survive Turbulent Telecom Sea," *Boston Globe*, May 26, 1999, C3; and Kimberly Blanton, "Massachusetts Seen [as] High-Tech Leader," *Boston Globe*, July 22, 1999, C1, C14.

74. See Meyer, *The Five Dollar Day*, 2, regarding the remarkable increases in the number of Ford Motor Company employees hired and cars manufactured between 1903 and 1921. In this regard, see also Rae, "Why Michigan?" 436–44. Kuhn (*GM Passes Ford*, 6) even argues that "the early automobile business constituted America's first major high-tech industry."

75. Daniel Gavron, *The Kibbutz: Awakening from Utopia* (Lanham, Md.: Rowman & Littlefield, 2000), 4. See also, for example, Yonina Talmon, *Family and Community in the Kibbutz* (Cambridge, Mass.: Harvard University Press, 1972); Tom Bethell, "Is the Kibbutz Kaput?" *Reason* 22 (October 1990): 33–37; Alan Cooperman, "A Socialist's Worst Nightmare: Wealth," *U.S. News and World Report* 122 (March 10, 1997): 41–42; Ilene R. Prusher, "Zionist Dream of Kibbutz Fades in 1990s Lifestyle," *Christian Science Monitor*, December 5, 1997, 6–7; and Jessica Steinberg, "In Soy Food, Kibbutzim Find Manna for a Modern Age," *New York Times*, April 20, 2004, W1, W7. My statistics derive from Gavron, from Steinberg, and from various reports issued by the University of Haifa's Institute for Research on the Kibbutz and the Cooperative Idea.

76. Gavron, *The Kibbutz*, 221; and Steinberg, "In Soy Food."

77. David E. Lilienthal, "Lost Megawatts Flow over Nation's Myriad Spillways," *Smithsonian* 8 (September 1977): 83–84.

78. But see the persistent legacy of TVA and other large-scale power systems in the United States, the former Soviet Union, and other countries, as detailed in Paul Josephson, *Industrialized Nature: Brute Force Technology and the Transformation of the Natural World* (Washington, D.C.: Island Press, 2002).

79. John McPhee, "Minihydro," in his *Table of Contents* (New York: Farrar Straus Giroux, 1985), 203.

80. Ibid., 215.

81. Richard F. Hirsh, *Power Loss: The Origins of Deregulation and Restructuring in the American Electric Utility System* (Cambridge, Mass.: MIT Press, 1999), 116; see also chap. 6.

82. On these points and those of the preceding paragraph, see Howard J. Brown, ed., *Decentralizing Electricity Production* (New Haven, Conn.: Yale University Press, 1983), esp. 37, 109, 243, summarizing the essays by David Morris, Bent Sorenson, and E. F. Lindsley. The definition of cogeneration in this paragraph comes from Brown's introduction (15). Interestingly, the book is dedicated "To R. Buckminster Fuller, whose ideas, lifetime work, and belief in individual initiative provide the inspiration to 'dare to be naive'" (v). On the American electric power industry's reluctant technological innovations, see Hirsh, *Technology and Transformation in the American Electric Utility Industry* (New York: Cambridge University Press, 1989). On current opportunities for greater use of solar, water, and wind power, see Jane Holtz Kay, "Wind, Solar Give Us a Chance to Capitalize on a Crisis," *Boston Sunday Globe*, March 11, 2001, E4; Scott Dionne, "Harness Ocean Waves," *Bangor Daily News*, March 20, 2001, A9; Rich Hewitt, "Maine Has Potential for Renewable Energy, Report Says," *Bangor Daily News*, February 22, 2002, A9; Stephen H. Burrington, "Our Energy Future Is in the Wind," *Boston Globe*. July 13, 2002, A15; Barbara Claire Kasselmann, "Plugging into the Sun: Even on the Coast of Maine, a House Can Be Entirely Solar Powered," *Boston Globe*, May 1, 2003, H1, H6; "Boosting Solar Power" (editorial), *Boston Globe*, June 30, 2003, A12; Misty Edgecomb, "Mars Hill to Harvest Wind Power," *Bangor Daily News*, July 19–20, 2003, A1, A6; and Barnaby J. Feder, "G.E. Signals a Growing Interest in Solar," *New York Times*, March 13, 2004, B1, B2. But see also Heather Clark, Associated Press, "Solar Movement of the 1970s Stalled," *Boston Globe*, July 16, 2002, A5; Richard C. Hill, "Forget Wind and Solar" (letter to the editor), *Maine Times*, April 4, 2002, 15; Edgecomb, "Threat to Wildlife Becalms County Wind Power Plan," *Bangor Daily News*, July 8, 2004, A1, A2; and Beth Daley, "Wind Farms Find Unlikely Foe in Environmentalists," *Boston Sunday Globe*, August 1, 2004, B1, B5. For historical perspectives on developments in Maine, see the very balanced account by Evan Rallis, "Solar and Wind Energy Development in Maine: 1973–1997" (M.A. thesis, University of Maine, 2003).

83. John McPhee, "The Control of Nature: Farewell to the Nineteenth Century: The Breaching of Edwards Dam," *New Yorker* 75 (September 27, 1999): 44–53; and Daniel J. Michor, "People in Nature: Environmental History of the Kennebec River, Maine" (M.A. thesis, University of Maine, 2003), 24, 88–91. See also Jonathan Carter, "That Dam Duplicity," *Bangor Daily News*, July 3–4, 1999, A13; Linda Ashton, Associated Press, "Significance of Edwards Dam Removal Debated," *Bangor Daily News*, July 5, 1999, A1, A2; Glenn Adams, Associated Press, "162-Year-Old Dam Removed: Kennebec River Once Again Flows as It Did in Colonial Times," *Bangor Daily News*, November 2, 1999, B6; Daniel Ostrye, "Edwards Dam Removal Cited as 'Chartering New Territory,'" *Bangor Daily News*, February 19, 2000, S4; and "Future and the Dam," editorial, *Bangor Daily News*, July 8, 2000, A12. See also Dusti Faucher, "On the Presumpscot: Dam Removal Good for River, Fish, Anglers, and State," *Maine Sunday Telegram*, October 13, 2002, 5C.

84. "Wayne County Parks and Parkways," brochure, n.d. (but likely 1989), 1. The brochure was widely circulated in the Detroit area for several years from hotels to

airports to restaurants to travel agencies. The Wayne County Park System is the commonly used name for what is officially the Wayne County Department of Public Services, Division of Parks. My thanks to David L. Lewis for this clarification.

85. John Stewart, "Ford Heritage Trails," Wayne County Department of Public Services, Division of Parks, typed report, n.d. (but likely 1989), 1. The use of "laboratory" here is more positive than its use in 1924 by journalist Paul Kellogg (chapter 6). See also local newspaper accounts of the initial rosy prospects for the Phoenix and Plymouth trail sites in Wayne Pearl, "County Considers Plans to Improve Hines Lakes," *Observer and Eccentric*, March 2, 1989, n.p.; and Kevin Brown, "Township Donates to Heritage Trail," *Observer and Eccentric*, March 8, 1990, n.p. Compare these with Francis D. LeBlond's later, quite pessimistic "Assessment of Cultural Landscape: Ford Heritage Trail: Plymouth Mill and Phoenix Mill" (unpublished paper, Eastern Michigan University, Spring Term 1999). LeBlond has been president of the Plymouth Historical Society; its Plymouth Historical Museum is the source of his paper and of the two earlier newspaper articles.

86. See Diane Gale Andreassi, "Nankin Mills Center Will Lead Trail Back to Area's History," *Observer and Eccentric*, December 27, 1998, 2; George Hunter, "New Center Spotlights Rouge River: Interactive Exhibits Represent Historical Uses of Nankin Mills," *Detroit News*, January 12, 2001, D3; and Richard Pearl, "Dedicated Volunteers Realize Nankin Mills Center Dream," *Observer and Eccentric*, January 18, 2001, A10. My thanks to Nancy Darga, then Manager of Design, Wayne County Division of Parks, for these and other materials about the Nankin Mills Interpretive Center.

87. On the Plymouth Historical Museum exhibit, see Julie Brown, "Exhibit's Rich in History," *Observer and Eccentric*, April 27, 1989, 1, 3; Brown, "Plant Staffers Took Pride in Job Well Done," *Observer and Eccentric*, April 27, 1989, 1; and references to transcripts of interviews with former village industries workers (chapter 6).

88. On the proposed Women's Museum at the Phoenix Mill, see Laura Lucas, "Hines Drive: A Forgotten Treasure," *Your Community Crier: Plymouth's Only Weekly News Magazine*, February 22, 2002, 6, and March 1, 2002, 7; Lewis, "Ford Country" (column), *Cars and Parts* 45 (February 2002): 53; and Michael Strong, "Commissioner Works to Save Legacy," *Crain's Detroit Business: The Ford Legacy* (Summer 2003): 14.

89. On the MotorCities National Heritage Area's background and objectives, see its Web site—http://www.autoheritage.org—which is my principal source. My thanks to both Nancy Darga and Beth Stewart, director of the Plymouth Historical Museum, for this reference and for related printed materials that are part of the overall MotorCities project.

CONCLUSION

1. Press Release, Ford News Bureau, August 16, 1948, 4.
2. What Kleiman writes about E. F. Schumacher applies to Ford, notwithstanding the numerous profound differences between them: "Establishing the proper size of everything from political units to economic firms became one of his central

preoccupations. But Schumacher's concern over the issue of size was rooted in a more meaningful aim—the creation and maintenance of a thriving culture" ("Appropriate Technology Movement," 88–89).

3. Cameron, "Decentralization of Industry," 486. Thomas P. Hughes concurs with this assessment; see his *American Genesis*, 309. As Ernest Liebold recalled about these experiments, Ford "thought they were performing a wonderful service for [all] his various reasons" (*Reminiscences*, 577).

4. Kasson, *Civilizing the Machine*, 71.

5. Donald F. Davis, *Conspicuous Production: Automobiles and Elites in Detroit, 1899–1933* (Philadelphia: Temple University Press, 1988), 127. On the need to go beyond Ford's eccentricities in any serious evaluation, see also Drucker, "Henry Ford," 3.

6. The notable exception is the work of Bruce Pietrykowski, cited earlier.

7. See, for example, Piore and Sabel, *The Second Industrial Divide*; Amin, *Post-Fordism: A Reader*; Green and Yanarella, *North American Auto Unions in Crisis*; and Milkman, *Farewell to the Factory*.

8. Patrice Higonnet, review of *World of Possibilities*, ed. Sabel and Zeitlin, in *Journal of Interdisciplinary History*, 30 (autumn 1999): 309.

9. It is disturbing, though hardly surprising, that this interpretation is perpetuated in so relatively recent, if so unscholarly, a work as Collier and Horowitz, *The Fords*, 107–9, 131.

10. See Segal, "The 'Middle Landscape,'" 13–26. On the major writings of automobile historian James J. Flink and his eventual achievement of a balance between his originally uncritical acceptance and later critical rejection of the automobile, see Segal, "The Automobile and the Prospect of an American Technological Plateau," in Segal, *Future Imperfect*, 27–35; and Segal, review of Flink's *Automobile Age*, in *American Historical Review* 95 (April 1990): 608–9.

11. Huxley, *Brave New World*, vii–viii.

12. Among many illuminating studies of Walt Disney, the most pertinent one here is Steven Watts, *The Magic Kingdom: Walt Disney and the American Way of Life* (Boston: Houghton Mifflin, 1997).

13. The term is applied by Nevins and Hill in *Ford: Decline and Rebirth*, 73.

14. Tarbell, "Every Man a Trade and a Farm," 5, 79, 80.

15. H. G. Wells, *The Outline of Man's Work and Wealth*, 3d. ed. (Garden City, N.Y.: Garden City Publishing, 1936), 421, 421, 423. The book was originally published in the United States in 1931 and in Britain in 1932 as *The Work, Wealth, and Happiness of Mankind*, but these particular passages remain the same in all three editions except that the final sentence (beginning "The essential point") was added to the third edition. I am indebted to my colleague Professor of History Emeritus David C. Smith, one of the world's leading authorities on Wells, for bringing this book and its pertinent passages to my attention. Smith edited Wells's correspondence and found several positive references about Ford, whom Wells met in Dearborn in 1931 and quite liked both personally and intellectually. As Smith put it in a letter to me of November 18, 1999, "Wells apparently thought Ford was a wave of the future, or at least a significant ripple." One might nevertheless question Wells's judgment in characterizing Ford as allegedly still believing, in 1936, that

"work should be so planned as to provide the best possible life for the worker" (421). Still, the third edition has some additional comments on Ford that suggest a somewhat less positive overall assessment than that of the first and second editions.

16. Ames, introduction to Axelrod, *The Colonial Revival in America*, 14.

17. Ford is paraphrased in Wik, *Henry Ford and Grass-roots America*, 207; a slightly different version quotes Ford's own words in William Greenleaf, *From These Beginnings: The Early Philanthropies of Henry and Edsel Ford, 1911–1936* (Detroit: Wayne State University Press, 1964), 103. On Ford and history, see Burlingame, *Henry Ford*, 85, 95–96; Roger Butterfield, "Henry Ford, the Wayside Inn, and the Problem of 'History Is Bunk,'" *Proceedings of the Massachusetts Historical Society* 77 (1965): 57–66; Ford, "War and History," in *Henry Ford: Great Lives Observed*, ed. John B. Rae (Englewood Cliffs, N.J.: Prentice-Hall, 1969), 53–54; and Nye, *Henry Ford: "Ignorant Idealist."*

18. Ford and Crowther, *Today and Tomorrow* (Productivity Press 1988 reprint), 230–31.

19. Quoted in Denny, "Times Good, Not Bad, Ford Says," 1, 3.

20. Ibid., 1.

21. See Lewis, "Ford Country" (column), *Cars and Parts* 39 (March 1996): 52–53; 40 (February 1997), 24; and 45 (September 2002), 63. Later print ads for the Ford Taurus did not show Ford himself but said that "Henry Ford dreamed of 'making the desirable affordable'"—as with the Taurus. See, for example, the inside front cover of *Newsweek* 133 (December 28, 1998–January 4, 1999).

22. See, for example, G. Donald Adams, Steven K. Hamp, Randy Mason, and John L. Wright, *The Automobile in American Life* (Dearborn, Mich.: Henry Ford Museum and Greenfield Village, 1989); and Joseph J. Corn, review of both this exhibit catalog and of the exhibit it summarizes, "The Automobile in American Life," *Journal of American History* 76 (June 1989): 221–24. See also Leo O'Connor, "Back to the Future," *Mechanical Engineering* 115 (March 1993): 56–59.

23. *Newsweek* 133 (April 19, 1999): advertisment between 42 and 43, the start of a special section on national parks. Interestingly, another Ford Motor Company special advertising section headed "Conserving, Cataloging, and Complementing Nature," which appeared a year earlier (*Newsweek* 131 [May 18, 1998])—before William Clay Ford became chairman of the board—barely mentioned Henry Ford. See also Keith Bradsher, "Advertising: Ford Is Starting a Big Campaign to Establish a Common Image for Its Sport Utility Vehicles," *New York Times*, August 23, 1999, C12. On William Clay Ford, Jr., as himself a "passionate environmentalist" and consequent possible tensions with other top company executives and stockholders uninterested in any improvements that might cost the company money, see Bradsher, "The Top Spot at Ford Is Returning to a Ford," *New York Times*, September 12, 1998, C1, C2; Holusha, "Ford Thinks Green for River Rouge Plant," 42; Martha Sherrill, "The Buddha of Detroit," *New York Times Magazine*, November 26, 2000, 112–16; and Bradsher, "A Ford Heir Struggles for Control," *New York Times*, February 6, 2001, C1, C2. On Chairman Ford and corporate environmental policies, see also Kevin J. Sweeney, "Ford Has Better Global Idea," *Bangor Daily News*, December 10, 1999, A13. On Ford Motor Company's surprisingly frank admission that its sport utility vehicles are harmful to the environment and must be made more fuel-efficient, see Bradsher, "Ford's Admission Perplexes

the Neighbors in Henry's Hometown," *New York Times*, May 13, 2000, B1, B4; and Keith Naughton, "Ford Goes for the Green," *Newsweek* 136 (August 7, 2000): 62. A very different use of that famous photo with the ax was made in an utterly different publication just a month after the *Newsweek* advertisement. The politically provocative *Hightower Lowdown* (a newsletter of sorts edited by Jim Hightower and Phillip Frazer) 1 (May 1999): 3, as part of its major story on the positive uses of hemp (marijuana), had the following lines accompanying the photo: "The car's body was made of a cellulose plastic formed from hemp and sisal. He [Ford] also made cars powered by an alcohol fuel derived from hemp. It was a part of his vision to 'grow automobiles from the soil.'" See also Lewis, "Ford Country" (column), *Cars and Parts* 44 (October 2001): 67.

24. See chapter 11; and Holusha, "Ford Thinks Green," and Sherrill, "The Buddha of Detroit."

25. Lewis, "Ford Country" (column), *Cars and Parts* 44 (July 2001): 38; see also 41 (March 1998): 51, on Henry Ford's growing reputation beyond the Ford Motor Company as a conservationist. But see Danny Hakim, "Advertising," *New York Times*, June 13, 2002, C4, regarding the Sierra Club's recent criticism of the younger Ford for siding with the automobile industry's traditional and ongoing "lobbying against toughening fuel-economy regulations" and so allegedly betraying his own environmental values. See also the Sierra Club's ad in the *New York Times*, June 13, 2003, C3, using Ford's centennial celebration to demand that the company "do better—use existing technology to make cleaner cars that go farther on a gallon of gas, save your customers money and time at the pump, clean up the environment, and cut our country's need for oil. Begin your second century with innovation truly worth celebrating."

26. See Hakim, "Ford Family Takes the Helm," *New York Times*, October 31, 2001, C1, C9; Hakim, "Left in Nasser's Exhaust at Ford," *New York Times*, November 1, 2001, C4; Keith Naughton, "Hit the Road, Jacques," *Newsweek* 138 (November 12, 2001): 44; and Alex Taylor III, "Bill's Brand-New Ford," *Fortune* 149 (June 28, 2004): 68–76.

27. "Ford on Ford," advertisement in *New York Times*, March 13, 2002, C5, and in *Newsweek* 139 (March 18, 2002): 49. On this 2002 advertising campaign, see Hakim, "Advertising," *New York Times*, February 20, 2002; Naughton, "Bill Ford, Pitchman: 'If You Don't Like Me, Get Someday Else,'" *Newsweek* 139 (March 4, 2002): 8; and Michelle Krebs, "Ford Puts On Its Best Face to Build Confidence in Brand," *Boston Globe*, March 14, 2002, G7.

28. "Ford on Ford," advertisement in *New York Times*, March 20, 2002, C7. Related "Ford on Ford" advertisements appeared in, among other places, *New York Times*, March 6, 2002, C5.

29. Michelle Krebs, "The Winner Is You: Ford Celebrates 100 Years," *Parade Magazine*, October 6, 2002, 6.

30. See Lewis, "Ford Country" (column), *Cars and Parts* 45 (November 2002): 63.

31. See Steven K. Hamp, "Subject over Object: Interpreting the Museum as Artifact," *Museum News* 63 (December 1984): 33–37, for a perceptive elaboration of this interpretation of Ford's efforts in the village industries and elsewhere. Burlingame, *Henry Ford*, 85, 95–96, implicitly offers a similar interpretation but never spells it out. So, too, does Benson, *The New Henry Ford*, 10–11, 290–91, a work that

nevertheless epitomizes the Ford hagiography popular in 1923. On Ford's sense of history, see also Greenleaf, *From These Beginnings*, chap. 3; Nye, *Henry Ford*; and Kammen, *Mystic Chords of Memory*, 352–58. On Ford as a social engineer even in the industrial area, see Drucker, "Henry Ford," 1–8; Peter F. Drucker, *The New Society* (New York: Harper & Row, 1950), 19–20, 22–25; Banta, *Taylored Lives*; and Prettyman, "Criticism, Business, and the Problem of Complicity," 49–66. But see also the advertisement in, among other places, *Sports Illustrated Women* 3 (July/August 2001): 63, of Ford's historic 1901 race against champion Alexander Winton for its emphasis on Ford as a conventional (if de facto) "engineer" with a "passion" for technical advancements.

32. Ford and Crowther, *Today and Tomorrow*, 272–73.

BIBLIOGRAPHICAL ESSAY

I have identified and grouped here those primary and secondary works of greatest usefulness to my book and to any future research on the village industries. Save for a few, I do not evaluate their individual scholarly worth but rather accord all of them some basic scholarly significance.

Among Henry Ford's own writings, Ford and Samuel Crowther, *My Life and Work* (Garden City, N.Y.: Doubleday, Page, 1922) and *Today and Tomorrow* (Garden City, N.Y.: Doubleday, Page, 1926), are the most useful for comments on the village industries. Ford's usually worshipful contemporary biographers often mentioned the village industries but rarely devoted much space to them. An exception is Allan L. Benson, *The New Henry Ford* (New York: Funk & Wagnalls, 1923), chaps. 18, 19.

For detailed statements by Ford and his official spokesmen regarding "decentralization," see Henry Ford and Samuel Crowther, "Management and Size," *Saturday Evening Post* 203 (September 20, 1930): 24–25, 150, 153–54, 157; W. J. Cameron, "Decentralization of Industry," *Mechanical Engineering* 59 (July 1937): 483–87; "Ford Aide Tells Rural Plant Gains: Cameron in Paper Written for Management Congress Urges Advantages to Employees," *Sunday New York Times*, August 21, 1938, sec. 3, 7. Cameron's paper was reprinted in *Proceedings, Seventh International Management Congress*, Production Section (Washington, D.C., 1938), 36–38. On the contemporary need for greater precision about decentralization in the context of technology, society, politics, and culture, see Langdon Winner, "Decentralization Clarified," in Winner, *The Whale and the Reactor: A Search for Limits in an Age of High Technology* (Chicago: University of Chicago Press, 1986), 85–97.

Representative extended interviews with Ford by leading contemporary journalists are Wilbur Forrest, "The Secret of an Interview with Henry Ford; Lucky Reporter Had Appearance of a Mechanic," *New York Herald Tribune*, February 20, 1921, sec. 7, 1; Bruce Barton, "'It Would Be Fun to Start Over Again,' Said Henry Ford," *American Magazine* 91 (April 1921): 7–9, 121–22, 124; Paul V. Kellogg, "The Play of a Big Man with a Little River, Part I," *Survey Graphic* 52 (March 1, 1924): 637–42, 658, 661, 664, and "Part II" (April 1, 1924), 13–19, 52;

Drew Pearson, "Ford Predicts the Passing of Big Cities and Decentralizing of Industry," *Motor World* 80 (August 28, 1924): 9–11, also published as "Henry Ford Says Farmer-Workmen Will Build Automobile of the Future," *Automotive Industries*, August 28, 1924, 389–92; Ida M. Tarbell, "Every Man a Trade and a Farm," *McCall's* 54 (July 1927): 5, 79–80; Harold N. Denny, "Times Good, Not Bad, Ford Says: Sees the Dawn of a Bright Future," *New York Times*, February 1, 1933, 1, 3; Denny, "Small-Unit Plants Ford's Final Goal," *New York Times*, February 5, 1933, 1, 22; and Arthur Van Vlissingen, "The BIG Idea behind Those SMALL Plants of Ford's," *Factory Management and Maintenance* 96 (April 1938): 46–48, 50, reprinted as "Ford's Little Plants in the Country," *Reader's Digest* 32 (July 1938): 62–64.

Given the considerable circulation and importance of the two publications in which they appeared, it is likely that "America's Ruggedest Individual Takes a $35,000,000 Crack at Depression," *Life* 4 (May 30, 1938): 9–13, and John Bird, "One Foot on the Land," *Saturday Evening Post* 216 (March 18, 1944): 12–13, 46, 48, brought the village industries to the attention of thousands of readers throughout America and elsewhere.

On the need to take seriously Ford's ideas and writings (despite their frequently having been articulated by Crowther), see Martha Banta, *Taylored Lives: Narrative Productions in the Age of Taylor, Veblen, and Ford* (Chicago: University of Chicago Press, 1993); and Gib Prettyman, "Criticism, Business, and the Problem of Complicity: The Case of Henry Ford," *Interdisciplinary Literary Studies: A Journal of Criticism and Theory* 2 (fall 2000): 49–66. In addition, Reynold M. Wik, *Henry Ford and Grass-roots America* (Ann Arbor: University of Michigan Press, 1972), remains a first-rate analysis of Ford's persistent ideological appeal to rural America.

On Ford and history, see Roger Burlingame, *Henry Ford* (New York: Knopf, 1954), 85, 95–96; William Greenleaf, *From These Beginnings: The Early Philanthropies of Henry and Edsel Ford, 1911–1936* (Detroit: Wayne State University Press, 1964), chap. 3; Roger Butterfield, "Henry Ford, the Wayside Inn, and the Problem of 'History Is Bunk,'" *Proceedings of the Massachusetts Historical Society* 77 (1965): 57–66; Henry Ford, "War and History," in *Henry Ford: Great Lives Observed*, ed. John B. Rae (Englewood Cliffs, N.J.: Prentice-Hall, 1969), 53–54; and David E. Nye, *Henry Ford: "Ignorant Idealist"* (Port Washington, N.Y.: Kennikat Press, 1979).

On the broader context of Ford's anti-Semitism, see Leo P. Ribuffo, "Henry Ford and *The International Jew*," *American Jewish History* 69 (June 1980): 437–77, revised and reprinted in Ribuffo, *Right Center Left: Essays in American History* (New Brunswick, N.J.: Rutgers University Press, 1992), 70–105; and Neil Baldwin, *Henry Ford and the Jews: The Mass Production of Hate* (New York: Public Affairs, 2001). Ribuffo and Baldwin alike cite both Cameron and Ernest

Liebold (see next paragraph) as readily embracing and promoting Ford's anti-Semitism.

Illuminating primary sources include several "reminiscences" in the Oral History Section, Ford Motor Company Archives, Benson Ford Research Center, The Henry Ford, Dearborn. Those listed here contain either specific information about or insights into Ford and the village industries, or both: Edward J. Cutler, *The Reminiscences of Mr. Edward J. Cutler*, March 1952; Ernest G. Liebold, *The Reminiscences of Mr. E. G. Liebold*, January 1953; F. W. Loskowske, *The Reminiscences of Mr. F. W. Loskowske*, November 1951; Stanley Ruddiman, *The Reminiscences of Mr. Stanley Ruddiman*, October 1951; Mrs. Stanley Ruddiman, *The Reminiscences of Mrs. Stanley Ruddiman*, March 1952; Roscoe M. Smith, *The Reminiscences of Mr. Roscoe M. Smith*, April 1954; Charles Voorhess, *The Reminiscences of Mr. Charles Voorhess*, November 1952.

Two helpful books about the Ford Motor Company are *The Ford Industries: Facts about the Ford Motor Company and Its Subsidiaries* (Detroit: Ford Motor Company, 1924); and Hartley W. Barclay, *Ford Production Methods* (New York: Harper, 1936).

For secondary sources, Allan Nevins and Frank E. Hill's *Ford: Expansion and Challenge, 1915–1933* (New York: Scribner, 1957), and *Ford: Decline and Rebirth, 1933–1962* (New York: Scribner, 1963), are the starting points. Along with Nevins and Hill, *Ford: The Times, the Man, the Company* (New York: Scribner, 1954), they constitute a de facto official history of the Ford Motor Company and the Ford family, though the first two hardly devote adequate space to or offer broader context for the village industries.

By contrast, David L. Lewis, *The Public Image of Henry Ford: An American Folk Hero and His Company* (Detroit: Wayne State University Press, 1976), is in several respects more useful: not because Lewis devotes greater space to the village industries (he does not) but because he discusses them as integral parts of Ford's broad if admittedly unsystematic vision of America's past, present, and future, rather than (as with Nevins and Hill) merely marginal phenomena reflecting Ford's quirky personality. No less important are two collections of Lewis's "Ford Country" monthly columns from *Cars and Parts* magazine: *Ford Country* (Sidney, Ohio: Amos Press, 1987), and *Ford Country 2: The Family, the Company, the Cars* (Sidney, Ohio: Amos Press, 1999). I cite many of these columns with their original publication dates, but the two collections are invaluable to scholars of nearly every aspect of Ford and the Ford Motor Company.

Like Lewis's writings, none of Ford R. Bryan's four books on Ford, his family, and his business associates focus on the village industries but all contain extremely useful information to any serious researcher: *The Fords of Dearborn*, rev. ed. (Detroit: Harlo, 1989); *Henry's Lieutenants* (Detroit: Wayne State University Press, 1993); *Henry's Attic: Some Fascinating Gifts to Henry Ford and*

His Museum, ed. Sarah Evans (Dearborn, Mich.: Ford Books, 1995); and *Beyond the Model T: The Other Ventures of Henry Ford*, rev. ed. (Detroit: Wayne State University Press, 1997); A distant relative of the Ford family and an amateur historian, Bryan is also an utterly professional scholar in terms of research, analysis, and objectivity.

Four scholars have written at least one invaluable shorter study of the village industries: (1) John R. Mullin, "Henry Ford and Field and Factory: An Analysis of the Ford Sponsored Village Industries Experiment in Michigan, 1918–1941," *Journal of the American Planning Association* 48 (autumn 1982): 419–31; (2) John Tobin, Jr., "Henry Ford and His Village Industries in Southeastern Michigan" (M.A. thesis, Eastern Michigan University, 1985), plus several articles that I cited in the notes; (3) Rusty Davis, "Ford Motor Company Village Industries, Part 1," *V-8 Times* 20 (July/August 1983): 24–29, and "Part 2," (September/October 1983): 28–34; (4) Bruce Pietrykowski, "Fordism at Ford: Spatial Decentralization and Labor Segmentation at the Ford Motor Company, 1920–1950," *Economic Geography* 71 (October 1995): 383–401; and Pietrykowski, "Gendered Employment in the U.S. Auto Industry: A Case Study of the Ford Motor Co. Phoenix Plant, 1922–1940," *Review of Radical Political Economics* 27 (September 1995): 39–48.

On the "heroic theory" of the history of technology and its application to Ford, see Louis C. Hunter, "The Heroic Theory of Invention," in *Technology and Social Change in America*, ed. Edwin T. Layton Jr. (New York: Harper & Row, 1973): 25–46; Peter F. Drucker, "Henry Ford: Success and Failure," *Harper's Magazine* 195 (July 1947): 1–8; John Kenneth Galbraith, "Was Ford a Fraud?" in Galbraith, *The Liberal Hour* (Boston: Houghton Mifflin, 1960), 141–65; and James J. Flink, "Henry Ford and the Triumph of the Automobile," in *Technology in America: A History of Individuals and Ideas*, ed. Carroll W. Pursell, Jr. (Cambridge, Mass.: MIT Press, 1981), 163–75.

On the radically revised treatment of Henry Ford and the Ford Motor Company at the Ford Museum in Dearborn, which Ford founded, see Steven K. Hamp, "Subject over Object: Interpreting the Museum as Artifact," *Museum News* 63 (December 1984): 33–37; G. Donald Adams, Steven K. Hamp, Randy Mason, and John L. Wright, *The Automobile in American Life* (Dearborn, Mich.: Henry Ford Museum and Greenfield Village, 1989); and Joseph J. Corn, review of both Adams et al.'s exhibit catalogue and of the exhibit it summarizes, "The Automobile in American Life," *Journal of American History* 76 (June 1989): 221–24.

On the development of Detroit and its relationship to the automobile industry, see Thomas J. Ticknor, "Motor City: The Impact of the Automobile Industry upon Detroit, 1900–1975" (Ph.D. diss., University of Michigan, 1978); Donald F. Davis, "The City Remodelled: The Limits of Automotive Industry Leadership in Detroit, 1910–1929," *Histoire sociale/Social History* 13 (November 1980):

451–86; Davis, *Conspicuous Production: Automobiles and Elites in Detroit, 1899–1933* (Philadelphia: Temple University Press, 1988); Thomas J. Sugrue, *The Origins of the Urban Crisis: Race and Inequality in Postwar Detroit* (Princeton, N.J.: Princeton University Press, 1996); and Heather Ann Thompson, *Whose Detroit? Politics, Labor, and Race in a Modern American City* (Ithaca, N.Y.: Cornell University Press, 2001).

On the development of "Fordism" and the decades-long struggle for unionization in the automobile industry, see Carl Raushenbush, *Fordism: Ford and the Workers; Ford and the Community* (New York: League for Industrial Democracy, 1937); Stephen Meyer III, *The Five Dollar Day: Labor Management and Social Control in the Ford Motor Company, 1908–1921* (Albany: State University of New York Press, 1981); John Barnard, *Walter Reuther and the Rise of the Auto Workers* (Boston: Little, Brown, 1983); David Gartman, *Auto Slavery: The Labor Process in the American Automobile Industry, 1897–1950* (New Brunswick, N.J.: Rutgers University Press, 1986); Nelson Lichtenstein and Stephen Meyer III, eds., *On the Line: Essays in the History of Auto Work* (Urbana: University of Illinois Press, 1989), especially the articles by Wayne Lewchuk ("Fordism and the Moving Assembly Line: The British and American Experience, 1895–1930"), Thomas Klug ("Employers' Strategies in the Detroit Labor Market; 1900–1929"), and Meyer ("The Persistence of Fordism: Workers and Technology in the American Automobile Industry, 1900–1960"); Karel Williams, Colin Haslam, and John Williams, "Ford versus 'Fordism': The Beginnings of Mass Production?" *Work, Employment and Society* 6 (December 1992): 517–55; Elizabeth A. Fones-Wolf, *Selling Free Enterprise: The Business Assault on Labor and Liberalism, 1945–60* (Urbana: University of Illinois Press, 1994); Kevin Boyle, *The UAW and the Heyday of American Liberalism, 1945–1968* (Ithaca, N.Y.: Cornell University Press, 1995), 93–97; and Nelson Lichtenstein, *The Most Dangerous Man in Detroit: Walter Reuther and the Fate of American Labor* (New York: Basic Books, 1995).

On African American workers in the automobile industry, see Lloyd H. Bailer, "Negro Labor in the Automobile Industry" (Ph.D. diss., University of Michigan, 1943); Bailer, "The Negro Automobile Worker," *Journal of Political Economy* 51 (October 1943): 415–28; August Meier and Elliot Rudwick, *Black Detroit and the Rise of the UAW* (New York: Oxford University Press, 1979); Joyce Shaw Peterson, "Black Automobile Workers in Detroit, 1910–1930," *Journal of Negro History* 64 (Summer 1979): 177–90; and Sugrue, *Origins of the Urban Crisis.* The foremost study on Mexican labor is Zaragosa Vargas, *Proletarians of the North: A History of Mexican Industrial Workers in Detroit and the Midwest, 1917–1933* (Berkeley: University of California Press, 1993).

On post-Fordism, see Michael J. Piore and Charles F. Sabel, *The Second Industrial Divide: Possibilities for Prosperity* (New York: Basic Books, 1984); Joseph J. Fucini and Suzy Fucini, *Working for the Japanese: Inside Mazda's*

American Auto Plant (New York: Free Press, 1990); Ash Amin, ed., *Post-Fordism: A Reader* (Cambridge, Mass.: Blackwell, 1994); William C. Green and Ernest J. Yanarella, eds., *North American Auto Unions in Crisis: Lean Production as Contested Terrain* (Albany: State University of New York Press, 1996); Ruth Milkman, *Farewell to the Factory: Auto Workers in the Late Twentieth Century* (Berkeley: University of California Press, 1997); Bruce Pietrykowski, "Beyond the Fordist/Post-Fordist Dichotomy: Working through *The Second Industrial Divide*," *Review of Social Economy* 57 (June 1999): 177–98; and James M. Rubenstein, *Making and Selling Cars: Innovation and Change in the U.S. Automobile Industry* (Baltimore, Md.: Johns Hopkins University Press, 2001).

On European adoptions of Fordism (and Taylorism), see Charles S. Maier, "Between Taylorism and Technocracy: European Ideologies and the Vision of Industrial Productivity in the 1920s," *Journal of Contemporary History* 5 (1970): 27–61; and Kjetil Jakobsen, Ketil G. Andersen, Tor Halvorsen, and Sissel Myklebust, "Engineering Cultures: European Appropriations of Americanism," in *The Intellectual Appropriation of Technology: Discourses on Modernity, 1900–1939*, ed. Mikael Hard and Andrew Jamison (Cambridge, Mass.: MIT Press, 1998), 101–27.

On the transition from the "cottage industries" in England and on the Continent to the English Industrial Revolution, see Franklin F. Mendels, "Proto-industrialization: The First Phase of the Industrialization Process," *Journal of Economic History* 32 (March 1972): 241–61; Peter Kriedte, Hans Medick, and Jurgen Schlumbohm, *Industrialization before Industrialization* (New York: Cambridge University Press, 1981); and Robert S. DuPlessis and Martha C. Howell, "Reconsidering the Early Modern Urban Economy: The Cases of Leiden and Lille," *Past and Present* 94 (1982): 49–84. But also see the critiques of "proto-industrialization" in Lawrence Stone, "The New Eighteenth Century," *New York Review of Books* 31 (March 29, 1984): 42–48; and David Herlihy, review of *Peasants, Landlords, and Merchant Capitalists: Europe and the World Economy, 1500–1800* by Peter Kriedte, *Business History Review* 59 (autumn 1985): 530–31.

On the complex, often painful transition from predominantly agrarian to partially industrialized societies in many Third World countries in recent decades, see Gavin Kitching, *Development and Underdevelopment in Historical Perspective: Populism, Nationalism, and Industrialization*, 2d ed. (London: Routledge, 1989). On the related "appropriate technology" movement in the United States and abroad, see Jordan B. Kleiman, "The Appropriate Technology Movement in American Political Culture" (Ph.D. diss., University of Rochester, 2000). The key work of this movement is, of course, E. F. Schumacher, *Small Is Beautiful: Economics as If People Mattered* (New York: Harper & Row, 1973).

Among the many studies of the American automobile industry and of American industry overall, those most useful for studying the village industries (even if they do not actually mention those enterprises) are Alfred D. Chandler, Jr., *Strategy and Structure: Chapters in the History of the American Industrial Enterprise* (Cambridge, Mass.: MIT Press, 1969); Chandler, *The Visible Hand: The Managerial Revolution in American Business* (Cambridge, Mass.: Harvard University Press, 1977); Chandler, *Scale and Scope: The Dynamics of Industrial Capitalism* (Cambridge, Mass.: Harvard University Press, 1990); David A. Hounshell, *From the American System to Mass Production, 1800–1932* (Baltimore, Md.: Johns Hopkins University Press, 1984); Arthur J. Kuhn, *GM Passes Ford, 1918–1938: Designing the General Motors Performance-Control System* (University Park: Pennsylvania State University Press, 1986); James J. Flink, *The Automobile Age* (Cambridge, Mass.: MIT Press, 1988); Thomas P. Hughes, *American Genesis: A Century of Invention and Technological Enthusiasm, 1870–1970* (New York: Viking, 1989); James Rubenstein, *The Changing US Auto Industry: A Geographical Analysis* (London: Routledge, 1992); Lindy Biggs, *The Rational Factory: Architecture, Technology, and Work in America's Age of Mass Production* (Baltimore, Md.: Johns Hopkins University Press, 1996); Philip Scranton, *Endless Novelty: Specialty Production Industrialization, 1865–1925* (Princeton, N.J.: Princeton University Press, 1997); and Richard R. John, "Elaborations, Revisions, Dissents: Alfred D. Chandler's *The Visible Hand* after Twenty Years," *Business History Review* 71 (summer 1997): 151–200.

Of the growing number of studies about technology and American values, those most pertinent to the village industries (despite their rarely mentioning those experiments) are Morton White and Lucia White, *The Intellectual versus the City: From Thomas Jefferson to Frank Lloyd Wright* (New York: New American Library, 1964); Warren Susman, "The Thirties," in *The Development of an American Culture*, ed. Stanley Coben and Lorman Ratner (Englewood Cliffs, N.J.: Prentice-Hall, 1970), 179–218; Alfred H. Jones, "The Search for a Usable American Past in the New Deal Era," *American Quarterly* 23 (December 1971): 710–24; John F. Kasson, *Civilizing the Machine: Technology and Republican Values in America, 1776–1900* (New York: Grossman/Viking, 1976); T. J. Jackson Lears, *No Place of Grace: Antimodernism and the Transformation of American Culture, 1880–1920* (New York: Pantheon, 1981); David L. Lewis and Laurence Goldstein, eds., *The Automobile and American Culture* (Ann Arbor: University of Michigan Press, 1983), especially the articles by Mark Foster ("The Automobile and the City"), Joseph Interrante ("The Road to Autopia: The Automobile and the Spatial Transformation of American Culture"), John B. Rae ("Why Michigan?"), and Reynold M. Wik ("The Early Automobile and the American Farmer"); David E. Shi, *The Simple Life: Plain Living and High Thinking in American Culture* (New York: Oxford University Press, 1985); Richard Guy Wilson, Dianne H. Pilgrim, and Dickran Tashjian, eds., *The Machine Age in America, 1918–1941* (New York: Brooklyn Museum/Harry N. Abrams, 1986); Michael Kammen, *Mystic Chords of Memory: The Transformation of Tradition in Amer-*

ican Culture (New York: Knopf, 1991); Daniel Joseph Singal, "Towards a Definition of American Modernism," in *Modernist Culture in America*, ed. Singal (Belmont, Calif.: Wadsworth, 1991), 1–27; Terry Smith, *Making the Modern: Industry, Art, and Design in America* (Chicago: University of Chicago Press, 1993); Clay McShane, *Down the Asphalt Path: The Automobile and the American City* (New York: Columbia University Press, 1994); Amy Sue Bix, *Inventing Ourselves Out of Jobs? America's Debate over Technological Unemployment, 1929–1981* (Baltimore, Md.: Johns Hopkins University Press, 2000).

On the evolution of industrial and household power systems in the United States, see Louis C. Hunter, *A History of Industrial Power in the United States, 1780–1930*, vol. 1, *Waterpower in the Century of the Steam Engine* (Charlottesville: University Press of Virginia and Eleutherian Mills-Hagley Foundation, 1979), and vol. 2, *Steam Power* (Charlottesville: University Press of Virginia and Hagley Museum and Library, 1985); Hunter and Lynwood Bryant, *A History of Industrial Power in the United States, 1780–1930*, vol. 3, *The Transmission of Power* (Cambridge, Mass.: MIT Press, 1991); Jean Christie, "Morris L. Cooke and Energy for America," in *Technology in America: A History of Individuals and Ideas*, ed. Carroll W. Pursell, Jr. (Cambridge, Mass.: MIT Press, 1981), 202–12; Thomas P. Hughes, "The Industrial Revolution That Never Came," *American Heritage of Invention and Technology*, 3 (winter 1988): 58–64; Ronald C. Tobey, *Technology as Freedom: The New Deal and the Electrical Modernization of the American Home* (Berkeley: University of California Press, 1996).

On the "regionalist" movement in twentieth-century America, see Daniel T. Rodgers, "Regionalism and the Burdens of Progress," in *Region, Race, and Reconstruction: Essays in Honor of C. Vann Woodward*, ed. J. Morgan Kousser and James M. McPherson (New York: Oxford University Press, 1982), 3–26; and Robert L. Dorman, *Revolt of the Provinces: The Regionalist Movement in America, 1920–1945* (Chapel Hill: University of North Carolina Press, 1993).

The definitive account of New Deal community programs remains Paul K. Conkin, *Tomorrow a New World: The New Deal Community Program* (Ithaca, N.Y.: Cornell University Press, 1959). See also Joseph D. Conwill, "Back to the Land: Pennsylvania's New Deal Era Communities," *Pennsylvania Heritage* 10 (summer 1984): 13–17.

PHOTO CREDITS

[p. 78] Cartoon from United Auto Workers Local #3 newsletter, August 23, 1939. (Walter Reuther Library, Wayne State University)

All other photographs are from the Collections of The Henry Ford and are identified below with negative number in parentheses.

[p. 8] "Locations of Ford Village Industries" (833-77015)

[following page 50]

Promotional illustration of original Nankin Mills plant (833-81079)
Ford Motor Company executives on 1937 tour (0-7880)
Exterior of original Northville plant, 1932 (189-9974)
Interior of Flat Rock plant, 1923 (833-152935-14)
Aerial view of Flat Rock plant, 1927 (189-4768)
Renovation of old grist mill from which Saline plant was built, 1936 (188-16301)
Exterior of Saline plant, 1938 (188-23330)
Interior of the Saline plant showing soybean processing machinery, 1946 (833-83112-1)
Interior of Sharon Mills plant during renovation of old grist mill, 1933 (188-9382)
Exterior of Sharon Mills plant, 1941 (188-29664)
Interior of hydroelectric powerhouse at Milan, 1939 (0-2489-A)
Exterior of hydroelectric powerhouse at Nankin Mills, 1937 (189-18485-A)
Exterior of Waterford plant, 1945 (188-73471)
Exterior of Phoenix plant, 1936 (188-70275)
Surrounding area of Phoenix plant, 1936 (833-66169-A)
Exterior of Ypsilanti plant hydroelectric powerhouse and waterfalls, 1932 (833-57216-4)
Exterior of Ypsilanti plant, 1936 (833-66176-H)

Exterior side view of Ypsilanti plant, 1936 (833-66176-E)
"Industrial Farming" (D-1226)

[following page 74]

A worker testing carburetors at Milford plant, 1938 (833-71163-A)
A Milford plant worker using a Morris drilling machine, 1945 (833-82315)
Workers at the carburetor final assembly line at Milford, 1946 (833-86903-11)
An engraver at the Waterford plant, ca. 1947 (833-88329-1)
Older workers at the Ypsilanti plant, 1937 (189-12239)
Women working on voltage regulators at Phoenix plant, 1942 (189-17000)
A woman calibrating voltage regulators at Phoenix plant, 1942 (189-17001)
A woman starting an engine at Tecumseh plant, 1941 (B-36907)
Workers at Ypsilanti plant, including one of the few African Americans, 1947
    (833-84087-6)

INDEX

HOWARD P. SEGAL was born and raised in Philadelphia. He earned a B.A. from Franklin and Marshall College, where he was elected to Phi Beta Kappa, and an M.A. and Ph.D. in history from Princeton University. He has taught at Franklin and Marshall, the University of Michigan, and Harvard University and is currently Adelaide and Alan Bird Professor of History and Director of the Technology and Society Project at the University of Maine in Orono. He has received numerous grants and awards, including a National Science Foundation Grant, an Earhart Foundation (of Ann Arbor, Michigan) Grant, a Rockefeller Archive Center Grant, a Walter Reuther Library of Labor and Urban Affairs Grant, and a Mellon Faculty Fellowship in the Humanities from Harvard University. Professor Segal is the author of numerous articles, essays, and books, including *Technological Utopianism in American Culture* (1985), *Technology in America: A Brief History* (coauthor, 1989; second edition, 1999), *Future Imperfect: The Mixed Blessings of Technology in America* (1994), and *Technology, Pessimism, and Post-Modernism* (coeditor, 1995). He lives in Bangor, Maine, with his wife, Deborah Rogers, and children, Ricky and Raechel.